WOMANIST JUSTICE,
WOMANIST HOPE

American Academy of Religion
Academy Series

edited by
Susan Thistlethwaite

Number 79
WOMANIST JUSTICE,
WOMANIST HOPE

by
Emilie M. Townes

Emilie M. Townes

WOMANIST JUSTICE, WOMANIST HOPE

Scholars Press
Atlanta, Georgia

WOMANIST JUSTICE, WOMANIST HOPE

by
Emilie M. Townes

© 1993
The American Academy of Religion

Library of Congress Cataloging in Publication Data
Townes, Emilie Maureen, 1955-
   Womanist justice, womanist hope / Emilie M. Townes.
      p. cm. — (American Academy of Religion academy series; no.
79).
   Includes bibliographical references.
   ISBN 1-55540-682-3 (alk. paper). — ISBN 1-55540-683-1 (pbk.:
alk. paper)
   1. Wells-Barnett, Ida B., 1862-1931. 2. Civil rights workers-
United States—Biography. 3. Afro-American women civil rights
workers—Biography.   I. Title.   II. Series.
E185.97.B26T69   1993
323'.092—dc20
[B]   92-45204
                                           CIP

Printed in the United States of America
on acid-free paper

In memory of

my grandfather
Mitchell McLain
(1897-1966)

my grandmother
Nora Jane McLean Jackson
(1902-1983)

my father
Ross Emile Townes
(1915-1990)

my uncle
Mitchell McLean
(1930-1991)

God's magnificent designs

TABLE OF CONTENTS

ACKNOWLEDGEMENTS

Young Black girls of my generation in the South spent most if not all of their early grade school years in all-Black schools. One of the features of these classrooms was a line of pictures of famous African-Americans on one classroom wall. In my third grade classroom, the pictures were accompanied by a brief biographical sketch. I do not recall my teacher ever requiring us to read the sketches or write a theme on any of the people she picked out for us. She did refer to them with regularity if we became unruly or failed to complete our homework assignments. We were chastised with "What do you think Booker T. Washington would say if he was here now?" or "Do you know how hard Harriet Tubman worked so we could be free? And here you are wasting that freedom."

They became our silent judges, our measure of excellence. They rejoiced with us when we got arithmetic problems right or a new spelling word mastered. They were relentless in their demand for excellence and cheerleaders for our education. I hold those pictures firm in my memory.

I am grateful to a cloud of witnesses who contributed to the completion of this project. Their guidance and support carried me through times of indecision and over-extension. They helped me clarify time and again my rationale for beginning such a project. They understood when pain of uncovering my heritage was almost too much to bear. They were my rock and guide.

I thank Professor Rosemary Skinner Keller for the steadying influence and inspiration as my advisor. Her willingness to help me find my voice and her model of collegiality and teaching rests well within my soul. I also want to thank my other advisor, Professor Josef Barton of the history department at Northwestern University. He helped steady me in my days of course work and clarify my direction and interest. His enthusiasm for my project was infectious and gave me the impetus to continue on. In addition I thank the other members of my dissertation committee, Rosemary Radford

Ruether and Richard Tholin. Both prodded me to greater clarity, encouraged my questioning, and challenged my fuzziness.

I am deeply indebted to Susan Ebersold for her support and encouragement through the many drafts of this project. Her willingness to read and re-read drafts, ask questions, pushed me to "make it plain" and relevant were a ministry and witness of God's justice and grace.

I thank the members and friends of Christ the Redeemer Metropolitan Community Church. They embraced me as their pastor and ministered to my soul during the good times and the bad. They served as cheerleaders for the journey and provided a place to gain perspective and wholeness. I write with the joys and defeats of their lives ever before me as a beacon of hope.

I thank the staff of the Office of Ministry Programs at Garrett-Evangelical Theological Seminary. Our work together on the nature of partnership and shared gifts of all the people of the church gifted me with models for learning that will last a lifetime. The members of the Department of Religious Studies at DePaul University offered me their collegiality, their insights, and their friendship. They encouraged my growth as a teacher and challenged me to view teaching as a craft and ministry. We are learners one and all.

I am deeply indebted to my student assistant, Gail Madson. Her careful attention to detail and form are matchless. My colleagues at Saint Paul School of Theology—administration, faculty, staff, and students give me new visions of community and hope.

My family is my home and hearth, they provided the words of wisdom and reality. They were ever-present with encouragement and humor and helped me to remember my commitment to finish and to do so with integrity and dignity. They sustain me with a legacy of love and care and family.

INTRODUCTION

One day, I realized that the pictures on the wall of my grade school were mostly men. The only exceptions were Ida B. Wells-Barnett, Harriet Tubman, and Sojourner Truth. Occasionally Mary McLeod Bethune was added, but the pantheon of women's lives was limited in comparison to the men. Like many young Black girls, I assumed that men were the doers of the great things and that only exceptional women ever became leaders of our race.

The Civil Rights Movement and the early Women's Liberation Movement drastically altered that perspective. I began to search with vigor for women's lives and work in African-American history and culture. My worldview expanded and the possibilities for the role of African-American women in this culture broadened immeasurably.

I was drawn to biographies and autobiographies to recapture my history as an African-American woman. One of those autobiographies was Ida B. Wells-Barnett's. As I read, a strong, determined, arrogant woman emerged. Here was a woman who lived her life and witness in one breath. However, I was puzzled by the biographies about her, for they ran the gamut from critical to affirming. Her critical biographers took a condemnatory tone and highlighted her abrasive character and inability to work within groups. Her more sympathetic biographers noted her character flaws but emphasized her contributions and gifts. Here was a complex woman, who, in her time, forged great friendships and great animosities. She was a leader, but often could not work with others. She was an active churchwoman her entire life, and used her Sunday school classes to launch social reform crusades. She held this nation and all its people to a high moral standard and challenged her contemporaries to breathe life into the ideals this country espoused.

Wells-Barnett is an entry point for what I envision as a substantial scholarly historical and ethical inquiry into the social and moral lives of African-American women in the contemporary church.

My aim is rudimentary: to aid in the recovery of an ignored and forgotten part of the African-American experience in the United States, the contribution of African-American women.

I begin this larger project with the nineteenth century. It is my belief that it was not until this century that African-Americans had been exposed to Christianity, through conversion, for a period long enough for them to develop a moral world that was a true blend of African survivalisms and white western Christianity.

However, the scope of this volume is confined to an investigation of the social and moral perspectives of Ida B. Wells-Barnett who lived from 1862 to 1931. Wells-Barnett's understanding and social critique of her times, through her perception of Christian duty, truth, and leadership, reveal a penetrating social critic and an astute and creative social researcher.

The recovery of the lives of African-American women remains a relatively new area of historical research. The difficulty in recovering Black history, and particularly the lives of Black women, lies in the diffusion of written records. The researcher must rely on interviews, letters, women's groups records, newspapers, and other similar materials to develop a picture of the world for Black people in the nineteenth and early twentieth century. The tools of the social historian are an absolute necessity.

Recent increasing interest and scholarly research has yielded a greater understanding of the world of Black women in the nineteenth century. Yet there remains much work to do in recovering their moral sphere: how they made decisions, how their religious and moral values informed their participation in social issues, and how their spirituality interacted with their social conscience. It is my belief that the disciplines of social history and social ethics will be enriched by further investigations into these questions.

I have chosen Ida B. Wells-Barnett as the focus of this work because of her strong commitment to social justice and to the church. Further, the disagreement among her biographers in their evaluation of Wells-Barnett makes greater research into her life and work much needed. Wells-Barnett was an active churchwoman and contributed to numerous church periodicals of her day. She was an intriguing woman. She was unable to work for any significant length of time in groups, preferring to go her own way and use her own methods to agitate for social change. Yet she was fiercely dedicated and worked tirelessly to eradicate the negative stereotypes, the discrimination, and the abuse directed toward the African-Americans of her era. The first chapter is a brief biographical sketch. The second chapter is methodological. The third and fourth chapters attempt to set the context for Wells-Barnett. The fifth and sixth chapters center on the person and work of Ida B. Wells-Barnett. The seventh chapter is theoretical in nature and seeks to examine the resources for a contemporary womanist Christian social ethic based on chapters three through six.

The biographical sketch in Chapter One is not a detailed, chronological reconstruction of the life of Ida B. Wells-Barnett. Rather, the biographical approach of this chapter sets the context of her social and moral perspectives which become resources for a womanist ethic of justice. Her life story brings out in bold relief the foundation for her perspectives, her writings, and her crusade for justice.

Chapter Two explores the key methodologies used to look at Wells-Barnett, her autobiography and the biographies of her. These sources will be used in this study in conjunction with her essays, speeches, newspaper articles, minutes of NAACP meetings, and various women's clubs with which she was affiliated, as well as letters, church journals, and a host of secondary sources. My approach suggests that autobiography and biography can be used to reconstruct a worldview that had previously been lost or obscured. However, autobiography and biography are volatile resources that must be used with great care. I will consider Wells-Barnett's autobiography as a tool for historical research and raise the cautions which the researcher must take in using any autobiography to reconstruct the social and moral perspectives of an individual.

Chapter Three examines the emerging social class structure and the nature of work for African-Americans in the nineteenth century between 1892 and 1920. The nineteenth century world of African-Americans was one of economic, social, and racial subordination. This subordination deepened during the profound transition in the United States from a rural republic to an industrial nation. In the midst of this transition, African-American women put forth a reform agenda.

Chapter Four attempts to recover the religious and social world of these reform-minded Black women through the use of autobiography and biography. These tools will be augmented by other sources from the era such as newspapers and diaries. In this chapter, I will construct the framework of women's spirituality as it drew from eighteenth century evangelical roots and the revived evangelical reform movements in post-Civil War United States. The women's club movement sought to transform African-American Christianity and, by extension, Black domesticity. These components form the general social setting in which Well-Barnett grew up and lived her adult life.

Chapter Five will look closely at Wells-Barnett's writings and speeches to glean the religious and moral dimensions behind her arguments on the subject of lynching. I will pay particular attention to her autobiography and the various biographies of her life. Previous researchers have made note of her strong social stand, but have not taken a careful look at Wells-Barnett's deep roots in the church and the extremely high moral standards she set for herself, other Black people, and even clergy in her day. My task in this chapter is to explore her writings from the angle of vision of the social ethicist. I will attempt to clarify her religious and moral thought, remaining open to the possibility that she was in no way systematic, but addressed the social issues of her day on a one-to-one basis.

Chapter Six examines Wells-Barnett's role in the anti-lynching campaign of the 1880s to the early 1900s. Included in this chapter is a discussion of her clash with Frances Willard on the subject of lynching. Wells-Barnett addressed the myths and stereotypes surrounding the white justification of lynching. She also had to educate as well as confront white women social reformers on the issue.

Chapter Seven will draw on the material in chapters two through five. My design is to consider the social and moral perspectives of Wells-Barnett as they provide the resources for a contemporary womanist Christian social ethic. I will explore such themes as authority, suffering, obedience, liberation, reconciliation, and power.

I have formulated several basic questions. What was the role of Black women's church groups in the nineteenth century world? How did religious women combine spirituality and social justice issues? What is the nature of leadership for Black women? How did Wells-Barnett embody this and what lessons does her method of leadership provide for the contemporary Black woman who is active in the church? What role does community have among Black women involved in social reform? Are the themes I begin the study with—liberation, reconciliation, authority—an accurate reflection of the moral sphere of Black women in the nineteenth century? If they are not, what themes more accurately reflect the lived experience of these women? If they are, how can they be or how are they translated for African-American women today?

This study of Wells-Barnett began when I first considered those few women on my classroom wall. The lives of those women, along with the men, have greatly enriched the culture of this nation. They provide a witness and a hope forged within the traditions and rhythms of African-American culture—a culture and a people who refuse to be discounted and devalued. Among those people, women such as Wells-Barnett emerge as a crucible for understanding the nature of leadership and prophetic voice within the African-American community and the African-American church. Her story, though unique, joins those of countless women and men who continue to live their faith and to challenge the nation to truly embody justice.

I

IDA B. WELLS-BARNETT: REGAL, INTOLERANT, IMPULSIVE

Born in 1862, most of the first three years of Ida B. Wells-Barnett's[1] life were spent in slavery in Holly Springs, Mississippi. She was the oldest child of Elizabeth and James Wells. James Wells, who was politically active during Reconstruction, exposed young Ida and the rest of his family to leading Black political figures such as Hiriam R. Revels and James Hill.[2] This initial period of Black participation in the public realm was dampened in 1875. In this thirteenth year of Wells' life, white Mississippians resorted to armed violence to drive the Republicans from power and to reestablish white hegemonic rule in the South. However, the irony of 1875 is that a federal civil rights act passed in this year outlawed segregation all over the country.

In the midst of this mixed but worsening climate, James Wells provided a comfortable home for his family. He was a carpenter and used his skills to buy a home and to send young Ida to Rust College.[3] Here Ida B. Wells progressed from the elementary department to the college department.

Her schools days ended tragically in 1878. Wells, at age sixteen, became the sole support for five brothers and sisters. A yellow fever epidemic killed her parents and one younger sister. Wells was able to support her siblings and herself by teaching in Memphis, Tennessee. Due to her status as a teacher, Wells became a part of the small emerging Black middle class in Memphis. She discovered her writing ability through her participation in a literary society which met weekly to sponsor literary exercises which included recitations, essays, and debates.

The literary society's meetings ended with the reading of the *Evening Star*, by its editor. Wells described this newspaper as a "spicy journal."[4] When the editor left Memphis to return to his previous job in Washington, D.C., Wells was elected to replace him. The paper grew in popularity. One of the men who came to hear it read aloud was the Reverend R.N. Countee, who published the weekly newspaper, the *Living Way.* He asked Wells to write for his paper and she accepted, using the pen name, Iola. In the format of letters, she observed the condition of the schools and churches and other general concerns of Blacks in Memphis.

Wells' career began in the 1880s, as Reconstruction came to a dramatic halt for Black people. Black voters were driven from the polls and Black lawmakers lost their seats in southern legislatures and in Congress. In 1883 the Supreme Court ruled the 1875 Civil Rights Act unconstitutional. The new laws barred Blacks from restaurants, parks, cemeteries and required railroads and steamboats to provide separate but equal accommodations for the two races. T. Thomas Fortune's response revealed the frustration of countless Black Americans as he described legalized discrimination on the railroads, in hotels, and in theaters:

> The colored people of the United States feel as if they had been baptized with ice water....One or two murders growing from this intolerable nuisance would break it up.[5]

Barely six months after the Fortune editorial, Wells boarded a train for the ten mile trip from Memphis to Woodstock to join her family. As was her custom, she seated herself in the ladies car. The conductor refused her ticket and ordered her into the smoking car with other Blacks. Wells refused to move and it took three men to pry her from her seat and throw her off the train when it stopped at the next station. As she tumbled down the stairs to the platform, white passengers stood up and applauded.

The same Supreme Court, which had ruled the 1875 Civil Rights Act unconstitutional, advised Blacks to apply to state courts for redress of maltreatment. Wells took this to heart, hired a lawyer, and sued the railroad for damages. She was awarded $500 in damages and the railroad appealed the decision. The case *Wells versus Chesapeake, Ohio and Southwestern Railroad* (1884) was the first case heard in the South after the demise of the Civil Rights Act. The city's leading newspaper, the *Memphis Daily Appeal,* ran the headline on Christmas Day, 1884: A DARKY DAMSEL OBTAINS A VERDICT FOR DAMAGES AGAINST THE CHESAPEAKE & OHIO RAILROAD.

One of her first published articles was a "write-up" of her suit for damages against the Chesapeake and Ohio Railroad for forcibly ejecting her from the train when she refused to ride in the smoking car designated for Black passengers only. In the article, she told Blacks to stand up for the rights granted to them in Reconstruction legislation.[6]

Wells was soon to find out that the retrenchment and repression process was much harder to conquer. The judge who originally awarded damages to Wells was a former union army soldier. The Supreme Court which heard the appeal was made up of southern men. Their ruling was in concert with the general mood of the South: "We think it is evident that the purpose of the defendant was to harass. Her persistence was not in good faith to obtain a comfortable seat for the short ride."[7]

The verdict was devastating to Wells. She placed her faith in the law and in justice but neither was served. Her cry of bitter disappointment, "O God is there no redress, no peace, no justice in this land for us?" reveals the depth of her disillusionment. Yet as she voiced her frustration, she appealed to God to "show us the way, even as Thou led the children of Israel out of bondage into the promised land."[8]

Late twentieth century readers may deem Wells naive. However as late as the 1880s, most Blacks believed that racial injustice was the work of the lowly white person and an aberration that could be challenged. African-Americans had faith in the system which allowed economic gains for many after the war and education for over a quarter million Blacks in more than 4,000 schools. The court decision prompted Wells to re-examine her expectations and to cast a critical eye on the events happening to and around Blacks.

Over time, Wells' articles in the *Living Way* were copied in other Black newspapers. Her fame as an honest and candid journalist grew and she received letters from Black editors across the country asking her to write for them. At an 1889 press convention, Lucy W. Smith wrote of Wells' ability to reach both men and women in her articles.[9] Smith credited Wells' touch with the political implications of the race question and her knowledge of household issues and concerns. Smith also considered Wells a role model for young writers.

By 1891, Wells was a regular correspondent for the *Detroit Plaindealer*, *Christian Index*, and *The People's Choice*. In addition, she was the editor of the "Home" department of *Our Women and Children*[10] and a regular contributor to *The New York Age*, *Indianapolis World*, *Gate City Press* (Missouri), *Little Rock Sun*, *American Baptist* (Kentucky), *Memphis Watchman*, *Chattanooga Justice*, and the *Fisk University Herald*.

In the midst of this notoriety, Wells lost her teaching job in 1891 after a particularly pointed article on the inequities of the Black schools in Memphis. Wells bought a one-third interest in the *Free Speech* and devoted her energies to making it a profit-making newspaper to support herself and her two new partners. Her efforts took her throughout the South. She found the position of Black people worsening and her editorials reflected her concern.

As Wells wrote, the racial climate in the South grew more tense. The number and frequency of white mobs lynching Black men, women, and children increased steadily. Memphis African-Americans never believed that the injustice of the lynch law would cast its shadow on their thriving community. This illusion was shattered by the 1892 lynching of Wells' dear and close friend, Thomas Moss. It also served to launch Wells into national and international prominence as she became a key leader in the anti-lynching crusade in this nation.

Wells viewed the anti-lynching struggle as a moral struggle. The Reverend Norman B. Wood, writing in 1897, described Wells in biblical terms as a modern Deborah "whose voice has been heard throughout England and the United States wherever it was safe for her to go, pleading as only she can plead for justice and fair treatment to be given her long-suffering and unhappy people."[11] Wood compared Wells to Lincoln and Grant but ends his description of Wells with a direct appeal to the prophet Isaiah of the Old Testament that she might "cry aloud, spare not, lift up thy voice like a trumpet, and show my people their transgressions and their sins."[12]

Wells was confident in the power of truth. She called on the reader to look at facts and persuade "all Christian and moral forces" to pass resolutions against lynching. In addition, she urged her readers to make southerners aware that businesses refused to invest capital in areas where mob violence ruled.[13] She did not allow the North to escape its responsibility in the anathema of lynching:

> Is not the North by its seeming acquiescence as responsible morally as the South is criminally for the awful lynching record of the past thirteen years?[14]

Wells noted that northern papers published, without question, southern press stories that Black men assaulted white women. However, northern newspapers refused her request and other requests by Blacks to print their responses and accounts of the horror and facts of lynching.

Wells' contribution to the anti-lynching campaign was crucial. She spoke out at a time when few voices challenged the horror and injustice of the lynch law. Her research, writing, and public speaking were designed to articulate the truth and to bring the facts before the public. She was convinced, that once the facts were known, the atrocity of lynching would be the antecedent of its demise.

Wells did not confine herself to agitating for the end of lynching. She organized the first colored woman's club in Illinois at the end of the controversial Chicago Exposition of 1893. This club is also referred to as the "mother of the woman's clubs" in Illinois.[15] The club met every Thursday to hear music and lectures, and to discuss current topics under Wells' leadership. One of the early projects of the club was to raise money to prosecute a police officer for killing an innocent colored man on the West Side of Chicago.

When Wells was in England in 1894, the club took out a charter and assumed the name of its absent president. Wells remained as president for five years until the demands of caring for two young children prompted her resignation. The club was instrumental in establishing the first Black orchestra in Chicago and opening the first kindergarten for Black children. It was also a charter member of the Cook County Women's Clubs, stopping the color line in clubs.[16]

12   Womanist Justice, Womanist Hope

In June of 1895, Wells married Ferdinand L. Barnett, a lawyer in Chicago. Together they parented five children.[17] She believed that marriage and motherhood signalled her retirement from public work. Her marriage caused protest by various social reform groups, including African-Americans who felt she had abandoned the struggle against lynching and other forms of injustice. She was enticed out of retirement by the Women's State Central Committee of the Republican Party which wanted her to travel Illinois on a speaking tour. They also promised to hire a nurse for her six-month old son.[18]

Now out of retirement, Wells-Barnett continued her tireless agitation for social change and civil rights. In a 1903 lecture entitled "The Colored Woman, Her Past, Present, and Future" delivered to the Political Equality League, Wells-Barnett noted "there was little employment for the Negro, and the average Negro scarcely exceeded the domestic scale."[19]   After the white listeners responded with expressions of sympathy, Wells-Barnett answered, "we ask only that the door of opportunity be opened to us."[20]

During the 1908 Springfield, Illinois Riot, Wells-Barnett organized the young men of her Bible class at Grace Presbyterian Church of Chicago into what evolved into the Negro Fellowship League.[21] The League established a Reading Room and Social Center for men and boys at 2830 South State Street. Wells-Barnett ran the League until 1920 when her health required an operation and a long confinement in the hospital and later in her home.

In 1909, Wells-Barnett led the fight against the reinstatement of Frank Davis as sheriff in Alexander County, Illinois. Davis allowed the lynching of a Black man in Cairo, Illinois. By law, this was official neglect of his duties. After investigating the incident in Cairo, Wells-Barnett brought out the facts of the case and, in what was characterized as a bitter fight, presented her case to Governor Charles Deneen. He subsequently refused to reinstate Sheriff Davis despite heavy political pressure on Davis' behalf.[22] Wells-Barnett was succinct in stating her conclusion of the effect of the case because "from that day until the present there has been no lynching in the state."[23]

Wells-Barnett was staunch in her mission. She used the lecture podium and newspaper articles to bring the injustices and outrage of bigotry before the public eye in an uncompromising and clear manner. Wells-Barnett was present for the founding of the National Association for the Advancement of Colored People (NAACP) in 1909. When she and other more militant African-Americans were not appointed to the Committee of Forty, who were to form the permanent organization, Wells-Barnett withdrew her time and interest from the organization. She was eventually added to the Committee, but had felt betrayed by W.E.B. DuBois. Without consulting Wells or any others present at the meeting, DuBois removed her name in favor of a representative from his Niagara Movement.[24]

In addition to these activities, Wells-Barnett was active in the women's suffrage movement. She formed the Alpha Suffrage Club, Illinois' first Black woman's suffrage organization, in 1914 when the Illinois legislature passed a law allowing women the vote in local elections.[25]

Wells-Barnett attacked discrimination wherever she found it. In 1915, she confronted President Woodrow Wilson for his tacit approval of segregation within his administration.[26] When African-American soldiers in Houston, Texas were provoked to violence against local citizens in August of 1917, Wells-Barnett vigorously protested the summary court martial and execution of the soldiers.[27] In the same year, she travelled to East St. Louis, Illinois to get the details of a riot that killed more than forty African-Americans.[28]

Wells-Barnett was in Chicago during its 1919 riots trying to set up a Protective Association and find out the facts of the situation for the investigation that would follow.[29] Later in the year, she travelled to the scene of a riot in Phillips County, Arkansas to gather information needed for the release of seven Black prisoners who were called "Black revolutionists."[30]

Wells-Barnett did not slow her pace. She was a candidate for the state senate in 1929. She lost the campaign in which she ran as an independent. With her usual candor, Wells noted "the independent vote is weak, unorganized and its workers purchasable."[31] When she died of uremia poisoning on March 25, 1931, the obituary in the *Chicago Defender* captured the essence of Wells-Barnett as a woman who was "elegant, striking, and always well groomed,...regal though somewhat intolerant and impulsive."[32]

14   Womanist Justice, Womanist Hope

NOTES

[1] Throughout the book, I refer to Ida B. Wells-Barnett as "Wells" when referring to her before her marriage to Ferdinand Barnett and when she uses this as her last name in her articles and essays. I will refer to her as "Wells-Barnett" for the period spanning her marriage. Wells-Barnett was not consistent about which last name she used in her articles and essays after her marriage. I have chosen not to drop "Barnett" for she was one of the earliest African-American women to hyphenate her last name. This early model of black feminism should not be lost.

[2] Dorothy Sterling, *Black Foremothers: Three Lives* (Old Westbury, New York: The Feminist Press, 1979), 64-65. Revels was the first African-American United States senator. In 1874, Revels moved to Holly Springs to become a presiding elder in the Methodist Episcopal Church. Also in 1874, Hill, who was a close Wells family friend and ex-slave, became Mississippi's secretary of state.

[3] Ibid., 65. W. Augustus Low and Virgil A. Clift, ed., *Encyclopedia of Black America* (New York: McGraw Hill, 1981; reprint, New York: Da Capo Press, 1981), 737. Rust College, at Holly Springs, Mississippi, was founded in 1866 by the Methodist Episcopal Church, North. Rust College is named for Richard Rust, a white anti-slavery advocate who was active in the Freedmen's Aid Society. Its early mission was to teach ex-slaves how to read and write. In later years it offered courses in agricultural and domestic sciences. Rust made it possible for many of its students to qualify for predominately white colleges.

[4] Ida B. Wells, *Crusade for Justice: The Autobiography of Ida B. Wells*, ed. Alfreda Duster (Chicago: University of Chicago Press, 1970), 23.

[5] Sterling, 71-72.

[6] Paula Giddings, *When and Where I Enter: The Impact of Black Women on Race and Sex in America* (New York: William Morrow and Company, 1984), 23.

[7] Sterling, 76-77. Source not given.

[8] Wells, Diary, 11 April 1887, Special Collections, Joseph Regenstein Library, University of Chicago, Chicago.

[9] I. Garland Penn, *The Afro-American Press, and its Editors* (Springfield, Massachusetts: Willey and Co. Publishers, 1891), 408.

[10] Ibid., 407-408.

[11] The Reverend Norman B. Wood, *The White Side of a Black Subject* (Chicago: American Publishing House, 1897), 381.

[12] Ibid.

[13] Herbert Shapiro, *White Violence and Black Response: From Reconstruction to Montgomery* (Amherst: The University of Massachusetts Press, 1988), 57.

[14]Arna Bontemps and Jack Conroy, *They Seek A City* (Garden City, NY: Doubleday, Doran and Co., Inc., 1945), 80-81.

[15]Elizabeth Lindsay Davis, ed., *The Story of the Illinois Federation of Colored Women's Clubs* (n.p., 1922), 26.

[16]Ibid., 27. See also Bontemps and Conroy, 79.

[17]The children's names in order of birth are Ferdinand, Charles, Herman, Ida, and Alfreda.

[18]Wells, *Crusade*, 243-44.

[19]Bontemps and Conroy, 81.

[20]Ibid.

[21]Wells, *Crusade*, 298-300.

[22]Ibid., 310-319.

[23]Ibid., 319.

[24]Ibid., 323-27. Sterling, 105.

[25]Wells, *Crusade*, 345-47. Sterling, 109.

[26]Ibid., 375-76.

[27]Ibid., 367-70.

[28]Ibid., 383-95.

[29]Ibid., 405-7.

[30]Ibid., 397-404.

[31]Sterling, 116. No source given.

[32]Bontemps and Conroy, 82.

II

THE USE OF BIOGRAPHY AND AUTOBIOGRAPHY TO RECONSTRUCT THE SOCIAL AND MORAL PERSPECTIVES OF AFRICAN-AMERICAN WOMEN

Biography and autobiography are the key tools used in this thesis to explore both the social and cultural milieu of the period between 1892 to 1931 for African-Americans and the life and work of Ida B. Wells-Barnett. Autobiography and biography, in particular, help reconstruct a worldview previously lost or obscured. This study uses as research tools the autobiography of Wells-Barnett, *Crusade for Justice*, and biographies of her. In addition, the autobiographical writings of her contemporaries and their biographies comprise a major section of the research data.

These resources are used in conjunction with Wells-Barnett's essays, speeches, newspaper articles, and minutes from the various women's clubs with which she was affiliated. The minutes of organizations like the National Association for the Advancement of Colored People (NAACP), letters, church journals, and a host of secondary sources also help enrich the worldview of this period.

The researcher must guard against a natural tendency to measure the past by the yardstick of contemporary knowledge and mores. Historical research on the subject of biography or autobiography requires a safeguard against importing contemporary attitudes and values through which the past becomes a distorted reflection of the present.

Biography

Biography is a genre that can reveal aspects of the past through the life of a person or institution. Biography is not the study of the past, rather it is the study of material that has survived and been uncovered from the past. It is valuable historical material when the researcher remains aware that in using biography, the particular view of the subject dominates the enterprise. However, it should not consume the context nor the era of which the figure is a representative. Biography provides a helpful entrance into periods and/or peoples who have not been examined closely.

James Olney's essay, "Some Versions of Memory/Some Versions of *Bios*: The Ontology of Autobiography" [1] offers a more precise definition for *bios*—"the course of life, a lifetime." Although the essay concentrates on autobiography, Olney provides a useful insight into the nature of biography. He notes that *bios* is the historical course of life and that it is a process and not a stable entity. The researcher who uses biography as a method must remain mindful of the nature of a life as process. Its fluctuations and its changing nature can be used as an entre to an understanding of the institutions and/or movements of which the subject of the biography may have been a part of or representative.

The life of Booker T. Washington is an illustration. Washington's life story can be used to understand the philosophy and operations of the Tuskegee machine as well as the personal philosophy of Washington. Washington was such an integral part of the Tuskegee machine that one could not give an accurate historical account of the stratagems of the Tuskegee machine without an in-depth look at the life and actions of Washington.

The disadvantages of using biography as a method are evident from this example. In concentrating on a single life, there is the danger that a false perspective of the particular period may emerge. This problem is not confined to biography, but is germane to all methods of historical inquiry. Another disadvantage is that the background of the individual could become unfocused and distorted. Biography has a two-fold purpose: the recovery of the individual or institution, and the illumination of the era in which that person or institution is a representative. The subject must be recovered in such a way that it does not become larger than the times of which it is a member. Neither the subject nor the era can be explored with great integrity without a constant dialogue between the two. Both function to shape each other.

The advantages of using biography as a method outweighs the disadvantages. Biography, the *bios*, allows the researcher to narrow the field of study to manageable dimensions. No one can handle all of the surviving evidence. This is born out by the various fields of historical inquiry: constitutional, economic, social, military, African-American, women, etc. Biography becomes another lens through which to understand a period. It allows the researcher to examine some of the philosophical as well as emotional underpinnings of an era. The subject can become a case study of the era and of its participants.

In using biography, a mass of surviving evidence must be available, including primary source material from the subject. Diaries, letters, speeches, and records from organizations in which that person was involved, are examples. The researcher can then examine how the subject viewed his or her world. Washington's records of his activities are illustrative of this. It is a recovery of historical value to learn that Washington did in fact control the media in an authoritarian and dictatorial manner. Contemporary Americans are allowed a larger perspective on Washington and his motivations and methods through the opening of his personal papers for research/examination. This material must be handled with care. It may be an excellent record of what the person believed when he or she wrote, but not accurate evidence about the past. The researcher must be careful in handling this material to develop skills which enable him or her to discern its nature: was it intended to be a record for posterity or was it a reflection or speculation on the situation in which the subject found him or herself?

Another source for the researcher is the body of material from people who knew the subject. This material shows how the larger world viewed the individual. Insights from spouse(s), friends, colleagues can help broaden the picture of the individual being studied as well as help expand the view of the times he or she represents. The subject of the biography should never be the only voice to which the researcher listens.

When placed within the particular context of African-American history, this discussion must take into consideration the dynamics of oppression peculiar to the cultural miasma of the United States. If the researcher is Black and approaches the study of African-American history from a self-conscious perspective, the researcher must hold this dynamic in careful tension. Within this enterprise is an overt element of subjectivity. The study of African-American history becomes the conscious exercise of examining the surviving evidence—some of which has been intentionally omitted, masked, and devalued.

The "truth" must be told with integrity in using biography as a method for Black historical recovery. This entails an intentional method of uncovering as much of the remnants of the historical epoch as possible. The researcher must take care to uncover the individual's reflections as well as the reflections of those around him or her. It is poor scholarship to use the biographical method to create larger than life (and inaccurate and untruthful) figures no matter how racist or oppressive history has been as a discipline. Little is served in "creating" an historical figure. The task of using biography must be to examine the surviving evidence and help fill out the actors and institutions which influenced the events and character of society.

Biography and autobiography can provide the critical tools for a fuller recovery of history. These genres/disciplines enable the researcher to expand his or her vision of society in a historical epoch. He or she can concentrate on individuals or events.   In using biography, the researcher is provided with one type of lens to enter a culture if not a society. Autobiography provides a similar lens. Both genres must be used carefully to expand the worldview of the subject and to place that worldview in its cultural and social context.

Autobiography

Autobiography, according to Olney, has been utilized by thinkers in other disciplines to help define and organize disciplines

such as American Studies, Black Studies, and Women's Studies.[2] He
states that the researchers in these fields claim that

> autobiography—the story of a distinctive culture written in
> individual characters from within—offers a privileged access to an
> experience...that no other variety of writing can offer.[3]

He further states that autobiography is a direct and faithful way to
transmit the experience and thoughts of a people. Hence, it is used
by groups seeking to recover history that has been lost or ignored.
In its own way, autobiography helps to democratize history. For
groups like African-Americans, the bulk of their history has been
preserved in autobiographies, as well as in oral history.

Autobiography blends history and literature. It is the dialectic
between what the writer wishes to become and what society has
determined that person to be. The autobiographer examines,
interprets, and creates the importance of his or her life in the context
of a particular historical period. Autobiography not only expands
history, it can influence history by providing a model for later
generations. Above all, autobiography asserts that human life has or
can have meaning. It provides evidence that our actions are worth
being remembered. We are agents of time and circumstances. We
are not only determined by the flow of events, but we can affect that
same flow through our act of being.

Georges Gusdorf recognizes that writing an autobiography
takes place within history. The writer examines the differences and
similarities of his or her experience from that of society as a whole or
from that of a narrow gender, racial, or class grouping. The
autobiographer believes that it is useful and valuable to fix his or her
image. Gusdorf believes that inherent in autobiography is a curiosity
about the self and the destiny of the self.[4]

History, memory, and the life of the writer are in constant
interaction. Olney states "...it is memory that reaches tentacles out
into each of these three different 'times'—the time now, the time
then, and the time of an individual's historical context."[5] This
constant weaving of time, or history, helps to place autobiography
into the genre of literature. The writer uses his or her imagination to

a certain extent, as he or she attempts to remember and recover, the past events of her or his life.

AFRICAN-AMERICAN AUTOBIOGRAPHY

C.E.E. Bigsby offers another way to view autobiography. For him, autobiography is a series of transformations.[6] It offers a retrospective self that has control over his or her experience, orders history, and presents a paradigm of the private acquisition of authority over events. Black autobiography becomes what Bigsby terms a "handbook on life." It is a testament to the fact that an individual can function in the midst of chaos and prevail over the chaos.[7] Bigsby terms autobiography as a process of reconstructing the past out of the psychological needs of the present.[8]   John Blassingame is more biting in his assessment. He views Black autobiography as "a counterweight to the white historian's caricature of black life..."[9]

Through the process of interaction with history, the individual seeks to establish identity. This process reveals the psychological needs that Bigsby refers to in Black autobiography. He believes that consciousness is a necessary element of identity and is a means of "confirming a significance to experience" beyond the simple level of sequential event.[10]   The act of remembering implies consciousness on the part of the writer. He or she does not give an objective recounting of a life, but through the process of remembering, the writer attempts to identify and define who she or he is in the present.

Most of the white western male concept of "self" presented in autobiography is that of the individual forging a career, reputation, business, and family out of the raw materials around him. It is a manual on how to achieve wealth, power, and fame. The exceptions to this are spiritual journals. However spiritual journals and standard autobiographies from white men depict the self singularly mastering society.

Autobiographies can take a linear or cyclical approach. Black autobiography spins off a circle and is carried by what Roger Rosenblatt calls the "centrifugal force of life."[11]   Rosenblatt believes that the force of this life leads to an anticipated state of grace. The Black autobiography anticipates a future that is not solely possessed by the writer, but is possessed by African-Americans collectively, and vested in national ideals which are more important than an individual life. The self, in Black autobiography, is a member of an oppressed group with ties and responsibilities to the members of that group. Autobiography is one way in which African-Americans have been able to assert their right to live and to grow. Political awareness, empathy for suffering, the ability to break down the dualism of "I" and "You", knowledge of oppression and the discovery of coping mechanisms, shared triumph, and communal responsibility are key elements in Black autobiography.

Slave Narrative

The slave narrative reached its peak in the twenty or so years before the fall of slavery, when the peculiar institution was most repressive. The slave narrative had two aims: to prove that the slave was a person and to convince the largely white audience of the truths of the narrative being told by the narrator.[12] The moral assumptions underlying most slave narratives were temperance, honesty, worship of God and Christ, and respect for hard work. Black narrators tried to justify to their white audience why they had to lie and steal in order to survive. This indicates that these writers defined themselves by how they expected to be judged by whites.

The slave narrative was treated with skepticism and resistance unlike other types of autobiography. The slave narrator assumed a literate audience, but first had to prove his or her intelligence before explaining what benefit freedom would have to a race of people who were considered subhuman and inferior. The nineteenth century white audience of slave narratives did not read them to discover more about the person or individual writing the narrative. The white audience read the narratives to gain a first-hand look at slavery. Hence, slave narratives typically made a blatant appeal to white pity and piety. The object was to dismantle the institution of slavery.

The most "trustworthy" slave narrative was one in which the writer hid him or herself behind the universally accepted facts about slavery.[13] The slave narrative was mimetism according to William

Andrews. The self was placed on the periphery instead of being the center of attention. The effect was that the narrator looked into his or her life to transcribe it rather than interpret it.[14] The slave or ex-slave became an odd brand of participant-observer of his or her own life.

The self identity that was revealed in the narrative came from the narrator's desire for freedom. The act of resistance was the basis of selfhood. The opinions, goals, politics, dreams, and accomplishments of the narrator resulted from the act of resisting the oppression of slavery. The most common means of dealing with the conditions imposed upon the slave was guile.[15] Irony and satire were also employed. However, education was vital to self-definition and could provide an entre into a world other than the one given to the slave by the slaveholder. Learning to read and write was considered revolutionary and a step toward freedom. Slave narratives reveal that literacy was not granted freely by the slaveholder, but had to be seized by rebellious slaves.

The struggle for abolition was an extension of the slaves' individual quests for freedom. As in other periods of Black autobiography, the constructed identity of the slave was a reflection of race and class oppression. The slave narrator attempted to throw off the ideology of the oppressor through the retelling of his or her life. The person tried to neutralize any guilt he or she might have about their resistance to the slave system. Their goals were to live as free persons and to acquire the knowledge and skills that could make that possible. Also, the narrator wanted to build pride and self confidence as the he or she escaped the master's control.

Postbellum African-American Autobiography

Rosenblatt sees four patterns within postbellum Black autobiography.[16] The first is the accomodationist represented by William Pickens' *Bursting Bonds*. Second are the stories of the talented tenth, of which *A Colored Woman in a White World* by Mary Church Terrell is representative. The third are those from the Harlem Renaissance, such as Zora Neale Hurston's *Dust Tracks on the Road*. Last is the literature of direct protest and social comment represented by W.E.B. DuBois' *Dusk of Dawn*. Rosenblatt believes that the polemics are similar in each genre. The use of argument to refute errors is consistent, but Rosenblatt sees no single orthodoxy in Black autobiography. The consistent theme is the desire to live as one chooses as far as possible. Inherent in this theme is a tacit or explicit criticism of the external conditions placed on Blacks that limited freedom of choice or nonexistence. Hence, there is a high degree of subjectivity in the Black autobiography. A protest against social norms is coupled with a depiction of the victimization of the narrator.

The slave narrative adapted the literary forms and traditions of white American culture. The Black postbellum autobiography follows no single literary structure. The question of how to resist becomes more complex in the increasingly industrialized society. The writers of this period begin with the assertion that blackness is the starting point for creating a free self. The enemy is no longer the institution of slavery. Now it is institutional racism. The values of education, work, resistance, and group loyalty are carried forward by these writers from the slave narratives. Religion has a much weaker influence upon these authors, but Christian assumptions are embedded in the rhetoric of several writers from this period.

The authors are proud of their blackness, but continue to struggle with the image of Black people portrayed by white writers, politicians, ministers—white society. The white audience of the slave narrators is now the emerging white capitalist class. This audience could manipulate the reception of Black writing to reinforce its power. An excellent illustration is the suppression of the writings of W.E.B. DuBois. His Pan-Africanism, and his radical critique of white power structures lost out to Booker T. Washington's blatant accomodationist stance that blamed Blacks for their condition and absolved whites of any blame in large measure.

The social basis of the Black autobiography remained the same as that of the slave narratives. Racial and class oppression, voting rights, restrictions on movement, the lack of legal redress, slavery-like working conditions, and white violence were a continuing concern. However, where the slave narratives dealt with these concerns on the level of politics and religion, the Black autobiography dealt with them on the level of culture. Their chief concern was to resolve the identity crisis of Black people and the Black individual.

In the contemporary framework, Andrews believes that Black autobiography redefines freedom as the power to integrate the unknown and known within the self.[17] This can be a dangerous enterprise for an African-American to undertake. In attempting to rid oneself of the doubleconsciousness inherent in Black existence, the autobiographer has the power to integrate the "two warring ideals."[18] He or she asserts the right to a clearly defined self and refuses to allow others, either within or outside the community, to define who the writer is. It is the revolutionary act of defining the self.

Andrews asserts that writing an autobiography implies that one takes his or her life seriously enough to find in it a significance that makes reconstructing it valuable to others. He sees the mode of Black autobiographical discourse to be two-fold.[19] First, it validates its own claims to reality and its author's claim to identity. Second, it authenticates the story and its author by documenting both according to their fidelity to the facts of human nature and experience which, historically, whites have assumed to be true. Rosenblatt's term "mirror principle"[20] is helpful to describe how Black writing shows Black people continually opposing the white society about them. Through autobiography, the Black writer demands that the white social and cultural structure reckon with the reality of Black life rather than the image white society holds of Black life. The search for identity ends with the Black autobiographer discarding the mask he or she wore to survive in the midst of oppression. The act of revealing who he or she is demonstrates selfhood and freedom.

According to Andrews, Black autobiography mediates between the historical, the rhetorical, and the factual within the discursive framework of the narrative patterns of life.[21] The definition of the *autos* is the definition of the self. For the Black autobiographer, this definition is representative of the supreme act of freedom and the right of self-definition.

African-American historians, as well as those seeking to recover Black history in the U.S., have concentrated on the testimonies of slaves and ex-slaves concerning their lives during slavery.

Antebellum Black existence is characterized as one under monolithic oppression. The slave narrative is made synonymous with early African-American autobiography. The slave becomes the archetypical autobiographer. However, this is at the expense of Black spiritual autobiographies which appeared in the late 1700s and early 1800s. These spiritual autobiographies predate the great body of slave narratives.[22]

WOMEN'S AUTOBIOGRAPHY

What then of the autobiography of Black women in these time periods? The recovery of women's personal narratives focuses on the restrictions that women encountered in the nineteenth century and dwells on the auction block or the pedestal. Both are seen as similar in form and function—the repression of women. This dynamic is certainly true, but a monolithic experience is presented as universal for women, regardless of color. When the autobiographies of Black women are carefully considered, a larger worldview is apparent. Writings such as Jarena Lee's are from the tradition of spiritual autobiography. Nancy Prince's work belongs to the genre of travel literature and Harriet Wilson's *Our Nig* is in the category of autobiographical fiction.[23] This variety in autobiography shows that Black women and men lived in a spectrum of classes and geographies and challenges the notion of a monolithic slave experience.

African-American Women's Slave Narrative

Deborah Gray White's *Ar'n't I a Woman* attempts to recover a description of the status of women slave women considered ideal.[24] White does not assume that Black slave women sought the ideal of the pedestal bestowed on white women of the South. She recounts the story of Black women who depended on themselves for protection against sexual attacks. Marriage offered them no security or protection. White conveys the battle of wits slaves and masters engaged in, as well as the hard labor Black slave women were forced to perform.

White's questions are intriguing and the answers to the questions she poses provide clues to the history of Black family and community life.

> American white women were expected to be passive because they were female. But black women had to be submissive because they were black and slaves. This made a difference in the sex roles of black and white women, as well as in the expectations that their respective societies had on them, but how? Surely biological and social motherhood had different implications for slave women than it did for white women. Did being a wife and mother anchor slave women to the position of inferiority in slave society as it did white women in American society at large? How did slave women maintain a sense of worth and what standards did they use to judge their own conduct?[25]

White believes that the reason few scholars have dealt with these questions lies in how the issues of slavery were defined and in the difficulty of finding source material. She credits Stanley Elkins' *Slavery, A Problem in American Institutional and Intellectual Life* as having a profound effect on the research and writing about slavery. His thesis of the "closed" nature of slavery spawned much needed research, but White believes that his description had more to do with male slavery than female.[26]

She also sees problems with Elkins' discussion of the Middle Passage in which he insisted that Blacks travelled in the holds of slave ships. This is true for Black men, but Black women made the journey on the quarter and half decks.[27] Elkins continues to omit women in his discussion of Latin American slavery and does not mention Harriet Tubman in his discussion of those who resisted slavery actively. White emphasizes again and again the exclusion of Black women in favor of Elkins' Sambo thesis.

White catalogs the various books that followed in Elkins' wake, each emphasizing the masculine role of Black slave men and imposing the Victorian model of domesticity and maternity on Black female slaves.[28] In searching for the ideal which Black slave women sought for themselves, White argues that slave women were not submissive, subordinate, or prudish and were not expected to be so.[29] This tradition is echoed by such contemporary Black women writers as Alice Walker, who states that her tradition has assumed that she is capable.[30] White also argues that mutual respect characterized the relationship between slave men and women. This position has been argued by historians such as Karen Lebsock in her work, *The Free Women of Petersburg*[31].

To test her assertions, White relies on inference and the Works Projects Administration's interviews with female ex-slaves. She terms them "the riches, indeed almost the only Black female source dealing with female slavery."[32] She also uses the research of others and the traditional sources of the social historian to recover the past: plantation records, traveler's accounts, newspapers, slaveowner letters and diaries, and pro and anti-slavery pamphlets. Her approach is cross-cultural, as she compares slave women to other women who were not slaves, but members of the preindustrial Black agricultural society.

White uses the words of Black men and women ex-slaves to bring into focus the nature of Black women's experience of slavery. Former male slaves and fugitive male slaves regarded the lot of Black slave women as one of dehumanization. Williamson Pease noted that "Women who do outdoor work are used as bad as men" and Green Wilbanks spoke of his Grandma Rose who "was some worker, a regular man-woman."[33] But White doubts that slave women on large plantations with sizable females populations lost their female identity. With constant interaction among women, it is more likely, in White's view, that slave women developed a female culture among themselves. Sylvia King, a slave on a Texas plantation, noted that women sewed together in the spinning and weaving cabins. On a South Carolina plantation, "old women and women bearin' chillun not yet born did cardin' wid hand-cards..." and women passed on the domestic skills they had learned "how to make clothes for the family...knit coarse socks and stockins."[34]

White is unable to determine the role which slave women played in shaping their domestic work. Frances Willingham noted that "woman's cleant up deir houses atter dey et, and den washed and got up early next mornin' to put de clothes out to dry." and another reported that "Those who were not successful in completing this work [spin one cut a night] were punished the next morning."[35]

White postulates that the only saving grace to this constant work was that women were able to interact with one another.

Health care was another means of bonding. White notes that the pregnant female slave could usually depend on her peers during delivery and recovery. Slave women depended on "doctor women" not only for pregnancy and delivery, but for a variety of ailments. Slave women resorted to abortion to prevent more Blacks from entering slavery. It is not clear to what degree and frequency women used abortion. The guilt resulting from these practices is evident in the words of Mollie when she first embraced Christianity:

> I was carried to the gates of hell and the devil pulled out a book showing me the things which I had committed and that they were all true. My life as a midwife was shown to me and I have certainly felt sorry for all the things I did, after I was convert-ed.[36]

Older women and women who were so assigned, took care of the children when mothers were busy with their chores. White reports that the reflections of many indicate that no child was ever truly motherless, even in the face of the slave auction or death. "Aunt Viney...had a big old horn what she blowed when it was time for us to eat, and us knowed better dan to git so fur off us couldn't hear dat horn, for Aunt Viney would sho' tear us up."[37] A few women distinguished themselves as work gang leaders. Men usually occupied positions of leadership—overseers, managers, foremen, and drivers. Women did have a measure of authority over the work on some plantations. White cites Louis Hughes observation that each plantation had a "forewoman who...had charge of the female slaves and also the boys and girls from twelve to sixteen years of age, and all the old people that was feeble."[38] Another Mississippi slave reported that his master's Osceola plantation had a "colored woman as foreman."[39]

White uses ex-slave testimony to illuminate the pecking order that existed among slave women. In some cases, the leadership of certain women disrupted plantation life. She makes note of the prophetess Sinda who was able to stop work on Butler Island in Georgia with her prediction that the world would come to an end on a certain day. Other narrators relate the laments of people such as

Bennet H. Barrow who knew that Big Lucy had more control over his female slaves than he did: "Anica, Center, Cook Jane, the better you treat them the worse they are. Big Lucy the Leader, corrupts every young negro in her power."[40]

White makes a compelling case for the stability of female relationships. Given the context of slavery, she believes that it was easier for slave women to establish stable relationships with one another than with slave men. White cites Marth Goodson's interviews with ex-slaves which revealed slaveowners were least likely to separate mothers and daughters.[41]

As White explores the various ways that the pecking order was upheld among slave women, she uses slave and ex-slave narrative to enlarge the worldview of the Black slave woman. She ends her discussion noting the dependency and cooperation network which existed among these women. On the Sea Islands during the Civil War, sick women relied on their peers to help them through illness and pregnancy, "the tasks of the lying-in women are taken care of my sisters and other friends in the absence of their husbands."[42] Again women in Port Royal cared for pregnant women regardless of their marital status. The missionary Elizabeth Hyde Botume noted the plight of an unmarried woman named Cumber, "...their readiness to help the poor erring girl made me ashamed."[43]

White's work is a fine example of the use of autobiography to enhance the understanding of the real lives of Black women in slavery. Her use of narratives shows many of the features of the slave narrative mentioned previously. One senses that the slave, but more so the ex-slave, sought to tell the story of slavery as she knew it. Unlike the strict slave narrative, these interviewees did not have to prove the abolitionist case. Freedom had been effected and now these women and men were free to tell the story of their lives.

White's use of narrative, interview, and secondary sources is a splendid blend of these forms to recover the lives of Black women during slavery. She takes care to read no more into the first person account than what is readily apparent. However, she does use imagination to draw inferences on the nature of the material she is examining.

Work with narrative on the level of White's contribution helps frame the use of autobiography by African-American women.

White's subjects were largely unaware that they would one day be the source of information and data for researchers seeking to uncover Black women's lives. In contrast, the late nineteenth century Black woman who sat down to record her story was fully aware of the need to chronicle history for future generations.

Postbellum African-American Women's Autobiographies

An interesting debate between Estelle Jelinek and James Cox helps illuminate the unique genre of African-American women's autobiographies. Cox maintains that the history of America and the history of autobiography developed together with the greatest periods of productivity in autobiography corresponding to the important events in United States history.[44] Jelinek counters this assertion by noting that such periods of increased diary writing are male specific. She suggests that events like the American Revolution, the Gold Rush, the Civil War show a decrease in women's autobiographical production.[45]

Jelinek also takes exception to the consensus among critics that good autobiography focuses not only on the author, but also reveals a connectedness to the rest of society as a mirror of the era. For her, women's autobiographies rarely mirror the era. Instead they emphasize the personal lives of women. She believes that women's stories reveal a "self-consciousness and a need to sift through their lives for explanation and understanding."[46] Jelinek finds that women often try to convince the reader of their self-worth and develop an authentic self-image. She finds that instead of glowing narratives, women tend to write in a straightforward and objective style.

Jelinek's observations partially describe African-American women's autobiographies. The straightforward style is evident, but little else is germane. Elizabeth Schultz brings this point to the fore. Schultz makes a distinction between what she terms the testimonial mode versus the blues mode in Black autobiography.[47] An external community is assumed and the writers also seeks to create community through shared experiences. Schultz does agree with Jelinek at the point of self-discovery, but self-discovery is done within the context of community. For Schultz, Black women writers did not draw distinctions between the individual and the community. Schultz finds that personal voice is subsumed to minimize self and maximize themes. Intimate personal history is omitted and lengthy documents or newspaper accounts are included to prove objectivity and historicity.[48] Further, Black writers shift chronology so that early events can be contemplated through the filter of later events.

Regina Blackburn expands Schultz's work. She notes that African-American women's autobiographies communicate to the world what both the Black and white world have done to them.[49] She goes on to note that as Black women first look at themselves as individuals, "then as individuals within the Black community, and finally within the general society, [they] determine what they do with their lives, how they look at life, what they demand of life, and perhaps, most important, what they demand of themselves."[50]

Blackburn notes three emerging themes: identity, assigning value to the self, and the double jeopardy of being Black and female. Hence, there is not one voice spoken in the various autobiographies written by Black women. Some writers focus on personal experiences rather than the larger society. Other writers feel weak and powerless. Still others are determined to make a difference or die trying. In short, Blackburn believes that African-American women autobiographers seek to define themselves to repair the damage done by other women and men, white and Black.[51]

The Autobiography of Ida B. Wells-Barnett

Ida B. Wells-Barnett's autobiography, *Crusade for Justice*, is representative of the various streams which embody the tradition of Black women's autobiographies.[52] Her writing was tied intimately to life in the community of African-Americans in the United States during the late nineteenth and early twentieth centuries. Wells-Barnett decided to write her historical memoir after a young Black woman attending a vesper service described her as having the traits of Joan of Arc. But the young woman could not explain why she felt this connection between the two women.[53] Wells-Barnett states:

...I realized that one reason she did not know was because the
happenings about which she inquired took place before she was
born. Another was that there was no record from which she
could inform herself. I then promised to set it down in writing so
those of her generation could know how the agitation against the
lynching evil began,...It is therefore for the young people who
have so little of our race's history recorded that I am for the first
time in my life writing about myself. I am all the more constrained to do this because there is such a lack of authentic race
history of Reconstruction times written by the Negro himself.[54]

Wells-Barnett wrote to preserve the history of African-
Americans from Reconstruction to the late 1920s. She wrote because
the Black youth of the 1920s had no record of the history and
struggles of their foreparents. There were no records of the period
immediately after the Civil War, of Black disenfranchisement, or of
lynching written from the African-American perspective. Wells-
Barnett understood the importance of an accurate written record by
an African-American for future generations of African-Americans
in United States society. She did not want the bravery of the Black
men and women who fought to gain due rights for themselves and
for future generations to be lost, forgotten, or ignored.

Although Schultz suggests that personal voice is subsumed to
minimize self and maximize themes, the character and self of Wells-
Barnett is vibrant in the pages of her autobiography. She remains
true to the general format of postbellum Black women's autobiography, for the reader gets few insights into the intimate, personal
history of Wells-Barnett.[55] However, the reader is treated to a full
range of her joys and disappointments with herself and those persons
and events that made up her public world. Her anguish and outrage
at lynching are painted in clear, broad strokes.[56] Her deep commitment to motherhood is articulate and given in her characteristic
straightforward style.[57] Her disappointment in other African-
Americans who fail to agitate and work for the betterment of the
African-American community is stated in stark language.[58]

Yet the work and struggle for racial uplift and dignity by
Wells-Barnett and other African-Americans remains the focus of her
autobiography. The reader is given only glimpses of personal
relationships. When Wells-Barnett speaks of her relationships with

her children, it is to illustrate her life of divided duty and to point to
the necessity of moral womanhood. Her tone is one of moral
instruction rather than personal reflection.[59] Her marriage to
Ferdinand Barnett is given three pages, a considerable portion being
the newspaper account of the wedding ceremony. Her description of
the wedding and marriage serves as the prologue for the chapter's
longer discussion of the negative reaction her marriage caused among
social activists and the launching of the Black woman's club
movement.[60] As she writes, Wells-Barnett's story is not only her
own, but the story of her times.[61]

Wells-Barnett's autobiography makes liberal use of lengthy
documents and newspaper accounts to provide the historical tenor.
In addition to using the newspaper account of her wedding, she
draws upon verbatim newspaper articles to describe her clash with
Frances Willard of the Women's Christian Temperance Union in the
1890s and to illustrate the letters and interviews both women gave to
the British press. She also uses verbatim newspaper articles to
describe the negative response made by some ministers to her work.
Whenever Wells-Barnett uses press clippings, she is adept at giving
the context and an analysis of the events. It is clear that she seeks to
provide some measure of objectivity and historicity for the reader.

Throughout her autobiography, Wells-Barnett wonders at the
injustices done to her by both African-American and white society.[62] She does not, however, engage in the introspective work that
Blackburn suggests. Wells-Barnett prefers to remain in the public
realm so that the "facts of race history which only the participants
can give"[63] are presented. Her lack of introspection is disappoint-
ing, but the personal view she provides of the events in which she
participated and which she shaped give the reader a rich lens to view
the nature of social agitation and protest by African-Americans in
the late nineteenth and early twentieth century.

Wells-Barnett founded a "legitimate black feminism" through
her work which addressed the twin concerns of Black uplift and
women's rights.[64] She was a woman of her times and a shaper of
events. She espoused an evangelical piety which was forged within
the Black Church and was molded by a strong sense of morality and
personal dignity as a woman. Her autobiography, a conscious
attempt to reconstruct and redeem the history of African-Americans

for future generations, is an excellent resource for relaying her social and moral perspectives.

The autobiography of Wells-Barnett and the other biographical materials used here are not employed to construct a biography of her. Rather, biography is used as a method to discern the social and moral perspectives of Ida B. Wells-Barnett. Her life story illuminates her writings and provides the foundation for an analysis of her work, writing, life, and her ability to effect social change and moral uplift for African-Americans and for the nation. Like any African-American woman of her era, however, the writings and social reform work of Ida B. Wells-Barnett cannot be fully appreciated without placing her in her historical contexts.

NOTES

[1] James Olney, "Some Versions of Memory/Some Versions of Bios: The Ontology of Autobiography," in *Autobiography: Essays Theoretical and Critical*, ed. James Olney (Princeton: Princeton University Press, 1980), 236-267.

[2] Olney, "Autobiography and the Cultural Moment," in *Autobiography*, 13.

[3] Ibid.

[4] Georges Gusdorf, "Conditions and Limits of Autobiography" in *Autobiography*, 30-31.

[5] Olney, "Autobiography and the Cultural Moment," 19.

[6] C.E.E. Bigsby, *The Second Black Renaissance: Essays in Black Literature* (Westport: Greenwood Press, 1980), 183.

[7] Ibid.

[8] Ibid., 187.

[9] Joanne Margaret Braxton, "Autobiography by Black American Women: A Tradition Within a Tradition" (PhD diss., Yale University, 1984), 170.

[10] Ibid.

[11] Roger Rosenblatt, "Black Autobiography: Life as the Death Weapon," in *Autobiography*, 179.

[12] William L. Andrews, *To Tell a Free Story: The First Century of Afro-American Autobiography, 1760-1865* (Urbana: University of Illinois Press, 1986), 1.

[13] Andrews, *Free Story*, 6.

[14] Ibid.

[15] Stephen Butterfield, *Black Autobiography in America* (Amherst: University of Massachusetts Press, 1974), 20.

[16] Rosenblatt, 170.

[17] Andrews, *Free Story*, 9.

[18] For a discussion of doubleconsciousness as it pertains to Afro-Americans, see W.E.B. DuBois, *The Souls of Black Folk* (New York: New American Library, 1969), 45-46. This is one of many reprint editions of this seminal work first published in 1903. The most accurate edition of this work is the 1973 edition from Kraus-Thomson of the 1953 McClurg and Co. edition. Various editions since the Kraus altered DuBois' intent and argument with incorrect words and lost phrases.

[19] Andrews, *Free Story*, 18.

[20] Rosenblatt, 174.

[21] Andrews, *Free Story*, 18.

[22] William L. Andrew has an important discussion of the black spiritual autobiography in *Sisters of the Spirit: Three Black Women's Autobiographies of the Nineteenth Century* (Bloomington: Indiana University Press, 1986), 1-4. Andrews states "Without the black spiritual autobiography's reclamation of the Afro-American spiritual birthright, the fugitive slave narrative could not have made such a cogent case for black civil rights in the crisis years between 1830 and 1865."

[23] The complete titles for Lee and Prince's works are *The Life and Religious Experience of Jarena Lee, A Coloured Lady* (1836) and *A Narrative of the Life and Travels of Mrs. Nancy Prince* (1853). *Our Nig; or Sketches from the Life of a Free Black* was published in 1859.

[24] Deborah Gray White, *Ar'n't I a Woman: Female Slaves in the Plantation South* (New York: W.W. Norton and Company, 1985), 16.

[25] Ibid., 17.

[26] Ibid., 18.

[27] Ibid., 19.

[28] The works White cites as revealing this bias are John W. Blassingame, *The Slave Community: Plantation Life in the Antebellum South* (New York: Oxford University Press, 1972); Robert Fogel and Stanley Engerman, *Time on the Cross: The Economics of American Negro Slavery* (Boston: Little, Brown and Company, 1974); Eugene D. Genovese, *Roll, Jordan, Roll: The World the Slaves Made* (New York: Vintage Books, 1976); and Herbert G. Gutman, *The Black Family in Slavery and Freedom, 1715-1925* (New York: Vintage Books, 1976).

[29] White, 22.

[30] David Bradley, "Novelist Alice Walker Telling the Black Woman's Story," *New York Times Magazine*, 8 January 1984, 36. Walker tells Bradley in the interview, "You see, one of the problems with white feminism is that it not a tradition that teaches white women they are capable. Whereas my tradition *assumes* I'm capable. I have a tradition of people not letting me get the skills,

but I have cleared fields, I have lifted whatever, I have *done* it. It ain't a tradition of wondering whether or not I could do it because I'm a woman."

[31] Karen Lebsock, *The Free Women of Petersburg: Status and Culture in a Southern Town, 1784-1860*(New York: W.W. Norton and Company, 1984), 87-111.

[32] White, 24.

[33] Ibid., 120.

[34] Ibid., 122.

[35] Ibid.

[36] Ibid., 126.

[37] Ibid., 127.

[38] Ibid., 129.

[39] Ibid.

[40] Ibid., 131.

[41] Ibid., 132. White believes that the constant movement of slaves from one plantation to another due to sale made it difficult for female and male slaves to form long-term stable relationships. She does not suggest that such relationships did not occur and were less fulfilling. She stresses that the "female network and its emotional sustenance was always there—there between an 'abroad' husband's visits, there when a husband or son was sent or sold off or ran away."

[42] Ibid., 139.

[43] Ibid., 140.

[44] Estelle C. Jelinek, "Introduction: Women's Autobiography and the Male Tradition," in *Women's Autobiography: Essays in Criticism* (Bloomington: Indiana University Press, 1984), 5.

[45] Ibid.

[46] Ibid., 15.

[47] Elizabeth Schultz, "To Be Black and Blue: The Blues Genre in Black American Autobiography," in *The American Autobiography: A Collection of Critical Essays*, ed. Albert E. Stone (Englewood Cliffs, NJ: Prentice-Hall, Inc., 1981), 110.

[48] Ibid., 113.

[49] Regina Blackburn, "In Search of the Black Female Self: African American Women's Autobiographies and Ethnicity," in *Women's Autobiography*, 134.

[50] Ibid.

[51] Ibid., 136.

[52] Braxton, 171. Braxton characterizes Wells-Barnett's autobiography as an historical memoir which she identifies as a sub-genre of autobiography.

[53] Ibid., 181.

[54] Ida B. Wells, *Crusade for Justice: The Autobiography of Ida B. Wells*, ed. Alfreda Duster (Chicago: University of Chicago Press, 1970), 3-4.

[55] Braxton, 218.

[56] Wells, *Crusade*, chapters 6-26.

[57] Ibid., 248-52.
[58] Ibid., 223; 333; 352; 355-56; 358; 397-98.
[59] Ibid., 250-52.
[60] Ibid., Chapter 29.
[61] Braxton, 182.
[62] Wells, *Crusade*, 258; 283; 352.
[63] Ibid., 5.
[64] Braxton, 221.

III

AFRICAN-AMERICAN WOMEN AND THE UNITED STATES ETHOS, 1892-1920: EMERGING SOCIAL CLASS AND THE NATURE OF WORK

No life exists in a vacuum. Ida B. Wells-Barnett must be placed within her context to understand how she interacted with her social setting. Nineteenth century United States society grew increasingly complex. The century saw the end of the slave trade, the rise of the Black Churches, the Negro Convention Movement, the Civil War, Reconstruction, Redemption, and the lynch law. The Second Great Awakening, a shift from an agrarian to an industrialized economy, a more rigidly defined class structure, and an emerging national identity were also features of this era. With such great social, political, economic, and religious upheavals in so condensed a time frame, the effects on individual lives were profound.

African-American Women and Work: From Slavery to Immigration

FROM SLAVERY TO RECONSTRUCTION

African-American women have struggled with racial and economic subordination and have existed in a narrow space and dark enclosure.[1] African-Americans were brought to the United States to work. This reality cut across gender lines.[2] There was little regard for family life, education, culture, political rights, or religion. The racism evident in this period denied the humanity of African-

American women and men and justified the exploitation of their labor.   Slave women were labor units, and as Kenneth Stammp notes, "the slave woman was first a full-time worker, and only incidentally a wife, mother, and homemaker."[3] In the world of work, slave women over the age of sixteen labored more than 261 days a year with eleven to thirteen hour work days.[4] Jacqueline Jones suggests that the outline of African work patterns endured among slave households in which African women played a major role in the production of food and household services for the family.[5] She further suggests that the sexual division of labor among slaves had less to do with perceived female physical weakness and more to do with a woman's childcare and domestic responsibilities. This pattern of Black female work within the home and in the public sphere continued after emancipation.

The journey to freedom did not bring with it economic prosperity for African-Americans. A more accurate understanding of emancipation is one of a process rather than an event. Emancipation was a process by which African-Americans terminated their labor as slaves for a master and began to provide directly for their livelihood and survival. For the vast majority of Black men, economic success meant owning land.[6] Accumulating wealth was not within the range of possibilities for the majority of Black folk, so Black men and women judged their economic success through their ability to provide the essentials for their families. African-American women, slave and free, were not able to participate in the Victorian family ideal which predominated in the South. Black southern women worked, either in the newly emancipated home or in the field.[7] Manual labor was the predominate form of work for urban southern Blacks. The majority of jobs were as servants, porters, and unskilled day laborers.[8]

Beginning in 1865, African-American women left the fields and the domestic labor force controlled by whites.[9] Their dual purposes were to escape the yoke of slavery and keep their families intact.[10] Black women continued to pick cotton and perform whatever labor was needed to keep their families alive. In the urban South, women were reluctant to accept domestic jobs within white homes. Women who accepted domestic work frequently refused to live in the home of their employer.[11] White women who remained in the home were the models of the domestic ideal while their Black sisters who remained in the home were ridiculed for "acting the lady."[12] The key to understanding this brief period of Black female labor history for both rural and urban African-Americans is that Black females (and children) worked, but it was the Black family that decided when females and children would work and in what occupation, in contrast to the period of slavocracy.[13]

REDEMPTION

By the early 1870s, sharecropping had become the dominant form of Black labor. Jones terms sharecropping a "compromise" between white planters determined to grow more cotton and African-Americans who were determined to resist the labor arrangements of the old slave system.[14] Sharecropping became the principal form of Black labor.[15] The concomitant credit system subverted the promise of Black economic autonomy and jeopardized the survival of African-American sharecropping families.

Gradually, African-American women were forced into the labor market to bring wages into the household for survival. This labor market presented gender and racial restrictions.[16] Women, especially daughters, left the farm to sell their labor. The only positions open to them were in low-paying household work.[17] African-American women worked to insure the survival of their families. They worked outside of the home in higher percentages than white women and were concentrated in the domestic and agricultural labor force.[18]

INDUSTRIALIZATION

Whether in the southern rural areas or in the urban centers, African-Americans and whites alike were responding to the emerging industrial order as it reached into the South. Although the advancing prosperity of the early 1800s made it possible for white middle class women to aspire to a status that was formerly reserved for wealthy upper class women, African-American women could not aspire to the same heights as their white counterparts. The Black class structure was not comparable to the white class structure in terms of the amount of property and wealth Black men could aspire to attain.[19]

Industrialization in the late nineteenth century and early twentieth century created new employment opportunities for women. However, these opportunities were limited to native-born white women. White immigrant families later experienced an openness for women in their group to enter the labor market in sales, teaching, clerical, and social work positions. African-American women and other women of color were denied upward mobility and were relegated to private household work, farm labor, laundries, canneries, and the lowest paying manufacturing jobs. This was the social, economic, and political reality of the African-American woman at the turn of the century.

The low wages of African-American men, the significant number of African-American women who were heads of families, and the greater gender equality among African-Americans were the key factors accounting for a greater number of African-American women than white women in the public workplace.[20] Also, more than seventy percent of the Black population in the United States before World War I was rural. Many of the farms owned by Black men were managed entirely by the women of the family while the men worked in other occupations to provide a liveable income for the family.[21] Most families assigned an available female the task of organizing the household and stretching the limited incomes of the wage earners.

For white middle class women, notions of propriety and role served as the organizing principles for women's work force participation. This created a reciprocally corroborating system in which successful job experiences for women were defined in terms of values which were appropriate to future home life: gentility, neatness, morality, cleanliness.[22] Women chose jobs that reflected home-based values which were regulated by social and cultural norms. Although middle class white women were severely restricted in the public workplace, they had a greater range of options and mobility in the emerging industrial order than did working class women and women of color.

In 1890, ninety percent of the women over 35 years old were married and lived with their husbands for most of their lives. Until 1890, the vast majority of these women remained outside the paid labor force and contributed to the family income in other ways. However, 1890 was a year that marked the explosion of women entering the public workplace in significant numbers. In the period between 1890 and 1919, the height of the progressive era, the number of women seeking professional training mushroomed.[23] The World War I enabled women to find paid work in all professional areas, thereby destroying myths that women lack the physical stamina or intellectual prowess for the most demanding jobs in the public sector.

Poor Black and white women did not benefit in a proportional manner from the vast gains made by white middle class women during the war. It was immaterial if Black women stayed in the south or migrated north. Wherever their location, Black women were routinely denied factory work and had to do domestic work to supplement family incomes until the dramatic change in public sector work unleashed by the World War I.

Until the early twentieth century, the radical economic inequality of Black working women in the urban north was not apparent. Before this time, disproportionate numbers of single and married Black women worked for wages, but they and Black men and white women were concentrated in the same job category of domestic service.[24] Black women wage earners remained outside the expanding industrial economics and the few who gained a foothold in factory work remained in the lowest-paying, most tedious, and dangerous positions.

The average Black woman of the late nineteenth century and very early twentieth century began self-sustaining work at the age of 15 and remained in the labor force after marriage because of her husband's inability to support the family on his wages alone. She continued to work through her middle years because her wage-earning children tended to hand over only part of their wages. Despite the significant shift in white working women's options, the paid labor of Black women did not fluctuate in the changing economy in either the North or South.[25] This stagnation arises from Black women's intricate link with the employment situation of Black men.

IMMIGRATION

Beginning in the 1880s, the arrival of large numbers of eastern European immigrants had a profound impact on the type and numbers of positions available to Black men. Black men had never been able to dominate a single type of work. By 1900, successive waves of immigrant groups displaced Black men from jobs such as artisans, apartment house doormen, barbers, elevator operators, waiters, and cooks in expensive hotels.[26]

Black men constituted a labor force of last resort and could not expect even gradual advancement. Most Black male workers suffered from chronic underemployment and sporadic unemployment. Thus, other household members, particularly Black women, had to supplement their irregular earnings. Black wives worked in greater proportion than white wives, even serving as wage earners more often than immigrant wives of the same socioeconomic class. Black wives bore fewer children than immigrant women and their children established independent households or at least retained their wages for their own use in greater proportion than children of immigrant families.[27] Overwhelmingly, African-American women were insignificant in industry until World War I when the influx of women of various racial/ethnic backgrounds as well as social class changed the nature and composition of public sector wage work.

The Great Migration

The Great Migration brought 300,000 to 400,000 Blacks to the North between 1915 and 1920. Black women migrated north or to the urban centers of the South in record numbers, with their families or alone, particularly between 1916-1918. The majority moved to northern cities.[28] These women were more likely to be younger and better educated than other Black women in the South. They were single or widowed. One barely literate woman in Biloxi, Mississippi wrote a letter to the *Chicago Defender* which the paper used to encourage the migration North:

> From a willen workin woman. I hope that you will help me as I
> want to get out of this land of sufring I no there is som thing that

I can do here there is nothing for me to do I may be able to get in some furm where I dont have to stand on my feet all day I dont no just whah but I hope the Lord will find a place now let me here from you all at once.[29]

New techniques and conditions increased opportunities for Black women migrants as trained nurses, teachers, boardinghouse keepers, laundry workers, and waitresses. The highest percentage increase was among hairdressers, manicurists, clerical help, and elevator operators.[30] The drive to leave the rural South for better conditions and job opportunities in the North was desperate. The September 18, 1902 edition of *The Independent* published in Indianapolis contained the following reflections from an unnamed Black woman:

> There is a feeling of unrest, insecurity, almost panic among the best class of Negroes in the South....Must we remain in the South or go elsewhere? Where can we go to feel that security which other people feel? Is it best to go in great numbers or only in several families?...Many colored women who wash, iron, scrub, cook or sew all the week to help pay the rent for these miserable hovels and help fill the many small mouths, would deny themselves some of the necessaries of life if they could take their little children and teething babies on the cars to the parks of a Sunday afternoon and sit under the trees, enjoy the cool breezes and breathe God's pure air for only two or three hours; all this is denied them.[31]

When Black women migrated north, they found that industrial employers preferred white immigrant labor to Black workers and only welcomed Blacks when the supply of immigrant labor diminished during the war period. This attitude prevailed although the daughters of Black migrant parents attained educational parity with second-generation immigrant women and native white women of native white parentage in the hopes of competing in the workplace as well as for the advancement of Black people in the United States. Black women struggled for self-improvement in as equally a persistent manner as the racist and sexist system worked to keep them from attaining any advancement or benefit for their determination.[32]

In 1905, one-fourth of all adult Black women in New York lived alone or in lodging houses. Ninety percent of the working women in the city were domestic servants. Black women detested domestic work. Writing from the South in early 1912, an unnamed Black woman in Georgia wrote to *The Independent*:

> I frequently work from 14 to 16 hours a day, I am compelled by my contract, which is oral only, to sleep in the house. I am allowed to go home to my own children...only once in two weeks, every other Sunday afternoon...I'm not permitted to stay all night....Of course, nothing is being done to increase our wages, and the way things are going at present, it would seem that nothing could be done to cause an increase of wages. We have no labor unions or organizations of any kind that could demand for us a uniform scale of wages for cooks, washwomen, nurses....So that, the truth is, we have to work for little or nothing or become vagrants.[33]

The depth of the distaste for domestic service resounds in the words of a young migrant Black woman who worked as a cook in Georgia. She went to the North, first working as a waitress before obtaining a job in a box factory:

> I'll never work in nobody's kitchen but my own any more. No, indeed! That's the one thing that makes me stick to this job. You do have some time to call your own, but when you're working in anybody's kitchen, well you're out of luck. You almost have to eat on the run; you never get any time off, and you have to work half the night usually.[34]

As the Great Migration increased, so did white bigotry. Of particular concern was white insistence that Blacks remain confined to a narrow geographic area. This caused a rapid increase of Black ghettos in northern urban centers. However, this increase was in inhabitants, not in geography. The result was a severe concern for housing. The critical lack of reasonable and decent housing was intensified because commercial entertainment and vice districts were located in or near Black residential areas in most large cities of the period.[35] White law officials sought to locate this activity along with its attendant drug and alcohol use and abuse, prostitution, gambling, and petty organized crime away from white neighborhoods. Jones suggests that this physical concentration of urban vice gradually created a disproportionate number of Black prostitutes.[36] Most domestic servants in brothels were young Black women. Black prostitutes represented the extreme form of victimization endured by all Black women workers in terms of their health, safety, and financial compensation.[37]

The period featured a lack of facilities and money to meet the increasing needs of the burgeoning ghetto. Waste and duplication of services was coupled with patronizing attitudes, causing many ghetto dwellers to reject various social service groups.[38] Few Blacks were invited to sit on the boards of these groups. One exception was The Flanner Guild, a settlement home and training center, which was founded and funded by whites but controlled by Blacks.[39] Blacks worked for ghetto welfare. The Hope Day Nursery for Colored Children was founded in 1902 by a group of Black mothers when their children were rejected by a white day nursery. The White Rose Industrial Association was founded by Victoria Earle Matthews, an ex-slave, in 1897. The Association operated the White Rose Working Girls' Home to "check the evil of unscrupulous employment agents who deceived the unsuspecting girls desiring to come North."[40] White Rose agents were stationed in Norfolk, Virginia to help Black girls heading north and to explain to them the dangers of the North. In New York city, White Rose agents met the boats and helped Black girls find a place to live or housed them in the White Rose Girls' Home temporarily.

DOMESTIC WORK

Despite the efforts of White Rose, Black girls and women did not escape the exploitation of domestics. This exploitation was a national and not a regional phenomenon confined to the South. No differences have been found between the South and the North in the personal dynamics of the employer-employee relationship. In Chicago, New York, and Philadelphia the total number of servants declined by 25%, but the proportion of Black women in that industry

increased by 10% to 15%.[41]   The percentage of Black women
working in domestic service declined significantly between 1910-1920
in the major cities like New York, Cleveland, and Chicago.[42] In this
period, Black women in industry increased in these same major cities
while in the smaller cities almost all Black women remained servants.
This shift from domestic service to industry in the major urban
centers did not happen simultaneously. In Philadelphia, before the
Great Migration, 80% of the jobs held by Black women were in day
worker domestic service. Only white women worked in the higher
paying domestic jobs that provided free room and board in the
employer's home. When these white women moved into factory jobs,
their old positions as live-in domestics were taken by northern born
Black women. Southern migrant Black women replaced the northern
born Black women as day workers. The first positions available to
most African-American women as they entered Philadelphia from
the South was in domestic work.[43]   Black women entered industry
slowly in Philadelphia and in other major northern cities.

Alice Kessler-Harris notes the desire of native-born white
women "for gentility over poor working conditions and low
wages."[44] White women set the tenor for all females. They worked
to achieve upward mobility and social status. The Boston Women's
Educational and Industrial Union encouraged white women to leave
overcrowded factory jobs for domestic work as early as 1898.[45]
This effort met with little success because higher wages could not
compensate for the social stigma attached to domestic service.
Waitresses often earned more than ordinary factory workers, but the
social disgrace of that job kept white women away from it. It is not
surprising that these jobs were open to African-American women.
Black women were confined to the bottom of the labor pool and
chose laundry and domestic work over field labor. The native born
white woman worker valued respectable surroundings in the work
place. One measure of a refined environment was the absence of
immigrant and/or African-American co-workers. Southern white
women would not work in laundries or in textile, glass or tobacco
factories with Black women.[46]

SOCIAL STANDING AND WORK

Categorizing jobs by respectability and adhering to the divisions created benefitted the employer. The employer could offer reduced wages to immigrant and African-American women who sought the privilege of working with native-born white women.[47] Poor women entered the labor market not as a result of the technology that prompted middle class women toward work, but because wages were necessary to purchase consumer goods. To maintain the appearance of propriety necessary to attract white women at low wages, southern employers severely restricted the occupations in which the region's Black women could find work. The stigma of race, sex, and class combined to force Black women into the lowest paying and least respected work. Their position was sanctioned not only by factory owners, but by white women as well.

Throughout the nineteenth and well into the twentieth century, Black married women participated in the work force at a rate several times greater than that of white married women. Four-fifths of Black married women were employed as domestic servants, farm laborers, or laundresses. By 1920, they constituted more than one-fourth of all married women in the work force.[48] The job most closed to Black women was that of salesclerk in a department store.

The department store began in the 1870s, and by 1920 was the arbiter of cultural and economic consumption.[49] The interior and exterior designs of these stores set the standard not only for consumption, but for good taste as well. This new world open to white women of all classes had the luxury and theatrical behavior of the rich available to them for the first time as they entered and could purchase the accessible lavish items. The department store brought a new world of fashion, glamour, and consumption to middle class and upper middle class society. However, this was available to white society, not African-American society. Due to the wage structure and racism, Blacks entered the department store as maintenance personnel and cleaners, not as customers.

FACTORY WORK AND TRADE UNIONS

For white women workers, factories were second to department stores as a desirable workplace. A caste mentality developed
among department store workers and factory workers.[50] Women
who worked in the department store believed themselves superior to
factory workers. Store workers sacrificed eating to dress well and
live in better neighborhoods than factory workers although both
groups were earning comparable wages. In turn, factory workers ate
better by giving up other amenities.

Despite a shortage of white workers, most southern plants
would only hire Blacks to do the most dangerous, tedious, and
demanding work. A 1910 United States Senate investigation of
women and child labor in the cotton textile industry reported that of
the 152 southern mills surveyed, only 18 mills employed any Black
women and children. Barely 5% of the total number of women
employed in those mills were Black.[51] The few Black women who
were employed were almost exclusively sweepers and scrubbers.

Black women workers were not passive in the emerging
industrial order, even as they were systematically excluded from the
chance of upward mobility. *The Norfolk Journal and Guide* ran a
story in the March 3, 1917 edition of a walkout staged by Black
women workers in a southern knitting mill.

> Declaring that they would not work under the manager, every one
> of the female colored operatives at the knitting mill here (Rocky
> Mount, NC) left their work at 11 o'clock last Thursday morning.
> The trouble arose when the white manager cursed one of the girls
> and attempted to otherwise abuse her....he(the superintendent)
> immediately began to visit the homes of the operatives asking
> them to return to work. The offending white manager was
> discharged and the girls returned to their work with no loss of
> time.[52]

The article concludes by noting "The mill is owned and managed
entirely by white people. They employ colored girls from some of the
best families in the city."

The organized labor movement did not enhance the position
of the Black woman worker. Rather, the movement helped to

perpetuate the low position of the Black woman worker. A young Black working woman tells of the strong opposition she faced when she attempted to enter the Civil Service.

> I am a graduate of the Cambridge Latin and High School. I studied bookkeeping and stenography at evening school after I had graduated. In 1912 I passed the Civil Service examination for the first time, and later tried for a position.... From 1912 until 1915, I tried for positions, tried desperately hard, and always I was refused. For three years I was forced to work for half the money I could get at the work for which I had been trained....Again and again I would be certified. Again and again, as soon as I had a personal interview, I would be refused...once in a while an exceptionally honest man would state his reason. It would always be because of my race; in every other particular I would have passed the requirement.[53]

By complaining to the governor of Massachusetts, she finally got a job in the hospital under Civil Service but was required to eat lunch in her office. She refused to do so and insisted on eating with other employees in the regular dining room. The young woman was fired. Under the rules, no reason had to be given for the dismissal of an employee during the six-month probation period and she could not get a statement for the grounds of her discharge.

When she took her case to court, she lost. Thus, the young woman ended where she began. Her feelings about her ordeal were mixed. On the one hand, she hoped "it will make the way easier for other girls of my race." On the other hand she was not optimistic:

> For the way things stand at present, it is useless to have the requirements. Color—the reason nobody will give, the reason nobody is required to give, will always be in the way. Which, in other words, is the state standing back of a class of its children and saying: "No, you cannot enter here. You may study; you may pass the requirements, but that is as far as you may go."[54]

The American Federation of Labor (AFL) showed no interest in the fate of unskilled workers. The local chapters of the Federation that had a potential constituency of Black workers, such as the Amalgamated Meat Cutters and Butcher Workmen and the International Ladies Garment Workers Union, perceived the elimination of Black women from the labor force to be in their best interest.[55] Black women workers lacked a bargaining agent like the men's Brotherhood of Sleeping Car porters. They resorted to absenteeism, high turnover, careless work habits, or spontaneous walkouts to resist exploitation through low wages and poor working conditions. Such methods of resistance were employed by white workers as well.

Three aspects of Black women's industrial employment during World War I foretold that progress made in employment during the war would be temporary.[56] First, only a small number of Black domestics and laundresses found alternative employment in manufacturing. Second, the few Black women who were employed in the industrial sector remained in the jobs with the lowest wages and poorest working conditions. In many factories, Black women's pay started at $1 less per week than whites simply because they were Black.[57] Black women who replaced white women, even if they worked as well, would receive $2.50 for the $3 per week earned by white women, $7 instead of $10, and $10 instead of $12.50.[58] Finally, demobilization eroded even these modest gains. Black women faced opposition from the employer, the unions, and white women.

The extent of white women's labor militancy and racial prejudice dictated hiring practices for Black women. A racially segregated workplace meant Black and white women would not compete for the same jobs at the same time. In the case of the Pennsylvania Railroad, in one terminal of the line, white women only counted clean laundry in an airy room on the ground floor while three Black women sorted soiled linen in a dark basement.[59] The racism of the unions which kept Blacks out, also operated to keep them ignorant of and unsympathetic to the goals of unionism. The role of Black women workers as a reserve labor force served to intensify the fear and animosity of white women workers. Henri posits that white women who would have been co-workers with Black women were more racially prejudiced than white men in the same situation. The chilling bigotry of native born and immigrant white women led them to violence against Black women co-workers during the 1917 East St. Louis, Illinois, riot which resulted in at least 50 deaths and 240 buildings destroyed in the Black ghetto. Property damage estimates ran as high as $1 million. In the first three hours of the rioting, Black women and children were spared. White women, some of whom were co-workers with Black women in the local factories, joined the angry mob as the rioting increased and began to direct their assaults on Black women. The dispatch from *the Norfolk Journal and Guide* revealed some of the horror.

> "Let the women have her," was the cry among the men, and white women began tearing the garments from their victim. The woman's cry, "Please, please, I ain't done nothing." was stopped by a blow to the mouth with the club which a woman swung like a baseball bat. Another white woman seized the victim's hand and the blow was repeated. Fingers tore at her hair and her waist was stripped from her. "Now let's see how fast she can run," suggested a woman, as the woman broke loose. The women were loath to leave her alone, but after following her with their blows for a short distance, they stopped and she ran crying down the street.[60]

The fluctuating economy fostered constant worry in many white women about their ability to retain a non-service job.

Black women were employed as strikebreakers. This sparked a heated debate in 1910 between two of the leading African-American newspapers of the era, *The New York Age* and *the Horizon*.[61] In a January 20, 1910 editorial entitled "The Waistmakers' Strike," *The Age* boasted that it recruited "colored girls as ironers with the firms whose employees are now on strike." The paper revealed that it had received a request to reject strikebreaking advertisements. This was to "help induced colored girls to join the union, and that we dissuade other colored girls from taking the places of those now on strike." *The Age* asserted "We have refused these requests both on general and specific grounds." *The Age* noted the exclusion of Black women from the unions and regarded it "safe to assume from past experience that waistmakers would demand the immediate discharge of Black women hired by employers."

Finally *The Age* reported that it asked a "philanthropic sponsor" of the strikers, presumably the New York Women's Trade Union League (WTUL), for assurances "unions would admit Negro girls in the future without discrimination as to employment, should

they refrain from taking the positions open." When such assurances
were not forthcoming, *The Age* asked its readers if it could

> in sense and justice advise competent Negro girls, being idle and
> until now denied employment, to turn down the opportuni-
> ty?...Why should Negro working girls pull white working girl's
> chestnuts out of the fire?[62]

According to *The Age*, the waistmakers strike brought to

> clearest light the issue of the Negro and the union....the Negro
> will continue to be the pivot upon which future strikes will turn so
> long as labor will ignore his right to work and thwart his ambition
> to advance in the mechanical world. The friends and the leaders
> of labor should consider the Negro in days of prosperity as well
> as in those of adversity.[63]

Margaret Dreier Robbins, national WTUL president, insisted
that the union had Black members—1 in New York and 2 in
Philadelphia—and that in Philadelphia "two of the most devoted
pickets are colored girls, for they have not only been able to persuade
the girls of their own race and color to stand by their sisters, but have
also been most successful in persuading the white girls to stand by
them."[64]   A Black woman in New York who joined the strike early
in battle was not only welcomed, according to Robbins, but is "now
chairman of the shop committee, elected by white girls to that
office."

   Elizabeth Dutcher, an officer of the New York WTUL, stated
publically that *The Age* distorted waistmakers' union's policy toward
Blacks. In a letter published in the March 1910 edition of *Horizon*,
she wrote:

> In New York, colored girls are not only members of the union,
> but they have been prominent in the union....The editor should
> also know that meetings were held during the strike at the Fleet
> Street Methodist Memorial Church (colored) in Brooklyn and St.
> Marks Methodist Church in Manhattan and that in both,
> members of the Ladies Waist Makers Union said definitely and
> publically that colored girls were not only eligible but welcome to
> membership.[65]

Horizon expressed it pleasure at the opportunity to publish Dutcher's letter and urged all Blacks to read and study it carefully, especially

> those persons and editors who, some unwittingly, are assisting in the present insidious effort to make our people Ishmaelites in the world of labor, or as someone has put it to make us "Cossacks" of America.[66]

There were bright spots between African-American and white women in the labor force. Mary McDowell, a young Black woman, detailed the admittance of a Black woman in a woman's local in the Chicago stockyards.

> The president, an Irish girl whose father...had left his job because a colored man had been put to work with him, was naturally expected to be prejudiced against the reception of a negro woman. Hannah, as doorkeeper, called out in her own social way, "A colored sister is at the door. What'l I do with her?" "Admit her," called back the president, "and let all of ye's give her a hearty welcome."[67]

For Black women, the limited opening of industrial opportunities during World War I was significant, in spite of their being given the least desirable jobs in factories and shops and lower wages than white women doing the same work. The segregationist stance of the Woodrow Wilson administration laid the groundwork for segregated facilities in war plants and arsenals. The Wilson administration instituted segregated toilets, lunchroom facilities, and working areas in a number of federal departments. In war plants and arsenals it was not unusual to find superior sanitary provisions for white women as Black women were segregated to the least desirable washrooms, lunchrooms, and lockers.[68] The federal government continued this attitude in other areas such as the United States Railroad Administration. The Railroad Administration filled the higher-paying jobs, usually held by men now fighting in Europe, with white women only. The lower-paying menial tasks were the domain of Black women.[69]

The 1919 Department of Labor report prepared by Helen B. Irvin on Black women in industry, documents both her patriotic impulse as well as a thorough picture of Black women in the industrial work force.[70]

> In several arsenals and munitions plants groups of Negro women were found mixing chemicals, loading shells, making gas masks, stitching wings for aeroplanes, and engaging in similar processes requiring great care, skillful fingers, patriotism, and courage.[71]

Black women worked in various occupations in stockyards, tanneries, factories which produced clothing for the armed forces, and rubber plants. They worked in transportation facilities as switchmen, flagmen, road repair crews members. Mrs. Irvin sounded an optimistic but vain hope when she wrote:

> Many of these industries being essentials in peace times, it is probable that large numbers of the Negro women who were drawn into them during the war emergency, and have made good, will find permanent occupations at more desirable work than heretofore.[72]

The Irvin report noted the varied conditions in the factories from least desirable to most desirable. In some plants there were no provisions for first aid, no lunchrooms or lockers, and scant bathroom facilities for Black workers. Other plants were well lit and heated, had low noise volumes, provided first-aid stations, lunchrooms and adequate bathroom facilities. Many observations by Mrs. Irvin, were tinged with an element of deprecation regarding Black women:

> The chief problem of industrial training is presented by the very obvious need for a more carefully thought out plan of education for Negro women, who are comparatively new to industry and who have no adequate standards upon which to base their estimate of their own worth or the requirements of their occupations.[73]

Later, regarding the industrial training of Black women workers she writes of the need for

...training for efficiency, with its contributing factors of personal hygiene, industrial sense, increasing skill, and realization of contractual obligation. It is the development of industrial consciousness through the fostering of pride in achievement, through increasing personal and family thrift and through encouraging an attitude of constancy toward a given task or locality.[74]

And finally,

...Negro women on entering industry have need of patient, careful training in all processes required of them and in the use of all machinery employed in the specific work assigned to them. Such training plus the opportunity to advance individually or in groups, as their increasing skill may warrant, has been found profitable by most of the employers who awake to the possibilities of Negro women as workers.[75]

In June of 1918, the War Labor Administration began a Woman-in-Industry Service to "meet the problems connected with the more rapid introduction of women into industry as a result of war conditions."[76] The purpose of the Service was: (1) information and data gathering relative to women in industry, (2) developing policies and methods in industry that would enhance women's participation and providing less dangerous conditions, (3) coordinating work for women in other departments of the Department of Labor, industry and other government departments, and (4) cooperating with state labor departments to coordinate efforts.[77]

Although many considered this new agency little more than a "glorified information bureau," the Women's Trade Union League (WTUL) hailed its creation as a victory in their struggle for such a government agency since 1902. Mary Van Kleeck was appointed the director. Foner suggests her appointment prevented the agency from degenerating into merely a conciliatory device for the government as had been the case with Samuel Gompers on the Council of National Defense.[78] Van Kleeck was aware that protective regulations were a two-edged sword. Denying women employment in particular jobs because of the physical demands inherent was not universally approved by many women in the war industries. The opportunity to earn a relatively high wage influenced women's attitudes toward this work. Protective regulations would forbid their employment in these high-wage positions.

Black women were faced with an even greater threat by protectionist regulations. They suffered from the absence of viable alternatives to the would-be forbidden employment. A young Black woman railroad trucker who had been in domestic service previously, spoke for many of her sisters:

> All colored women like this work and want to keep it. We are making more money at this than any work we can get, we do not have to work as hard as at housework,...What the colored women need is an opportunity to make money. As it is, they have to take what employment they can get, live in old tumbledown houses or resort to streetwalking, and I think a woman ought to think more of her blood than do that....We are not employed as clerks, as cannot all be schoolteachers, and so we cannot see any use in working our parents to death to get educated....Please don't take this work away from us.[79]

The war opened jobs in the textile industry for Black women. *The Norfolk Journal and Guide* carried the following story in its September 10, 1917 edition:

> The Hosiery Mills of this city that have heretofore employed white help...on account of the scarcity of labor opened their doors to Negro women and girls, as a result of which 12 young women went to work at Passage Hosiery and about 14 at the Lawrence St. Mill Monday.[80]

Northern mills began to bring young Black women North to work in the mills.

One response to the increased opportunities for Black women was the founding of the Woman's Wage Earners' Association in 1917 with Mary Church Terrell as treasurer. The main objective of this Association was the bettering of working hours, housing, and wage-earning conditions for Black women in all lines of work.[81] This Black middle class organization revealed the class bias of the organization. They believed betterment work must be promoted and done by public-spirited women of the race who had homes of their own and resources independent of working for others for wages.

They also believed lecturers on domestic arts and moral uplift were important to their purposes as well.[82]

Other goals were: to create better, more sympathetic and helpful relations between employers and employees, to promote efficient and faithful service, to provide homes in which to teach domestic science, and to be a clearinghouse for employers. "Our women wage-earners are a large factor in the life of the race. They are becoming moreso every day as the business interests of the race expand and demand for intelligent workers grows with the expansions."[83]

Post-War Years

In the demobilization and reconstruction following the war, women workers were unable to obtain the protection of trade unions in new post-war jobs. Male unionists were primarily indifferent to women's efforts to maintain the gains they made during the war. African-American women were the first to lose their jobs. Foner terms the year 1919 as the most militant year of United States labor history. Three thousand six hundred and thirty strikes were called involving 4,140,000 workers.[84] Within twenty four hours of the Armistice, a directive issued by the chair of the Shipping Board and the secretaries of the Navy and War called an immediate halt to all Sunday and overtime work on government supervised contracts. This directive meant a wage cut of as much as 50%.

Black workers suffered the most. The heavy unemployment of the Black community centered in northern ghettos. Pressure began to build as Blacks were crowded into substandard housing and forced to pay ridiculous rents and higher prices than any other social groups in the U.S. When Blacks tried to leave the ghetto, they were met with attacks, lynchings, and race riots in the North and South. From May to September, race riots swept through Washington, DC; Knoxville, Tennessee; Charleston, South Carolina; Longview, Texas; Omaha, Nebraska; and Phillips County, Arkansas. Although riots were not a new feature in American life, Blacks previously had not fought back against their white attacker. In a letter to the editor of *Crisis*, a southern Black woman wrote of her happiness when she

learned that Blacks in Washington fought back. It "gave me the thrill
that comes once in a lifetime....at last our men had stood like men,
struck back, were no longer dumb driven cattle..."[85]

As Black society resisted white violence, representative Black
women presented a memorial on behalf of Negro women laborers to
the WTUL at the First International Congress of Working Wom-
en.[86] Among the signers of this memorial were Nannie H. Burroughs and Mary Church Terrell.[87] The letter is a clear and a
concise history of Black women workers and an unambiguous call
for democracy in the workplace:

> The present generation of Negro laborers like other women
> laborers, had little or no opportunity for training and education
> at childhood or since. The present prospect of the world demand
> for the products of American agriculture and industry makes it of
> fundamental importance to American production that the
> potential capacity of Negro women workers should be developed
> to its limit....We, a group of Negro women, representing those
> two millions of Negro women wage-earners, respectfully ask for
> your active cooperation in organizing the Negro women workers
> of the United States into unions, that they may have a share in
> bringing about industrial democracy and social order in the
> world.[88]

In many ways, the Black woman worker lived Henry Highland
Garnet's admonition, "let your motto be resistance."[89] Black
women resisted the racist, sexist, and classist society in which they
lived. They met unrelenting prejudice, yet they pressed on through
poor working conditions, unemployment, meager wages, migration,
riots, and segregation in northern urban ghettos. Black women were
not passive in the face of systematic discrimination. They fought for
jobs and for their rights. Often they lost in the struggle, yet persisted
at being included in the new industrial order.

The country was undergoing tremendous social, economic,
racial, and cultural upheaval. The new middle class helped to set the
standard of living sought by those living in the lower and working
classes. African-Americans were not allowed to participate fully in
the drive for upward mobility and respectability. Black women
suffered in the midst of the inequities. Yet they resisted as they
seized advantage of the paltry opportunities open to them and took

halting steps into the new industrial society. They lived within the confines of their narrow space and dark enclosure as they fought for the survival of their families and themselves.

NOTES

[1] Gloria Wade-Gayles, *No Crystal Stair: Visions of Race and Sex in Black Women's Fiction* (New York: The Pilgrim Press, 1984), 3-4. Wade-Gayles notes that there are three major circles of reality in United States society which reflect the degree of power. White men predominate in the large circle. In a much smaller circle are African-Americans. "Hidden in this second circle is a third, a small, dark enclosure in which black women experience pain, isolation, and vulnerability. These are the distinguishing marks of black womanhood in white America."

[2] Chinese and Japanese immigrants experienced various forms of labor exploitation and racial hatred and violence. Mexican Americans were largely displaced and relegated to barrios. Native Americans underwent genocide and relocation and enforced settlement on the reservation.

[3] Kenneth Stampp, *The Peculiar Institution: Slavery in the Antebellum South* (New York: Vintage Books, 1956), 343; quoted in Angela Davis, *Women, Race, and Class* (New York: Random House, 1981), 5.

[4] Jacqueline Jones, *Labor of Love, Labor of Sorrow: Black Women, Work and the Family, From Slavery to the Present* (New York: Vintage Books, 1986), 18.

[5] Ibid., 39.

[6] Eric Foner, *Reconstruction: America's Unfinished Revolution, 1863-1877* (New York: Harper and Row, Publishers, 1988), 104-6; 403-4. White southerners vigorously opposed Black landownership. Jones, 63. Although Blacks sought their own homesteads, by the mid-1870s Jones estimates that no more than four to eight percent of all freed families in the South owned their own farms.

[7] Ibid., 85-87.

[8] Ibid., 396. Foner notes that African-Americans worked for subsistence wages and endured higher unemployment rates than whites.

[9] Ibid., 85.

[10] Jones, 51.

[11] Foner, *Reconstruction*, 85.

[12] Ibid.

[13] Ibid., 86-87.

[14] Jones, 61. Foner, *Reconstruction*, 409. Foner suggests that sharecropping was a transitional arrangement between slavery and wage labor. Wage labor, in Foner's view, became "synonymous with economic oppression and, in some cases, debt peonage."

[15] Foner, *Reconstruction*, 404.

[16] Jones, 62. The wage guidelines of the Freedmen's Bureau dictated that African-American women receive less compensation than African-American men. This was based on their sex rather than the work performed or ability to work.

[17] Ibid., 62.

[18] Foner, *Reconstruction*, 86.

[19] Ibid., 392-411. Foner notes "only in life-style and aspirations did this elite constitute a 'black bourgeoisie,' for it lacked capital and economic autonomy, and did not own the banks, stores, and mills that could provide employment for other blacks." (398).

[20] Florette Henri, *Black Migration: Movement North 1900-1920* (Garden City, New York: Anchor Press, 1975), 141. See also Suzanne Lebsock, *The Free Women of Petersburg: Status and Culture in A Southern Town, 1784-1860* (New York: W.W. Norton and Co., 1984); Jacqueline Jones, *Labor of Love, Labor of Sorrow: Black Women, Work, and the Family, From Slavery to the Present*; Deborah Gray White, *Ar'n't I a Woman?: Female Slaves in the Plantation South* (New York: W.W. Norton and Co., 1985).

[21] In "The Colored Woman as an Economic Factor," Addie W. Hunton writes using the 1910 census figures, "The 15,792,579 acres owed and cultivated by Negroes, which with buildings and equipment and rented farm lands reach a valuation approaching a billion dollars, represent not only the hardihood and perseverance of the Negro man but the power for physical and mental endurance of the woman working by his side." *The New York Call*, 27 February 1916; quoted in Philip S. Foner and Ronald L. Lewis, eds., *The Black Worker From 1900-1919* Vol V (Philadelphia: Temple University Press, 1980), 55.

[22] Alice Kessler-Harris, *Out to Work: A History of Wage-Earning Women in the United States* (New York: Oxford University Press, 1982), 128.

[23] Between 1890 to 1910, the number of trained nurses multiplied seven-fold and by 1920 3,000 women were trained social workers compared with 1,000 in 1890.

[24] Jones, 161.

[25] Ibid.

[26] Ibid.

[27] Ibid., 162.

[28] Philip S. Foner, *Women and the American Labor Movement: From World War 1 to the Present* (New York: The Free Press, 1980), 10.

[29] Ibid., 10.

[30] Henri, 142.

[31] Foner and Lewis, 7. This article was written by a black woman and published in *The Independent* 18 September 1902.

[32] Jones, 154.

[33] Philip S. Foner, *Women and the American Labor Movement: From Colonial Times to the Eve of World War I* (New York: The Free Press, 1979), 463-464.

[34] Foner, *World War I to the Present*, 11.

[35] Jones, 181.

[36] Ibid.

[37] Ibid., 182.

[38] Henri, 126.

[39] Ibid.

[40] Ibid.

[41] Jones, 164.

[42] Henri, 142.

[43] Foner, *World War I to the Present*, 11. The figures of the Armstrong Association of domestics in Philadelphia reveal the great influx of southern black women. From May 1915 to May 1916, 1,232 of the 1,413 black female domestics were from the South. From May 1917 to April 1918, the number of southern born domestics placed rose to 2,085.

[44] Kessler-Harris, 136.

[45] Ibid.

[46] Ibid., 137.

[47] Ibid., 139.

[48] Carl Degler, *At Odds: Women and the Family in American from the Revolution to the Present* (New York: Oxford University Press, 1980), 391.

[49] Lecture by Josef Barton, "The Transformation of American Society" 8 May 1987, Northwestern University, Evanston, Illinois.

[50] Kessler-Harris, 135.

[51] Ibid., 140.

[52] Foner and Lewis, 432.

[53] Foner, *Colonial Times to the Eve of World War I*, 464.

[54] Ibid., 465.

[55] Jones, 168.

[56] Ibid., 167.

[57] Foner, *World War I to the Present*, 13.

[58] Ibid.

[59] Ibid., 14.

[60] Ibid., 15.

[61] Foner, *Colonial Times to the Eve of World War I*, 339-41.

[62] Ibid., 340.

[63] Ibid., 341.

[64] Ibid., 340. Foner suggests that the national WTUL caught the irony of its

numbers in answering the charge. At a post-strike meeting of the National Executive Board, the organization passed a resolution pledging to do something about organizing black women.

[65] Ibid., 341.

[66] Ibid. Even *Horizon* could not escape the clutches of the Red Scare.

[67] Foner and Lewis, 429.

[68] Foner, *World War I to the Present*, 13.

[69] Ibid., 13.

[70] Helen B. Irvin, "Negro Women in Industry: Summary Reports Made by Mrs. Helen B. Irvin, Special Agent of the Women's Bureau in 1918-1919" in *The Negro at Work During the World War and During Reconstruction: Statistics, Problems, and Policies Relating to the Greater Inclusion of Negro Wage Earners in American Industry and Agriculture*, U.S. Department of Labor (Division of Negro Economics, George Haines, Director).

[71] Ibid., 126.

[72] Ibid., 127.

[73] Ibid., 130.

[74] Ibid, 130-31.

[75] Ibid., 131.

[76] Foner, *World War I to the Present*, 51.

[77] Ibid., 51-52.

[78] Ibid., 52.

[79] Ibid., 52-53.

[80] Ibid., 10.

[81] Foner and Lewis, 430-31.

[82] Ibid., 431.

[83] Ibid.

[84] Foner, *World War I to the Present*, 99.

[85] Ibid., 100.

[86] "A Memorial on Behalf of Negro Women Laborers To: National Women's Trade Union League of America From: Representative Negro Women of US" in *Proceedings of the First International Congress of Working Women, October 28 to November 5, 1919*, quoted in Foner and Lewis, 455.

[87] Nannie H. Burroughs, an educator, founded the National Training School for Girls in Washington, DC. She was also active in the National Colored Baptist Convention and held the office of secretary of the Women's Auxiliary. Mary Church Terrell was an author and civil rights activist. In 1895, when she was appointed to the District of Columbia school board, she became the first African-American woman to hold such an appointment. She was also the first president of the National Association of Colored Women, serving in that role from 1895 to 1901.

[88] "Memorial on Behalf of Negro Women Laborers," Foner and Lewis, 455.

[89] Henry Highland Garnet, "An Address to the Slaves of the United States of

America, Buffalo, N.Y., 1843," in *Let Your Motto Be Resistance: The Life and Thought of Henry Highland Garnet*, ed. Earl Ofari (Boston: Beacon Books, 1972), 153.

IV

AFRICAN-AMERICAN WOMEN AND THE UNITED STATES ETHOS, 1892-1920: SPIRITUALITY, DOMESTICITY, AND SOCIAL REFORM

The primary responses of the late nineteenth century African-American woman to her struggle with the narrow space and dark enclosure of racial and economic subordination were expressed through her commitments to religious and social organizations. African-American women of Wells-Barnett's era espoused a profound spirituality which was forged from the twin hearths of African cosmology and evangelical piety. This spirituality was distinct from white evangelical Christianity in form and practice. However both Black and white spirituality provided the framework for women's participation in social and moral reform in the public realm.

Wells-Barnett exhibited this profound spirituality. Through it she became active in the religious and the social organizations of her day. Her work, like that of her peers, was given impetus and support through the church and Black women's clubs. Much of her activity in social reform and agitation grew out of these two types of influential organizations within the African-American community in the United States. A further contextualization of Wells-Barnett must include a discussion of these kinds of organizations and how they functioned in nineteenth century society.

Background to Social Reform and Spirituality

One intriguing analysis of the world of the late nineteenth and the early twentieth centuries in relation to women and labor is based

on the class conflicts that existed between women. Chapter Three
has revealed deep divisions among white middle class women and
immigrant and working class women. Such class issues must inform
any analysis of the position of African-American women and the
labor force. Yet the additional issues of spirituality, domesticity, and
social reform arise and interact in the lives of African-American
women and work during this period. These issues were focused for
many African-American women in their work in the church and
Black women's clubs. A study of these issues of the organizations
complete the contexts of African-American women through which
they addressed the narrow space and dark enclosure of racial and
economic subordination.

The Emergence of African-American Religion

The spirituality of African-American women of the nineteenth
century had its roots in the religious worldview of West Africa. The
distinctive blend of African cosmology and evangelical piety
produced slave religion which was neither solely African nor
Christian in theology or practice. The African-American women of
the late nineteenth century were inheritors of this religion as it
matured into a distinctive African-American evangelical pietism with
a strong impulse toward Christian duty and moral action on the part
of the individual.

Spirituality, domesticity, and social reform were intricately
linked for the African-American woman who was religious. The late
nineteenth century ideology of domesticity and the rise of the Black
women's club movement within the African-American community
cannot be fully understood without a consideration of the evolution
of Black women's spirituality from its West African roots. Although
the nineteenth century saw the erosion of a conscious West African
cosmology for emancipated African-Americans, their understanding
of perfection, Christian duty, freedom, and a just society evolved
from the syncretization of West African survivalisms and evangelical
Christianity.

AFRICAN COSMOLOGY AND CHRISTIANITY

C. Eric Lincoln suggests that a viable religion is one which has a working reciprocity with the culture that produces it or with which it interacts.[1] Slave religion was a viable religion for the early Africans and African-Americans of the United States. Slaves interacted and adapted to a new land and a new religion. Their blend of West African cosmology and western Christianity produced a distinct religion which met the needs of those who sought the presence of the divine in the midst of their struggle to survive.

From 1619, when Africans first arrived on United States' shores at Jamestown, to 1701 when the Society for the Propagation of the Gospel in the Foreign Parts began to christianize slaves, Africans in the United States had little or no contact with Christianity. Slave conversions to Christianity did not begin in any significant, recorded numbers until the 1740s during the First Great Awakening.[2]

However, slaves in the South and free Blacks in the North were not without a religious life. With the constant influx of Black Africans because of the slave trade, the traditions and religions of Africa were constantly being renewed and revitalized in the Americas.[3] Slaves were able to maintain links with their African heritage through myths and traditions. Slaves, like those in Liberty County, South Carolina, kept the ways of Africa alive through their drumming at funerals and dances, their wood carvings, and the reed baskets and mats they produced. All were African in design and reflected the art of the Dahomey tribes of West Africa.[4]

The religious world of the slave was not that of the white master.[5] Ex-slave Simon Brown's description of how Black people worshipped in slavery[6] is a vivid description of Melville Herskovits' contention that at the very foundation of Negro religion, the African past exerts a strong influence. Like other slaves, Simon Brown's universe was crafted from a blend of West African religions with Christianity. Brown's unconscious was in touch with a cosmology that extended beyond what he saw as the symbols of white religion: pious worship, confinement to church structures, and slavocracy.[7]

Slave Christianity was not cold and proper like its white counterpart. Brown notes that slaves did not have a church structure like whites, but met in a cabin in cold weather or outdoors under a tree or a brush arbor in the summer.[8] This was not a worship style limited to Brown's geographic locale. Brown's description is representative of slave worship throughout the South. Fredrika Bremer's description of a Georgia camp meeting illustrates this point. She describes two significantly different religious scenes between Black and white. In the Black camp meeting "men roared and bawled out; women squealed about like pigs about to be killed; many, having fallen into convulsions, leaped and struck about them so that many had to be held down. Here and there it looked like a regular fight." In contrast, worship was a "quieter scene among the whites."[9]

Religious dancing and shouting were prohibited by white missionaries, but the slaves danced and shouted in their religious life beyond the watchful eye of white religious authorities.[10] The ring shout, also known as "running sperichils," consisting of circular motion, shuffling steps, stamping, gesturing, and exhorting was kept alive.[11] Bishop Daniel A. Payne of the African Methodist Episcopal Church wrote in 1878:

> After the sermon they formed a ring, and with coats off sung, clapped their hands and stamped their feet in a most ridiculous and heathenish way...."Sinners won't get converted unless there is a ring." Said I: "You might sing until you fell down dead, and you would fail to convert a single sinner, because nothing but the Spirit of God and the word of God can convert sinners." He replied: "the Spirit of God works upon people in different ways. At camp-meeting there must be a ring here, a ring there, a ring over yonder, or sinners will not get converted."[12]

When Brown describes slave worship style free of white people, he notes that "the Spirit would move in the meeting" that "there was a living faith in a just God who would one day answer the cries of His poor black children and deliver them from their enemies."[13] Brown ends the passage, "but the slaves never said a word to their white folks about this kind of faith."[14] Slaveholders perceived the power and threat of slave worship[15] and Brown notes that pater-rollers were on hand when slaves gathered for religious purposes.[16]

Slaves conformed to white standards when whites were present, but when left alone, their worship contained the West African belief in the forces of the universe, both evil and good, being at hand and available for consultation and for protection.[17] Also present was the Christian God who would send a man to set the slaves free as Moses had confronted Pharaoh to set the Hebrew slaves free. This God was not wholly transcendent, but immanent as well:

> [God was] right there in the midst of them. He wasn't way off up in the sky. He was a-seeing everybody and a-listening to every word and a-promising to let His love come down.[18]

Brown's description of slaves shouting and his description of religious conversions contain West African religious elements of initiation and possession.[19] When describing shouting, Brown states that "they'd break down and cry like babies or shout until they fell down as if they were dead,"[20] which meant a successful conversion. Conversion was contingent upon initiation. The mourner's bench resembles the initiation period Herskovits describes as the secluded training period that new devotees undergo among the Yoruba and other tribes of Dahomey, also called mourning.[21] Seclusion is necessary because it is dangerous for a person to be possessed without proper knowledge of how to cope with the god who enters his or her body.

The evangelical influence is evident as the minister in Brown's story exhorted the sinners to repent and pictured "the poor sinners a-suffering in the fires of everlasting torment,..."[22] The use of singing, praying, and clapping to help the mourners to "come through" have definite West African roots.[23] These are forms of religious instruction as well as acts of contrition or petition.

After the revival meeting, everyone looked forward to the baptisms on the first Sunday of the month.[24] Herskovits' observation that the river spirits are among the most powerful of those inhabiting the supernatural world in West African religion is pertinent.[25] Brown's description, "folks would get their passes and come from all around—on foot, in buggies and carts, and on mule-back,"[26] echoes Herskovits' description of the Yoruba and the

Ashanti as they visit water which is indispensable in their religious rites:

> a bedecked procession of worshippers left a shrine atop a high hill, followed a long path to the riverside over two miles away...[27]

Baptism is also reminiscent of the art from the tombs of Kongo culture. In Kongo culture, the cemetery is a door between the worlds of the living and the dead which takes its pattern from the circle of the sun around the earth. In the Kongo cosmogram, the cross is an emblem of spiritual continuity and renaissance.[28] The birth of the person is mirrored in the rising of the sun and his or her death and decline is symbolized by the lowering of the sun and its disappearance beneath the sea or earth.[29] In the world below, *mpemba*, the dead lose the impurities of life and acquire a new freshness and reenter the world as reincarnated spirits.[30] The sea of the world below in the Kongo cosmogram resembles water in Christian baptism in which all sins are washed away and a "new" person emerges from the water. The power of water found in the Kongo cosmogram could not have been so quickly forgotten by the slaves as they transformed the Christian meanings of rituals through their understanding of African ritual and religion.

Brown notes that singing is constant in the ritual of baptism. The deacon, dressed in white (which echoes *mpemba*, the land of things all white) walks to the appropriate spot with his staff acting as a sounding stick to find the proper depth. This staff is reminiscent of the sign of the elder/chameleon with his cane in Kongo cosmology. The cane of the elder/chameleon is a bridge that puts the living world in communication with the realm of the dead.[31] One could surmise that the deacon was a descendent of or representative of those acknowledged as the good leader, the elder/chameleon. The deacon finds and carries the convert to the spot of new life and also returns the convert to shore.

The Christian cross introduced to slaves may have evoked a religious response that was more African in nature than western. There were definite western elements in the response, but also present was a worldview that was African in content and character. The cross symbolized not only the resurrected Christ, but also a life's journey. The entire symbolic world of Africa did not enter directly into slave worship, but the memory of those symbols was not lost completely. Slaves may not have always been conscious of why certain things were done and how, but they kept those symbols alive through a living faith. Although Brown was a sinner in his young days, he had respect for all who "got religion" and those who kept praying for his salvation. This is far from surprising if, as Herskovits suggests, possession is a social phenomenon, then its slavery counterpart, conversion, can be considered a social phenomenon as well.[32]

The Evangelical Impact

The evangelical religion of the first half of the nineteenth-century provided a refuge for people who relied on their subjective experience rather than on objective knowledge. Evangelical preachers such as Charles Grandison Finney, Lyman Beecher, and Theodore Weld led the Second Great Awakening which climaxed in 1830-1831.[33] This was not a continuation of the First Awakening. The Second Awakening was more secular and more optimistic than the first. It popularized religion because it was larger than merely a manifestation of religion. This new evangelical fervor came at a crucial time in the social life of the country. The United States was emerging from a period of anti-clericalism and moving into a period of social and cultural disintegration.

The traditional connections and boundaries of society were no longer present for the populace. This left people in a marginal position and searching for new ways to integrate and participate in the growing U.S. society. Religion and religious communities helped ease the tension. Revivalists launched open attacks on the leisure activities of the new working class. The pious did not attack the workers, but the sins in which the workers participated. Drink and the theater were considered evil because they wasted time and blocked the millennium.[34] Evangelicals fought against these evils to prepare society for a new awakening.

As they attacked the leisure activities of the working class, evangelicals poured money into poor congregations and helped establish new churches in working class neighborhoods.[35]   By the middle 1830s, hundreds of working class people in Rochester, like their counterparts in other regions who were swept up in the evangelical impulse, were involved in churches.[36] All this activity was understood as an effort to build the Kingdom of God. It is not clear why so many of the working class willingly joined their masters in this religious revival. Many workers came from a tradition of republican skepticism which dated from the Revolution and openly opposed the churches.[37] Free-thought papers printed anti-evangelical invectives and formal disproofs of the existence of God. The papers supported strikes and suggested that workers needed education and self respect more than middle class temperance sermons.[38]

The chief social function of religion in the first half of the nineteenth century was to ease the marginality of various groups. Usually religion helped to instill and strengthen a sense of identity for the various groups. The folk beliefs and fetishes that had developed in the Black religious worldview blended with this evangelical enthusiasm.[39] Religion was felt personally and bodily and this was particularly true for Blacks.[40] Until the 1740s, Black slaves who were religious had little option but to cling to an African cosmology with its stress on body and spirit to order their religious and social worlds.[41] By 1790, the number of slaves raised within a fully developed African culture was only a small percentage of the slave population. More slaves were employing Judeo-Christian symbols to formulate their conceptions of their origin and destiny.[42] Mathews further suggests that in this emerging Black Christianity, social status, race, and illiteracy also performed many of the functions of dogma by channeling Black faith.[43]

SLAVE SPIRITUALS

The burst of revivalism helped Blacks and whites alike gain reference points in a society that was undergoing drastic change through immigration, the closing of the slave trade, and growing industrialization. On some levels, Black churches embraced a theology of liberation, self-determination, and Black autonomy.[44]

An image or understanding of what the second advent of Christ looks like to a people who were enslaved emerges. Slaves who gathered to worship could not reflect a concrete millennial impulse openly.[45] With whites keeping a watchful eye on slave religious gatherings, slaves were forced to be careful in their eschatological impetus, so that the untrained or ignorant eye and ear could not catch the this-worldly implications of songs like "Swing Low, Sweet Chariot."[46] On one level, slaves were singing about their coming glory in heaven, on another level they were letting each other know when a route to freedom to the North was found and informing others to prepare to make that journey as well.

Spirituals were drawn from the Bible, Protestant hymns, sermons, and African styles of singing and dancing.[47] The religious music of slaves expressed their faith in powerful and dramatic terms.[48] Albert Raboteau notes the hand-clapping and head-tossing which accompanied the music. Spirituals were not only sung, but shouted and often in the ring shout itself so that the lyrics could be acted out.[49]

CONVERSION AND SALVATION

African-American evangelicalism was a communal celebration, not an "isolating experience of awakening to a deep sense of guilt and sinfulness."[50] This is contrary to the white evangelicalism which stressed a polarization between the individualism and the community.[51] Also, white evangelicalism had a need to create powerful symbols of sinful worldliness. This resulted in a prohibition against dancing which was a central feature of the ring shout of Blacks.[52] Whites felt a need to find signs of redemption in abstinence, bodily inhibition, and withdrawal from the world. Such needs were not shared by slaves who lived in a world of sacred meaning and collective redemption.[53]

Among Black and white Baptists, salvation was the central focus, and human repentance and faith were not sufficient to guarantee salvation.[54] The emphasis on the conversion experience was also characteristic of the Congregationalists, the Presbyterians, and the Methodists. The revivals of the nineteenth century were not a *pro forma* ritual. They were a drama of personal salvation and freedom which demanded moral rectitude from the individual and the community of believers.

White evangelicals experienced conversion as an emotional outpouring of relief, for they were now saved from the wrath of God and aware of their imperfect nature.[55] They believed that only a person convicted of sin could receive true salvation. Believers were prevented from celebrating their salvation because of guilt and a persistent sense of sin.[56] Slaves did not share this sense of original sin. They prayed to be released from sin in the midst of a physical bondage which could be objectified and cast outside of their souls in a way that was unavailable to their white masters.[57] Donald Mathews notes "the emotional toll of slavery was much more effective than the doctrine of original sin in creating self-contempt."[58] Whites broke down and Blacks were lifted up in their respective experiences of conversion and salvation.

Blacks usually went through a period of personal anxiety concerning their salvation which lasted from days to weeks.[59] Raboteau states that sinners not only sat on the mourner's bench (also called the anxious seat), but some were moved when they were alone in the woods or fields.[60] The usual sequence of events began with a feeling of sinfulness, then a vision of the person's damnation, and finally an experience of acceptance and being reborn by God.[61] The converted man or woman believed that he or she had been with God or that God had been with them,[62] for this was an intensely personal inner-directed phenomenon. Among those slaves who followed the Baptist path, they could not become a member of a congregation of that faith if their soul had not been with God.[63]

The white evangelical concentration on sin and control of the body as a war between the spirit and the flesh were not central concerns for slaves. Both groups experienced conversion by crying out, falling down, and experiencing an ecstatic release. Rhys Isaac posits that slaves and white evangelicals had different connotations for their actions. Slave religion did not draw a sharp line between the religious and the secular. Conversion was desired and sought by slaves invested in their salvation. The goal was similar but the worldview and context for conversion between slaves and their white masters and mistresses differed greatly. By the 1830s, the emotional breakdown of whites under evangelical preaching became less common and was limited to revivals or camp meetings.[64]

THE MORAL SPHERE OF BLACK EVANGELICALISM

Burdened with the yoke of slavery, Blacks could resign them-selves to their fate without struggle, or they could make a conscious effort at self-determination.[65] Slaves who showed open resistance to white slaveholders challenged the theological as well as sociologi-cal dynamics that held slavery in place.[66] Slaves possessed a theo-logical perspective that helped them stand against their whites masters and mistresses and could provide them with the means to question the authority of slavocracy.

Most slaves, like Simon Brown, were silent on the subject of the hypocrisy of white Christianity. Slaves believed in the ultimate condemnation of slaveholders and any minister who preached a gospel of subjugation. William Humbert, a fugitive slave from Charleston, South Carolina captures the thoughts of many slaves:

> I have seen a minister hand the sacrament to the deacons to give the slaves, and, before the slaves had time to get home, living a great distance from the church, have seen one of the same deacons, acting as patrol, flog one of the brother members within two hours of his administering the sacrament to him, because he met the slave...without a passport, beyond the time allowed him to go home.[67]

From evangelicalism, Blacks inherited a belief system which valued a disciplined person who lived within a disciplined communi-ty.[68] Blacks believed that by submitting to such discipline they were in a position to demand that whites deal with them according to standards which transcended the master-slave relationship.[69]

The experience of Charles Colcock Jones, a white missionary to the slaves, illustrates this point. Jones reveals in his journal his attempts to appeal to the authority of Paul in preaching to slaves against running away. The effect of his admonishments, according to Jones, is that half of his audience walked off and those remaining looked dissatisfied. Jones shares that the remaining slaves expressed their anger and contempt at the close of the service with such passion that they told him that there was no such gospel in the Bible or that his sermon was not the gospel. Others took the bold tact of telling him that he was preaching to please the masters and that they would not return to hear any more of his preaching.[70]

Slaves used a variety of methods to reject the slaveholders' gospel. One method was rejection of the master's denomination. Another was a refusal to obey the moral precepts of whites such as the prescriptions against stealing, lying, and deceit. These were held as virtues by many slaves in their dealings with whites.[71] Another subtle form of protest was the decision by some slaves to devote themselves to a life of virtue in which they developed a sense of dignity and moral superiority to their masters.[72]

Rebellion was also practiced by pious slaves. Nat Turner's understanding of his call to free his people came directly from his religious life. His sense of mission and appointed time have clear and unambiguous religious roots.[73] Rebellion was more than sabotage, revolt, or flight. Raboteau sees religion itself as an act of rebellion.[74] Religion and its practice was a way slaves could assert their independence from white dominance and control.

Protest and accommodation were the two poles open to slaves in their religious as well as secular lives. Evangelical Christianity supported both, at times enabling slaves to choose protest and at other times calling slaves to accept their fate.[75] The protest tradition of the Black Church faded as the century wore on. The militancy represented by Blacks such as David Walker and Henry Highland Garnet diminished as the independent Black evangelical churches began to institutionalize and take on many of the characteristics of their white evangelical counterparts.[76]

Many Black churches maintained a policy of silence or apathy on the issue of slavery and equal rights to win public approval and acceptance. Some Black leaders began to reject the establishment of separate Black churches because they believed such churches served to maintain prejudice and a Christian caste system.[77]

Yet there were voices like that of Martin Delany, a supporter of the missionary outreach to Africa, who believed it was better to send Black missionaries than white ones to convert the continent.[78] However, Delany was biting in his criticism of religion in the Black community. He felt that Black churches were imitating the pietism of Protestant evangelicalism which gave Blacks the impression that they were miserable because suffering was a precondition to entry into the Kingdom. Delany believed that God helps those who helped themselves and he thought prayer was a foolish means to gain power in the midst of death-dealing structures. He faulted the Black Church's other-worldly stress and saw God as a liberator to Blacks who would claim their future through actions rather than pious platitudes and accommodationist behavior.[79]

Raboteau suggests that the revivalistic, inward impetus of evangelical Christianity called forth an egalitarian tendency on the part of Blacks and whites. This sometimes led to genuine religious mutuality in preaching, praying, and conversion.[80] However the words of Mathews ring a sad note on the promise and the reality:

> The tragedy of southern Evangelicalism was not that its institutions were unable to make white men behave as they should have, but that they could not allow black people full liberty in their Christian profession.[81]

The sense of evangelicalism elevated a disciplined self within a disciplined community. Both Blacks and whites strove to meet this goal with earnestness and passion. However the catastrophe known as slavery and its companion, racism, prevented Blacks and whites from carrying the evangelical impulse to its logical conclusion.

Nevertheless, Blacks continued the struggle for full humanity and salvation. Wells-Barnett joined with other African-American men and women who sought to proclaim their right to freedom which came from their religious understanding of freedom and a just God. African-Americans who responded to the evangelical impulse of the late nineteenth century sought to maintain their dignity and to shape a cosmology that affirmed their personhood and self-worth.

African-American Women's Spirituality

African-American and white women of the nineteenth century were the products of the religious revival that began in the late 1700s. Women were extremely active in practicing their religious lives.

Among white women, Nancy F. Cott notes that by the mid-seventeenth century, women outnumbered men in New England churches and that by the early nineteenth century, New England ministers took for granted that women were the majority of Christians.[82] Cott's research shows that female converts in New England during the late 1790s to early 1820s outnumbered males by three to two.

African-American and white women's religious expression and their spirituality were intensely personal matters. Yet they were able to expand their concern for their own moral development to their families, and ultimately take this concern to the larger society through associational work and moral reform societies as well as preaching and exhorting.

Black women who were active in the church had a deep, personal relationship with God and Jesus. This was similar to the experience of Black men who were active in the church. Jesus was not only Lord and Savior, he was brother and friend. Through this personal relationship with Jesus, Black women were able to transcend the inhuman structures that surrounded them in the slave South and the repressive North.

At the beginning of the nineteenth century, worship and spirituality were expressed in groups as people gathered to worship in a form that blended African survivalisms and white evangelical Christianity. One's spiritual life was shared experience—conversion, baptism, communion. Increasingly as time passed, the joy and release of the ring shout, the spontaneity of spirituals, the appeal to the interrelatedness of humans with nature were lost. African-American Christians began a personal journey in their faith.

African-American women, however, took an intriguing avenue in expressing their spirituality. Evelyn Brooks notes that Black women in religious circles did not depict themselves as the larger society portrayed white women—fragile and impressionable with little capacity for rational thought.[83] Rather, Black women viewed themselves as having a capacity to influence men and consistently described their power of persuasion over men as historically positive.[84] Black women's biblical hermeneutics revealed women in dual images, just as men were portrayed, and they affirmed their likeness to men and their oneness with men in a joint quest for salvation.[85]

Black women took pride in the mothers of the Bible who became their role models for motherhood. The mothers of Isaac, Moses, Samson and others gave Black women a view of women as more than bodily receptacles through whom great men were born. They saw these mothers as being responsible for raising sons who would deliver Israel from its oppressors.[86] They drew the obvious parallels to their lives and the lives of Black people in the nineteenth century.

African-American women did not break from the orthodoxy of the Black church, but restated that orthodoxy in what Evelyn Brooks characterizes as a "progressive and liberating language for women."[87] Black women took the roles of wife, sister, daughter, and mother, combined them with a personal spiritual experience of God in Christ, and understood themselves to be ministers in their homes. With that step, Black women were able to move beyond the image and role of domestic comforter to a greater call. This was possible by their intense evangelical spiritual drive to live a higher and better life and by their concern to shape families and a society that reflected Christian morals and precepts. Black women took the citations of Phoebe, Priscilla, and Mary as co-workers with Paul and translated them to their own work. They stressed an ultimate allegiance to God, and not to men.[88]

This drive toward Christian moral perfection by Black women did not readily translate into ordination. Jarena Lee travelled well over 2,000 miles and delivered 178 sermons to spread the gospel, yet she was never ordained.[89] Lee took the path of soul-saving rather than social reform. She felt salvation forged an armor against slavery and racial oppression and prepared Black folk for a future life.[90]

Lee was concerned about social issues, but they were not at the forefront for her. Like many other Black and white women, she experienced an ecstatic religious experience in her call,[91] but within herself she fought against the traditional notions of women's image. She did not argue against the high ideals women were held to, but she did argue for a freer interpretation of piety, purity, submission, and domesticity.

O how careful ought we be, lest through our by-laws of church government and discipline, we bring into disrepute even the word

of life. For as unseemly as it may appear now-a-days for a
woman to preach, it should be remembered that nothing is
impossible with God. And why should it be thought impossible,
heterodox, or improper, for a woman to preach? seeing the
Saviour died for the woman as well as the man. If a man may
preach, because the Saviour died for him, why not the woman?
seeing he died for her also. Is he not a whole Saviour, instead of
half one? as those who hold it wrong for a woman to preach,
would seem to make it appear.[92]

Black women's religious experience in the nineteenth century
integrated the idealization of the home and motherhood with the
secular woman's movement attack on sexually exclusive spheres.
Brooks notes that the dual image of Christ as "feminine and
masculine, passive and aggressive, meek and conquering," emerged
to inform "their self-perceptions and self-motivations."[93] Brooks
goes on to note that these women shifted back and forth from
feminine to masculine imagery as they described their role in the
evangelical crusade. They described themselves both as homemakers
and soldiers.[94]

African-American women, like white women, could not remain
within their homes and fully answer God's call to repentance and
salvation. Women's associational activities were in direct response
to the Great Awakening in which Protestants tried to counteract the
religious indifference, rationalism, and Catholicism of the day to
create an enduring and moral social order.[95]

Black and white women developed a spirituality which took
them beyond their daily prayer and reflection time and into the
world. Their public work was deeply wedded to their inner and
intense reflection. The goal was salvation on earth. Because of their
unique role in shaping the moral fiber of society through the family,
women took up the challenge to spread the promise of salvation.
Religion provided a way to order one's life and priorities. It also
enabled women to claim an authority beyond the world of men.[96]

African-American and white women formed maternal societies
in response to the cultural and religious elevation of the role of
motherhood.[97] The focus of moral reform societies was on the
family as an arena in which to solve larger social problems. Their
members gathered to prepare themselves to guide children properly

and to raise a generation of Christians. Moral reform societies were begun to eliminate the sin of licentiousness expressed in the lust of men and the prostitution of women.[98] They sought to reform and resurrect fallen women and to publicize and ostracize men who visited prostitutes. It was not unusual for the women of these societies to portray females as sacrificial victims of male lust in language designed to evoke women's power to avenge this treatment.[99]

African-American women began with an intense personal experience of the divine in their lives and took that call to salvation into the public realm to reform a corrupt moral order. Their spirituality, which at first viewing resembles a self-centered piety with little relation to the larger context, is an excellent example of the linking of personal and social transformation to effect salvation. These women sought perfection and advocated social reform in the framework of a spirituality that valued life. They took seriously the responsibility to help create and maintain a just and moral social order. These women of the nineteenth century lived their spirituality. They were able to accept the traditional roles handed to them, yet shape and bend them to reflect their understandings of their ultimate relationship to God.

The Ideology of Domesticity in the Lives of African-American Women

The ideology of domesticity had a profound impact on the world of African-American women in the nineteenth-century, but it was not the only source of Black women's subordination in nineteenth-century culture. The ideology of domesticity affected African-American women in their cultural, organizational, and religious spheres. Further, the effects of slavery and racism, as well as an emerging class structure, combined with domesticity to place African-American women in a narrowly defined sphere in nineteenth-century culture.

NINETEENTH CENTURY CULTURE

Nancy Cott provides an excellent overview of domesticity. Although her study concentrates on New England between 1780 to 1830, she gives a broad overview of the nature of domesticity, providing a framework in which to consider the place of Black women in society. Cott notes that most of the literature constituting the cult of true womanhood, the epitome of domesticity, originated in New England.

The early nineteenth-century was a world of tremendous upheaval. Women's economic participation, public activities, and general social visibility increased in the midst of a changing economy, wars, and the beginnings of the reordering of work roles. Although unable to participate directly in the political process, white middle class women used the power of the petition to demand legislation that would enable wives to retain the rights to their property within marriage. Women participated in a variety of social reform movements, for reasons of self-interest as well for moral reform.

In the midst of this whirlwind, a strong sense arose that women's proper role was in the domestic sphere. Cott notes that male and female authors created a new popular literature that ran the gamut from advice books to sermons. They all advocated or restated women's subordinate role in society. Cott calls this the "women's sphere." This notion of women's sphere has been interpreted three ways by later historians and feminist theorists.[100] One interpretation is that women were victims or prisoners of this idea. This interpretation stems from what Cott terms the didactic literature about women's place and home. This literature adopts the nineteenth-century feminist emphasis on the disabilities of women simply because of their sex and draws domesticity and feminism as opposites.

A second interpretation observes that women used domesticity to advance their own agenda. This includes educational opportunities as well as avenues for expressing animosity toward men. This interpretation uses the published works of women authors in a search for the roots of feminism in domesticity.

A third interpretation is that the women's sphere was the basis for a subculture among women that formed a source of strength and identity affording supportive relations among women. This interpretation is based on the private documents of women such as diaries. The second and third interpretation are pertinent to African-American women.

CULT OF TRUE WOMANHOOD AND AFRICAN-AMERICAN WOMEN

The cult of true womanhood arose in the shift from a rural republic, in which work had non-sexual connotations, to an economy with an industrial and urban base. The subordination of Blacks, through an ideology of the Black savage, and the confinement of white women in the cult of womanhood were interdependent and mutually supporting. The effect of these two ideologies had a tremendous impact on the lives of African-American women.

The development of "true womanhood" within the African-American community began in the mid-1870s with the emergence of a southern Black middle class. Although the post-Civil War Black urban community did not have a well-established elite of bankers and merchants, in a few cities the Black upper class was large enough in numbers to comprise a well-defined portion of society.[101] These Blacks developed their own life-style and forms of entertainment. In Washington, the elite included barbers, caterers, professors at Howard University, political appointees, and a few lawyers and doctors.[102] In New Orleans, the elite was made up of wealthy members of the old free elite (composed mostly of mulattoes) and some newcomers. The Rollins sisters of Columbia, South Carolina were the mulatto daughters of a prominent slaveholder who educated them in Boston before the war. Their home was a Republican focal point and gathering spot for the colored elite of that city.[103]

However, when considered within the aggregate of Southern society, the Black middle and upper classes were small in number and had negligible economic impact. Eric Foner writes, "only in life-style and aspirations did this elite constitute a 'Black bourgeoisie,' for it lacked capital and economic autonomy..."[104] The cult of true womanhood was a status symbol for the African-American women of this small elite group. These women were true to the cardinal

tenets of domesticity—piety, submissiveness and purity—as they
sought to be true moral guardians of the home.[105] Black women
like Sarah Pettey believed that only educated, intelligent women
should head households to insure that young Black men received the
best training[106] and Rosetta Douglass Sprague believed that educated Black women could be most effective in the home.[107]

Central to the idea of the cult, for Black women, was domesticity. Even as Black women fought alongside Black men for social
reform of slavery in the South and racism in the North, they were not
allowed full participation in the convention movement[108] until after
1848. Even then, men reluctantly shared decision-making power
with women. Josephine Washington (spouse of Booker T. Washington) reflected the general attitude among Black women—woman
must take her place beside man, but a women must never forget she
is a woman.[109] No matter how active a Black woman might be in
social reform through the club movement, she was constantly
reminded to remain within the woman's sphere in her activities.
Hence, Black women were active in founding "women's" projects
such as kindergartens for children of working mothers. The
changing nature of work for Blacks as they reached emancipation
necessitated childcare. The organization of childcare facilities for
working parents was considered the woman's role in social reform
and racial uplift.

FEMALE SUBORDINATION

W.E.B. DuBois' essay on women in *Darkwater* helps provide
the larger context for the subordination of African-American women
in nineteenth century society. According to DuBois, Black women
existed for Black men and not for themselves in nineteenth-century
culture.[110] In what he called the "damnation of women" he saw
that women sacrificed their intelligence and a chance to do their best
work to have children.[111] He advocated not only economic independence for women, but also the right of women to make their own
decisions about having children. He did so with an appeal to the
effects of constant breeding on the mortality of slave women.[112]

DuBois presented a fascinating argument containing elements of the cult ideal with penetrating social analysis. He was not completely free from the prejudices of domesticity as evidenced when he calls Black women the foundation of the Black Church.[113] He then noted that "perhaps even higher than strength and art loom human sympathy and sacrifice as characteristic of Negro womanhood."[114] Yet DuBois pointed out that because Black women must work to support their families, the family as the ideal of this culture

> is not based on the idea of an economically independent working mother. Rather it harks back to the sheltered harem with the mother emerging at first as nurse and homemaker, while the man remains the sole breadwinner. What is the inevitable result of the clash of such ideals and such facts in the colored group? Broken families.[115]

For him, the break up of families was the result of economics, modern working conditions, and sex roles that hit Black male and female workers. The majority of work available to Black men was below standard pay while Black women had numerous openings in domestic work and industry.[116] He decried any attempt to force African-American women to return to the home.

> We cannot abolish the new economic freedom of women. We cannot imprison women again in a home or require them all on pain of death to be nurses and housekeepers.
>   What is today the message of these black women to America and to the world? The uplift of women is, next to the color line and peace movement, our greatest modern cause.[117]

His point was to maintain the family unit, but he did not want to do so at the expense of the new economic freedom that he saw Black women enjoyed.[118]

Race, sex and class are key elements of DuBois' argument. They are interconnected with domesticity and the ideals of the cult of true womanhood. DuBois offered a final tribute to the strength of Black womanhood as he observes

no other women on earth could have emerged from the hell of
force and temptation which once engulfed and still surrounds
black women in America with half the modesty and womanliness
that they retain.[119]

Yet DuBois longed for the day

when we will no longer pay men for work they do not do, for the
sake of their harem; we will pay women what they earn and insist
on their working and earning it; we will allow those persons to
vote who know enough to vote, whether they be black or female,
white or male and we will ward race suicide, not by further
burdening the over-burdened, but by honoring motherhood, even
when the sneaking father shirks his duty.[120]

African-American Women's Club Movement and Social Reform

Black club women, like their white sisters, placed a great
emphasis on the sanctity of the home and a woman's place in it.
There was little direct contradiction of the church's doctrine that
females were essentially domestic beings.[121] Also like white women
active in the club movement, Black women enlarged the concept of
domesticity to include area interests of club women.[122] They held
mothers' meetings involving discussions on "child culture" and
"social purity." Their religious beliefs revolved around a "woman's
true calling is to make peoples' lives better." This led to an aggressive campaign to convert the "fallen woman" and public denounce-
ment of any man who frequented her company. African-American
women also verbally accepted the idea that women were the moral
guardians of the community.

Both inside and outside the club movement, motherhood
enjoyed the greatest sanctity. Black women saw Mary, the mother
of Jesus, as the personification of the highest expression of womanhood.[123] Although motherhood was dominant, these women also
referred to their roles as wives, sisters, and daughters. Male
conversion and the minister's moral rectitude were attributed to "a
mother's influence, a sister's guidance, or to the tender persuasion of
a devoted wife or daughter."[124]

The effects of domesticity were present in the forming of literary clubs and even night schools for those who worked during the day. The education of the young was the province of women. This responsibility was then extended through the emerging economic and class structure of Blacks to service the entire age range of the Black community. All of the educational activities Black women engaged in did not change the prevailing attitudes about the proper role and proper jobs for women.

One strong effect of domesticity on the lives of women was the shift in understanding leisure time and industriousness. With the shift toward industrialization and the increasingly narrow notion of women's proper arena as the home, leisure time became an indicator of one's social standing. Middle class white women, and a much smaller number of Black middle class women, who once contributed to the economy of their families, now became models of consumption. White men found the cult of womanhood convenient in an increasingly industrial economy where more men were forced to leave farming and enter occupations that had been previously held by middle class white women.[125] When the cult's notion of domesticity began to dominate, native-born middle class white women were replaced by poorer immigrant women as a cheaper, more permanent and exploitable work force. Black women were systematically denied easy access to jobs other than domestic work. The cult preached that women's place was in the home at a time when increasing numbers of poor women and Black women began to enter the wage-labor force.

Yet, Brooks argues, woman's uplift was:

> within an evolutionary framework that repeatedly referred to the degraded status of women in ancient civilizations and in contemporary non-Christian cultures, and they argued that the standard of womanhood evolved to a higher plane with the spread of Christianity.[126]

The combined efforts of Black and white women were essential for the progress of Blacks and peaceful race relations. Women believed that Christianizing the home and education were key to solving the race problem.[127] Black women identified with Esther who acted as an intermediary for her race. They saw their role as being similar to hers. Through them, the race would be saved and lifted to greater heights. African-Americans would receive deliverance.

There was also a clear, strong voice within the Black Church that carried the mild rhetoric of Black women to its farthest extension. For women like Mrs. G.D. Oldham of Tennessee, women were to be ministers, not slaves to their home.[128] Lucy Wilmot Smith, speaking in 1886 to a predominately male audience in a church stated:

> It is one of the evils of the day that from babyhood girls are taught to look forward to the time when they will be supported by a father, a brother, or somebody else's brother.[129]

The image of woman as loyal and comforting spouse fostered by the cult of true womanhood, was transcended to embrace woman's relationship with Jesus. The stress was on ultimate allegiance to God, not to men. In a strictly biblical appeal, women yoked their faith, with its requirement for support and kindness, with women's domestic image as comforter, to support a public responsibility to prophesy and spread the Gospel.[130]

In her 1908 book, *The Work of the Afro-American Woman*, Mrs. N.F. Mossell gave yet another image of leadership for turn of the century African-American women. She believed that the home should be founded on right principles, morality, Christian living, and a "due regard to heredity and environment that promise good for the future."[131] In her truly remarkable work, she deftly handled the social location of women in African-American culture while advocating for a wider range of possibilities for male and female interaction and roles.

> Man desires a place of rest from the cares and vexations of life, where peace and love shall abide, where he shall be greeted by the face of one willing to provide for his comfort and convenience—where little ones shall sweeten the struggle for existence and make the future full of bright dreams. Woman desires to carry into effect the hopes that have grown with her growth, and strengthened with her strength from childhood days until maturity; love has made the path of life blend easily with the task that duty has marked out.[132]

In biting advice to newly married women (and perhaps those who had not yet given up on reforming their spouses), Mossell stated:

> ...keeping a clean house will not keep a man at home; to be sure it will not drive him out, but neither will it keep him in to a very large extent. And you, dear tender-hearted little darlings, that are being taught daily that it will, might as well know the truth now and not be crying your eyes out later.[133]

Further,

> The men that usually stay in at night are domestic in their nature, care little for the welfare or approval of the world at large, are not ambitious, are satisfied with being loved, care nothing for being honored....A man who aspires to social pre-eminence, who is ambitious or who acquires the reputation of being a man of judgment and knowledge, useful as a public man, will be often out at night even against his own desires, on legitimate business.[134]

She did not maintain that women should always greet their spouses with a smile, though they should not allow the list of trials Mossell gave to deter them from maintaining themselves in some semblance of dignity and beauty:

> Women must not be blamed because they are not equal to the self-sacrifice of always meeting husbands with a smile, not the wife blamed that she does not dress after marriage as she dressed before; child-birth and nursing, the care of the sick through sleepless nightly vigils, the exactions and irritations incident to life whose duties are made up of trifles and interruptions, and whose work of head and heart never ceases, make it an impossibility to put behind them at all times all cares and smile with burdened heart and weary feet and brain.[135]

Mossell's rhetoric is astounding and even more so given the period in which she wrote. She not only addressed African-American society, she also addressed white women of her day:

> Hath not the bonds-woman and her scarce emancipated daughter done what they could? Will not our more favored sisters,

convinced of our desires and aspirations because of these first few feeble efforts, stretch out the helping hand that we may rise to a nobler, purer womanhood?[136]

Mossell's writings represent in clear terms the ideology of the Black women's club movement. Her concentration on the home, with its foundation of morality and Christian living, represents the influence of evangelical Christianity and the cult of true womanhood. Her remarkable ability in providing piercing social commentary, while maintaining her role as wife, mother, and supporter of Black social uplift, is a key characteristic of the Black women who were active in the club movement. Mossell, like her Black sisters, was trained to strike this balance by Black evangelical Christianity and its demand for a disciplined person and a moral lifestyle. This demand extended from a personal spirituality to a concern for the moral fiber of the African-American community and United States society. This concern on the part of African-American women took its organizational form in the club movement.

The National Federation of African-American Women had great impact on Black social and political life. This organization was composed of 85 groups scattered throughout the country with the greater number of located in the South. In the August 1, 1895 session held in Charles Street AME Church, the organization adopted a two-fold agenda:

> (1) concentration of the dormant energies of the women of the Afro-American race into one broad band of sisterhood: for the purpose of establishing needed reforms, and the practical encouragement of all efforts being put forth by various agencies, religious, educational, ethical and otherwise, for the upbuilding, ennobling and advancement of the race;
> (2) to awaken the women of the race to the great need of systematic effort in home-making and the divinely imposed duties of motherhood.[137]

After 1896, and the formation of the National Association of Colored Women, the various women's clubs made no move to standardize their activities. Groups and programs evolved out of the needs of the immediate communities, with common themes being education and care for the aged.[138] Sharecroppers, housewives,

students, salesgirls, dressmakers, artists, teachers, and school
principles all came together to form women's clubs for community
uplift and support.

One such club was the Washington Colored Woman's League,
which was organized in 1892. It paid tuition for two nurses in
training, contracted to pay one half of the salary of the instructor for
a kindergarten, and established a sewing school.[139] Club women
established night schools, worked with prisoners, cared for aged ex-
slaves, created insurance-type funds for illness benefits, educated
females, and established community facilities.[140] These clubs were
the latter-day equivalents of the YMCA, the public library, and the
Department of Social Services.

The Belle Phoebe League of the twins cities of Pittsburgh and
Allegheny, Pennsylvania provides another vital emphasis for
women's clubs. In the League's report to the 1896 convention of the
National Association of Colored Women, it described its objectives
as

> Self culture, and to advance the interest of the women of our race
> on all lines pertaining to the development of a nobler womanhood
> and the securing of our rights in every legitimate way, and to
> second the efforts of our leading women such as Mrs. Ida B.
> Wells-Barnett and others....[141]

Wells-Barnett was not unusual for the women of her period.
Her strong church ties provided the basis for social change and civil
rights. Most club members were active church workers or at least
attended church. Churches were the major benevolent, spiritual, and
social institutions of the African-American community.[142] The
Black Church opened its doors for the women of the club movement.
The 1896 convention of the National Association of Colored Women
was held at Nineteenth Street Baptist Church in Washington, DC.
Of the fifteen national meetings between 1901 to 1930, eight were
held in churches.

A second women's organization effecting Black club women on
a national level was the National Association of Colored Women.
This organization focused on the uplift of the Black peasant woman
and the improvement of Negro family life.[143] As Wilson Moses
notes, one of its goals was to introduce the standards of Victorian

domesticity into the cabins of Georgia and Alabama sharecroppers. There was a decided class bias in the organization because most of the influential and dominant members were from the emerging Black middle class. Josephine St. Pierre Ruffin was a major force in this organization and in the Black woman's club movement in general.

Ruffin founded the Women's Era Club on the belief that the Black women's club movement should be involved in temperance, morality, higher education, and hygienic and domestic questions.[144] The club founded a newspaper, *The Woman's Era*. The paper reflected concerns of the club and, in particular, Ruffin's concerns. It was uncompromising in its defense of Black womanhood and in its condemnation of lynching. In the first issue of *The Women's Era*, it made clear the bias and program of the club:

> Up to their [white lynchers] ears in guilt against Negro women, they offer as their excuse for murdering Negro men, Negro women, and Negro children, that white women are not safe from the Negro rapist....We are told that Frances [sic] Willard of America and Laura Ormiston Chant of England, have entered the lists of apologists....Why did not the slaves, when their masters were away trying to shoot the Union to death and keep them forever slaves, out-rage the wives and daughters of these traitors confided in their care?[145]

Black women were no more immune to the nativist sentiments of the period than any other group in the United States. The pages of *The Era* reflected this state of affairs:

> The audacity of foreigners who flee their native land and seek refuge here, many of them criminals and traitors, who are here but a day before they join in the hue and cry against the native born citizens of this land is becoming intolerable....self defense and self protection will force this government to protect its own people and to teach foreigners that this land is for Americans black or white and that other men are welcome and come here only by behaving themselves and steering clear of plots and schemes against the people and the citizens who are here by right.[146]

The Black women's club movement came of age when Ida B. Wells-Barnett was attacked by Mr. Jacks, the editor of a Montgomery City, Missouri, newspaper and the president of the Missouri Press Association.[147] Jacks was both a Sunday School superintendent and the son of a slaveholder. His attack on Wells-Barnett, and then on Black womanhood, was vitriolic and sensationalist. In a letter he sent to Florence Belgarnie of England he claimed:

Out of some 200 [Negroes] in this vicinity it is doubtful if there are a dozen virtuous women or that number who are not daily thieving from the white people. To illustrate how they regard virtue in a woman: one of them, a negro woman, was asked who a certain negro woman who had lately moved into the neighborhood was. She turned up her nose and said, "the negroes will have nothing to do with 'dat nigger', she won't let any man, except her husband sleep with her, and we don 'sociate with her."[148]

Ruffin enclosed this letter in her call to the first conference. However, Moses notes, also enclosed was Ruffin's warning not to give out Jacks' letter for general circulation or publication. The fear was that the letter was so inflammatory that it would spark violent protest.

Jacks also attacked the character of northern women and British women involved in the anti-lynching campaign:

Your pleas seem to us to take the form of asking us to make associates for our families of prostitutes, liars, thieves, and lawbreakers generally, and to especially condone the crime of rape if committed by a negro. Respectable people in this country not only decline to form such associates, but naturally infer that those who ask them to do so and place themselves on a level with such characters must either be of the same moral status themselves, or else wholly ignorant of the condition of affairs here, and consequently do no know what they are talking about.[149]

Reaction to the Jacks letter was swift and filled with outrage in the various women's clubs. In a letter signed by one thousand women of Bethel Church in New York, the writers acknowledge that Jacks had spurred a deeply felt need by the various women's clubs to come together and begin to strategize on how to better effect the uplift of the race:

> We are sorry that the "Jacks' letter" should seem to be the prick which stung to activity. We would not have it appear that we are aroused to action only by the irritation of external circumstance, but would be glad for the world to know that, in reality, our women are taking intelligent cognizance of the inner life of the race, and that the desire to be actually noble is more potent than the impulse to resent insult and seek vindication. What we think of ourselves is always more important than what others think of us, that is to say, self-respect based upon truth is the foundation we seek to lay.[150]

When the women met, they passed a resolution defending Wells-Barnett's character and her anti-lynching work:

> ...That we, the representative women of our race in United States, have witnessed with great admiration the noble and truthful advocacy of Mrs. Ida B. Wells Barnett, defending us against the lying charge of rape, and we take this opportunity of congratulating her upon her recent marriage, and are glad to hail her, in the face of all her assailants, as our noble "Joanna of Arc."[151]

Ruffin's presidential address captures the vision and scope of the Black women's club movement. The movement focused on both individual and community. It also focused on questions of national importance. These women were vitally concerned with racial uplift, but they were also cognizant of the national debates of temperance and morality:

> In the first place we need to feel the cheer and inspiration of meeting each other; we need to gain the courage and fresh life that comes from the mingling of congenial souls, of those working for the same ends. Next, we need to talk over not only those things that are of especial interest to us as colored women, the training of our children, openings for our boys and girls, how they can be prepared for occupations and occupations may be found or opened for them, that we especially can do in the moral education of the race with which we are identified, our mental elevation and physical development, the home training it is necessary to give our

children in order to prepare them to meet the peculiar conditions in which they shall find themselves, how to make the most of our own, to some extent, limited opportunities, these are some of our own peculiar questions to be discussed. Besides these are the general questions of the day, which we cannot afford to be indifferent to: temperance, morality, the higher education, hygienic and domestic questions....[152]

These concerns were also Ida B. Wells-Barnett's concerns. Like the majority of the women in her day, she upheld the need for women to be the moral guardians of African-American society. She was far from immune to the ideology and rhetoric of the cult of true womanhood. Temperance, morality, education, domesticity, social uplift were of deep concern to her as she wrote and agitated for justice in the United States in the late nineteenth and early twentieth centuries.

NOTES

[1] C. Eric Lincoln, *Race, Religion, and the Continuing American Dilemma* (New York: Hill and Wang, 1984), 60.

[2] Sydney E. Ahlstrom, *A Religious History of the American People*, vol. 1 (Garden City, New York: Image Books, 1975), 425-26; F.L. Cross and E.A. Livingstone, *The Oxford Dictionary of the Christian Church*, 2d ed. (Oxford: Oxford University Press, 1974), 590. The First Great Awakening was a religious revival in the United States beginning in 1726 and peaking in New England in the 1740s. There was a stress on visible conversion. The beginnings of the movement were in the Dutch Reformed Churches of New Jersey and spread to the Congregationalists and Presbyterians.

[3] Erskine Clarke, *Wrestlin' Jacob: A Portrait of Religion in the Old South* (Atlanta: John Knox Press, 1979), 7-8; Gayraud Wilmore, *Black Religion and Black Radicalism: An Interpretation of the Religious History of Afro-American People*, 2d. ed., rev. and enl. (Maryknoll, New York: Orbis Books, 1983), 15-17. Wilmore notes that the religion of West Africa entailed a highly involved ontological and ethical system. There was no rigid demarcation between the natural and supernatural. Africans appealed to animals as symbolic representations of the environment in which humans exist. These may have been related to the spirits of ancestors, but above all were related to a Supreme Being. This

Supreme Being or God was above all gods and was known to the slaves as creator, judge, and redeemer.

[4] Clarke, 8.

[5] Rhys Isaac, *The Transformation of Virginia: 1740-1790* (Chapel Hill, North Carolina: The University of North Carolina Press, 1982), 70; Albert J. Raboteau, *Slave Religion: The "Invisible Institution" in the Antebellum South* (New York: Oxford University Press, 1978), 291-311; Lincoln, 63.

[6] William John Faulkner, ed. "How the Slaves Worshipped," *The Days When the Animals Talked: Black American Folktales and How They Came to Be* (Chicago: Follett Publishing, 1977), 52-59.

[7] Isaac, 70. Isaac notes that Afro-Virginians were not caught in a tension between church-centered sacred celebrations and home-centered profane styles. Such English Christian distinctions had little meaning for blacks who came from an integrated cosmos.

[8] Faulkner, 53; Raboteau, 212.

[9] Adolph B. Benson, ed., *America of the Fifties: Letters of Fredrika Bremer,* (New York: The American-Scandinavian Foundation, 1924), 117.

[10] Raboteau, 66; Isaac, 70.

[11] Raboteau, 71; Stuckey, 62-63.

[12] Raboteau, 68-69.

[13] Faulkner, 54.

[14] Ibid.

[15] Raboteau, 212-15.

[16] Donald G. Mathews, *Religion in the Old South* (Chicago: University of Chicago Press, 1977), 224. Beginning in 1822 with the Stono Rebellion of Denmark Vesey to the 1831 Nat Turner revolt to the Civil War, whites tried to keep in direct contact with all black religious activities. Pater-rollers were groups of white men who patrolled the slave quarters (and later the freed Black community) to frighten and intimidate the slaves. Their chief function was to ensure white hegemonic rule.

[17] Melville J. Herskovits, *The Myth of the Negro Past* (Boston: Beacon Press, 1958), 214.

[18] Faulkner, 54.

[19] There are two schools of thought concerning the linkages between African spirit possession and the shouting found in revivalist American evangelicalism. Herskovits, 215-23 and Zora Neale Hurston, *The Sanctified Church* (Berkeley: Turtle Island Press, 1981), 91-92 argue for a close association between the two. Raboteau, 63-64 questions this link. Raboteau suggests that it is the Holy Spirit who mounts the worshipper, not African Gods. This is a valid point, however Raboteau fails to appreciate fully the depth of blending between African and Christian cosmologies. The state of possession was familiar to slaves. Their acceptance of a Christian God replaced the myriad gods of Africa as the object who enters and renews the person.

[20] Faulkner, 54.

[21] Herskovits, 222.

[22] Faulkner, 55.

[23] Herskovits, 216; 223.

[24] Faulkner, 56. Isaac, 171. Through baptism, black converts were told by white (and black) preachers of their responsibility to maintain godly conduct and to internalize strict Protestant Christian values and norms.

[25] Herskovits, 232.

[26] Faulkner, 56.

[27] Herskovits, 233.

[28] Robert Farris Thompson and Joseph Corner, *The Four Moments of the Sun: Kongo Art in Two Worlds* (Washington: National Gallery of Art, Washington, 1981), 44. The Christian cross resembles the Kongo cross. The horizontal line, *kalunga*, which is the name of God, is interpreted as water—either river or sea. Above the line extends heaven, and below it is found the earth. Between earth and heaven stands the mount of the living and the mount of the dead. This parallels the Christian understanding of baptism as a dying and rising to new life.

[29] Ibid., 43.

[30] Ibid.

[31] Ibid., 35.

[32] Hurston, 91.

[33] Paul E. Johnson, *Shopkeeper's Millennium: Society and Revivals in Rochester, New York 1815-1837* (New York: Hill and Wang, 1978), 4.

[34] Ibid., 110.

[35] Ibid., 116.

[36] Ibid., 102-108.

[37] Ibid., 120.

[38] Ibid., 120-121.

[39] Isaac, 70.

[40] Ibid.

[41] Donald G. Mathews, *Religion in the Old South* (Chicago: University of Chicago Press, 1977), 208.

[42] Isaac, 306.

[43] Mathews, 213. Mathews elaborates this point by explaining that black religious experience was incapable of being represented in doctrines and was only hinted at by talking about "hope, faith, courage, power, celebration, expectation, and freedom as ultimate vindication."

[44] Darlene Clark Hine, "Lifting the Veil, Shattering the Silence: Black Women's History in Slavery and Freedom," in *The State of Afro-American History: Past, Present, and Future*, ed. Darlene Clark Hine (Baton Rouge: Louisiana State University Press, 1986), 228.

[45] Mathews, 208. Mathews notes that in the process of conversion to Chris-

Womanist Justice, Womanist Hope

tianity, the wrath of Denmark Vesey and Nat Turner—the dialectic of white mission and black piety—gave impetus to a faith of liberation through an apocalyptic event.

[46] Raboteau, 250-51.

[47] Raboteau, 243; Hurston, 79-80; Isaac, 300.

[48] Hurston, 79-80; Lawrence W. Levine, "Slave Songs and Slave Consciousness: An Exploration in Nineteenth Century Social History," ed. Tamara K. Hareven (Englewood Cliffs, New Jersey: Prentice-Hall, 1971), 99-130; Lawrence W. Levine, *Black Culture and Black Consciousness: Afro-American Folk Thought From Slavery to Freedom* (New York: Oxford University Press, 1977), 30-55; John Lovell, Jr., *Black Song: The Forge and the Flame, The Story of How the Afro-American Spiritual Was Hammered Out* (New York: The Macmillan Company, 1972), 24-88.

[49] Raboteau, 244-45.

[50] Isaac, 172.

[51] Ibid.

[52] Ibid., 308.

[53] Ibid.

[54] Mechal Sobel, *Trabelin' On: The Slave Journey to an Afro-Baptist Faith* (Princeton: Princeton University Press, 1988), 90.

[55] Mathews, 214. Conversion was also a release from the tension between God's expectation of perfection and human inability to achieve it.

[56] Ibid., 215.

[57] Ibid.

[58] Ibid.

[59] Raboteau, 267.

[60] Ibid.

[61] Ibid.

[62] Sobel, 95.

[63] Ibid., 96.

[64] Mathews, 214.

[65] Lincoln, 62.

[66] Clarke, 41.

[67] Raboteau, 293.

[68] Mathews, 224.

[69] Ibid., 225.

[70] Clarke, 40.

[71] Raboteau, 294-96.

[72] Ibid., 301.

[73] Mathews, 231-36; Sobel, 159-66; Raboteau, 164.

[74] Raboteau, 305.

[75] Ibid., 304.

[76] Henry Highland Garnet, *Walker's Appeal, With a Brief Sketch of His Life*

(New York: J.H. Tobitt, 1848). Walker's *Appeal to the Coloured Citizens of the World* written in 1829 was steeped in religious imagery and prophecy. He predicted bloody retributive justice on white slaveholders as a necessary outcome unless emancipation was immediately declared. Earl Ofari, *Let Your Motto Be Resistance* (Boston: Beacon Press, 1972), 144-53. Henry Highland Garnet's "Address to the Slaves of the United States of American" written in 1843 built on Walker's *Appeal*. Garnet's address is stunning in its dissection of slavery as an evil in the sight of God and submission to slavery as sinful. For him, it was better to die than live in submission.

[77] Leon F. Litwack, *North of Slavery: The Negro in the Free States 1790-1860* (Chicago: University of Chicago Press, 1961), 211-12.

[78] Wilmore, 110.

[79] Ibid., 111-13.

[80] Raboteau, 314.

[81] Mathews, 247.

[82] Nancy F. Cott, *The Bonds of Womanhood: "Woman's Sphere" in New England, 1780-1835* (New Haven: Yale University Press, 1977), 126-28.

[83] Evelyn Brooks, "The Women's Movement in the Black Baptist Church, 1880-1920" (PhD diss., The University of Rochester, 1984), 146. Although Brooks concentrates on women of the Black Baptist church, her observations ring true for black women across denominational lines during this period of African-American religious history and experience.

[84] Ibid.,145. Black Christian society did allow exceptions to the rule. The characters of Delilah and Jezebel were not models for female behavior.

[85] Ibid.

[86] Ibid., 146.

[87] Ibid., 140.

[88] Willie Mae Coleman, "Keeping the Faith and Disturbing the Peace Black Women: From Anti-Slavery to Women's Suffrage" (Phd diss., University of California, Irvine, 1982), 88. Coleman notes that Black women took the *Virginia Baptist* to task for a series of articles which claimed that women who aspired to preach or desired suffrage were in violation of God's law. These Black sisters reminded church men that women outnumbered men in most churches and were crucial for the financial health of the church and noted "when there is a question as to legislation or expenditure, then the men arise in their majesty and delegate to women the task of remembering that St. Paul said 'let the women keep silence'."

[89] Bert James Loewenberg and Ruth Bogin, ed., *Black Women in Nineteenth-Century American Life: Their Words, Their Thoughts, Their Feelings* (University Park: The Pennsylvania State University Press, 1976), 135 and Andrews, *Sisters of the Spirit: Three Black Women's Autobiographies of the Nineteenth Century* (Bloomington: Indiana University Press, 1986), 29.

[90] Loewenberg and Bogin, 135.

[91] Andrews, *Sisters of the Spirit*, 29 and 35.

[92] Ibid., 35.

[93] Brooks, 165.

[94] Ibid.

[95] Ibid., 133.

[96] Ibid., 139.

[97] Ibid., 149.

[98] Ibid., 151-52.

[99] Ibid., 153.

[100] Cott, 197-98. Barbara Welter, "The Cult of True Womanhood, 1820-1860," *American Quarterly* 18 (1966):151-74 and Gerda Lerner, "The Lady and the Mill-Girl: Changes in the Status of Woman in the Age of Jackson," *Mid-Continent American Studies Journal* 10 (1969):5-15 are representative of the first interpretation. The second interpretation Cott suggests is represented by the works of Glenda Riley, "The Subtle Subversion: Change in the Traditionalist Image of the American Woman," *The Historian* 32 (1970):210-27 and Ann Douglas Wood, "Mrs. Sigourney and the Sensibility of Inner Space," *New England Quarterly* 45 (1972): 163-81. The best representative of the third interpretation Cott cites is Kathryn Kish Sklar, *Catharine Beecher: A Study in American Domesticity* (New Haven: Yale University Press, 1973).

[101] Eric Foner, *Reconstruction: America's Unfinished Revolution 1863-1877* (New York: Harper and Row, Publishers, 1988), 397.

[102] Ibid., 397-98. Foner describes these as the "mostly light-skinned 'elite of colored fashion and high life'." The majority of the elite in most southern cities were mulattoes. Former slaves challenged the old elite for positions of political leadership and community position and power.

[103] Ibid., 398. Their names were Catherine de Medici, Charlotte Corday, and Louisa Muhlbach.

[104] Ibid.

[105] Paula Giddings, *When and Where I Enter: The Impact of Black Women on Race and Sex in America* (New York: William Morrow and Company, Inc., 1984), 47.

[106] Cynthia Neverdon-Morton, "The Black Woman's Struggle for Equality in the South, 1895-1925," in *The Afro-American Woman: Struggles and Images*, ed. Sharon Harley and Rosalyn Terborg-Penn (Port Washington, New York: Kennikat Press, 1978), 43.

[107] Ibid.

[108] The convention movement was a series of meetings held in the nineteenth century by leading African-American social reformers. The purpose of the movement was to agitate for racial and social reform. It also had strong anti-slavery rhetoric. Black reformers meet to discuss the conditions of the day and also plot strategy for effective social and moral change.

[109] Ibid.

[110] W.E.B. DuBois, "The Damnation of Women" chap. in *Darkwater: Voices from Within the Veil* (New York: Schocken Books, 1920), 163.

[111] Ibid., 164.

[112] Ibid., 164-69.

[113] Ibid., 174-79. He cites Mary Still as one of the "early mothers of the church" and refers to her "quaint" observation: "For the purpose of mutual aid, they banded themselves together in society capacity, that they might be better able to administer to each other's sufferings and to soften their own pillows. So we find the females in the early history of the church abounding in good works and in acts of true benevolence."

[114] Ibid., 177.

[115] Ibid., 180.

[116] Ibid.

[117] Ibid., 181.

[118] Ibid., 184. He writes, "God send us a world with woman's freedom and married motherhood inextricably wed,..."

[119] Ibid., 186.

[120] Ibid., 185.

[121] Coleman, 83.

[122] Ibid.

[123] Brooks, 146.

[124] Ibid., 147.

[125] The textile and clothing industries are examples of this. Women traditionally did the weaving and spinning to create the cloth necessary for clothes. Both these forms of production passed into the factory where men controlled both hiring and production.

[126] Brooks, 166.

[127] Ibid., 168.

[128] Ibid., 148. It is not clear from Oldham's rhetoric that she was advocating for the ordained ministry. It is most likely she was speaking in the broadest terms possible for ministry.

[129] Ibid., 153.

[130] Ibid.

[131] Mrs. N.F. Mossell, *The Work of the Afro-American Woman*, 2nd ed. (Philadelphia: Geo. S. Ferguson, Company, 1908; reprint, New York: Oxford University Press, 1988), 125 (page references are to reprint edition). Mrs. Mossell published using her husband's initials (Nathan F.). Her full name was Gertrude Bustill Mossell.

[132] Ibid., 115.

[133] Ibid., 120.

[134] Ibid.

[135] Ibid., 121.

[136] Ibid., 47.

[137] *A History of the Club Movement Among the Colored Women of the United States of America, As Contained in the Minutes of the Conventions, Held in Boston, July 29, 30, 31, 1895, and of the National Federation of Afro-American Women, Held in Washington, D.C., July 20, 21,22, 1896* (n.p., 1902), 34-35.

[138] Coleman, 69-70.

[139] Ibid., 71.

[140] Ibid., 77-78.

[141] *A History of the Club Movement*, 27.

[142] Coleman, 78.

[143] Wilson Jeremiah Moses, *The Golden Age of Black Nationalism, 1850-1925* (New York: Oxford University Press, 1978), 103.

[144] Ibid., 107.

[145] Ibid., 109.

[146] Ibid., 113.

[147] Moses, 116. The editors of *The Christian Educator*, sponsored by the Freedmen's Aid and Southern Education Society, told the *Era* that Jacks "has never printed a disrespectful word in his paper here against colored people. It is safe to say from what is known about the man, that he would never be even courageous enough to print the whole letter in his own paper, and look his neighbors in the face the same week."

[148] Ibid., 115.

[149] Ibid., 115-16.

[150] *A History of the Club Movement*, 18-19.

[151] Ibid., 11-12.

[152] Ibid., 31.

V

IDA B. WELLS-BARNETT:
HER SOCIAL AND MORAL PERSPECTIVES

Ida B. Wells-Barnett was an active participant in the women's club movement and other programs for social changes of her time. Her deep and abiding spirituality was forged in the Black Church of the South. Her rebellion against the traditional roles assigned to women emerged in her career as activist and newspaper journalist. She bowed to societal conventions surrounding domesticity and took time away from the socio-political world to raise her children, returning to her work as quickly as time and circumstance allowed. Her concern for decent jobs and wages for African-Americans found voice and action in the Negro Fellowship League.

Wells-Barnett responded to and helped shape her era. The greatest contribution she made to United States society as a whole was her untiring work in the anti-lynching movement. Her work in this movement was shaped by the political, social, cultural, and economic movements of her day. She attempted an integrated analysis of discrimination and violence, and sought to call the nation to task for violating its social principles regarding race.

Early Years: Religious Commitment and Social Criticism

Wells created a standard for herself, her people, and United States society. Her earliest writings reflect a woman with a strong sense of Christian duty. The first of her two surviving diaries was written between 1885 and 1887. This early diary illustrates a young woman in her early twenties wrestling with her faith and her culture. It reveals some of the intensity of her internal struggle for moral rectitude and agency. The early diary also contains reflections on some of the later issues with which Wells would wrestle: clerical leadership, the mission of the church, lynching, Black unity, interracial marriage and sexuality, and Black womanhood.

CHRISTIAN DUTY

Wells' understanding of Christian duty was rooted in her belief in an immanent God in Christ. The mission of her Jesus was to offer salvation for sinners. She revealed much of her personal theology in commenting on Dwight Moody's preaching at a revival held in Memphis.

> His style is so simple, plain and natural. He told the old, old story in an easy conversational way that charms the listener ere he is aware and the secret of his success is, I think—that he does not preach a far-away God—a hard to be reconciled Savior but uses a natural earnest tone and tells in a natural way without long drawn doctrine or finely spun theology or rhetoric the simple truth that Christ Jesus came on earth to seek and save that which was lost.[1]

Wells' understanding of God and Christ was typical of both slave and free Blacks of her day who saw God as personal and just. Writing after a watch meeting at one o'clock in the morning, she gave the reader a lucid picture of her intensely personal experience of God and its importance for her integrity:

> ...and I felt lifted up and I thank God I opened my mouth and told of His wonderful mercies to me and my heart overflowed with thankfulness....and tonight I came away after greeting them all and finding their hearts warm and inclined to me—with a lighter and more peaceful forgiveness with all mankind and I thank God for it....[2]

Wells' words echo the rhythm and motion of slave worship and its evolution into the Black evangelical Christianity of the late nineteenth century. The slave tale told by Simon Brown also reveals an immanent God:

The folks would sing and pray and testify and clap their hands,
just as if God was right there in the midst of them. He wasn't way
off up in the sky. He was a-seeing everybody and a-listening to
every word and a-promising to let His love come down.[3]

A strong sense of God's judgment and the necessity of right
action in relation to God's will also pervades Wells' writing. Her
commitment to Christian duty and responsibility is evident in her
early years. In the midst of deciding whether she would remain in
California with her aunt and sisters, Wells writes:

I know not if I will ever have another chance yet I try not to be
rebellious but extract consolation out of the thought that my
Heavenly Father will reward and bless me for doing what is right
and just. And if I did nothing, sacrificed nothing in return for all
that has been done for me, I could not expect his blessing and
sanction. Help me and bring success to my efforts I pray.[4]

Her diary entries of January, 1887 reveal a fully developed and
unequivocal understanding of moral action and Christian duty.
Wells decided to teach a Sunday school class as a way to begin to
work for God who had done much for her. She was disappointed
with the way the Bible was taught and preached and hoped to
influence her charges "in a small degree to think of better things."
She concluded her entry with a covenant plea and commitment.

God help me to try. I shall begin this year with that determination, so that another year may find me with more to offer the
master in the way of good works. God help me to be a Christian!
To so conduct myself in my intercourse with the unconverted. Let
it be an ever present theme with me, and O help me to better
control my temper! Bless me for the ensuing year; let me feel that
Thou art with me in all my struggles.[5]

By January 18, she had organized a class of young men who
promised to come regularly on Sundays. However, her relationship
with her brother who was in the class was strained. Some of the
difficulties she would encounter in later life, as she tried to work with
others toward her understanding of justice and moral rectitude, were
revealed in her analysis of her relationship with her brother. Wells

understood that she alternated between harshness, indifference, and repulsion in his regard. She asks, "God help me to be more careful and watchful over my manners and bearing toward him. Let not my own brother perish while I am laboring to save others!"[6]

In another set of entries during February, Wells encountered her humanity and her responsibility in a direct manner. After asking God to bless her in her undertakings and guard her against evil,[7] she was brought up short by Mr. Dardis (apparently an authority figure to the young Ida Wells) who gave her a severe lecture on going to the theater. In reflecting on herself as both leader and role model, Wells revealed her humility as well as her resolve to put teaching and deed in harmony:

> I had not placed so high an estimate on myself. He [Dardis] certainly gave me food for thought and hereafter when I grow weary or despondent and think my life useless and unprofitable, may I remember this episode, and may it strengthen me to the performance of my duty, for I would not willingly be the cause of one soul's being led astray. O thou, Help of the weak and helpless! Help me be firm and strong for the right and watchful for my own conduct.[8]

Later, as Easter neared and she heard a sermon on the cost of religion, she resolved to put away her plans for fun and pleasure during the Easter season. She would fast for her "many sins of dereliction and remain home to work, watch and pray, and praise for the wonderful goodness of my Father to an unworthy servant."[9]

In an entry near the end of this diary, Wells reflected on her life and her future as she celebrated her twenty-fifth birthday. She found herself falling short of the mark, particularly where her education was concerned. She noted her "hunger and thirst after righteousness and knowledge" but felt that she was not as persistent as she should be in her pursuit of both. She asked God for the "steadiness of purpose" to acquire both and hoped that in ten years hence she would be "increased in honesty and purity of purpose and motive!"[10]

Wells was clear about the correct behavior God expected from a faithful Christian. She had a strong sense of personal sin and personal salvation. However, she did not remain individualistic in her approach to religion. Rather, she blended this forceful sense of personal responsibility for moral agency with a larger critique of worship and the role of clergy. She held her personal standard as the model of authentic moral action and Christian witness.

ROLE OF INSTITUTIONAL RELIGION

Wells could not accept segregated worship. After listening to Dwight Moody[11] preach in 1885, she was moved by his simple, yet eloquent message, and wrote:

> I intended writing Mr. Moody a letter asking him why ministers never touched on that phase of sin—the caste distinction—practiced even in the churches and among christianity (?) but rather, tacitly conniving at it by assenting to their caste arrangements, and accepting it as a matter of course, instead of rectifying it—but I had no chance, and he left the city yesterday; so I know not where to address him.[12]

Wells echoed the words of Simon Brown again when he saw "so much pretending in the white man's religion that I felt better off being an honest sinner."[13] For Wells, even though she admitted to hearing a good sermon, she also "witnessed practical evidence of 'white folks' Christianity,' in the haste with which they passed us by when choosing a seat."[14] The reference to being "passed by" is an allusion to the fact that Blacks, both slave and free, were relegated to the back of the church or into the balcony in churches where whites and Blacks worshipped.

Like other African-Americans of her day, Wells could not understand or accept a Christianity which separated the people of God from one another on the basis of race. Wells held a high view of religion. For her, religion and the church constituted a *living* faith in a just God, faith in which the believer's action must conform to the teachings of the Bible. She did not suppose that the true believer made exceptions to the demands of the word of God. Rather, he or she lived the word and sought to embody God's presence in the world.

Her strong sense of moral agency extended to the clergy as well. She was biting and uncompromising in her estimate of a young preacher she encountered:

> Went to service yesterday morning and found a very slender, puerile-looking, small specimen of humanity occupying the pulpit. His "talk" was premature somewhat, and yet applicable; his peculiarities and oddities certainly have the spice of novelty and daring which surprises too much for demur and carries one by storm almost against the judgment....[15]

She returned that evening to hear him *preach* (her emphasis) and reached a conclusion about his fitness for ministry. Her evaluation was negative and to the point. She found his discourse to be:

> A constant arraignment of the negro as compared to the whites, a burlesque of Negro worship, a repetition of what he did not believe in, and the telling of jokes together with a reiteration of his text "ye must be born again" made up his "sermon."[16]

Further,

> ...he lacks some of the essential elements that compose a preacher; he *seems* to be wanting in stability, and there seems also, to my mind, to be a lack of reverence in touching and dealing with holy things; a disregard of the Father's command to "take off thy shoes; for the ground on which thou standest is holy."[17]

In Wells' estimation, for a person to become an ordained minister demanded a serious commitment to adhere to the word of God and to be a model for the worshipper. She extended her personal high standards of moral rectitude further for the preacher than for the layperson.

As biting as she could be in her condemnation, she also could be magnanimous in her praise. Writing over a year later, she wrote with delight about the preacher of her church. She found him to be "the most energetic man I know. He has made the waste places blossom as a rose and the church is beginning to look up." Wells marveled at his ability to handle difficult congregants and keep them involved in the life of the church. She ends this entry with the observation that "he is certainly a splendid judge of human nature."[18]

Wells' words reveal her standards for leadership. Ultimately, the preacher needed to be a good judge of human nature who could lead the church in its mission. The preacher must show stability to provide the members of the church with a firm model of moral agency. The preacher could not shy away from belligerent behavior. He must address it directly while bringing the difficult person or persons into fellowship with the whole church. Wells held the ordained minister in high regard. Her personal code of moral conduct demanded much of herself and others.

LYNCHING

Wells' early diary also reveals her growing concern against lynching and the brutalization of Blacks by whites. Writing in March of 1885, she reflected on the shooting of thirteen Black men in Carroll County, Mississippi:

> O, God when will these massacres cease—it was only because they had attempted to assassinate a white man (and for just cause I suppose). Colored men rarely attempt to wreak vengeance on a white one unless he has provoked it unduly.[19]

A year and one half later, Wells expressed her outrage in print when she learned of a Black woman who was accused of poisoning a white one. The Black woman was:

> taken from the county jail and stripped naked and hung up in the courthouse yard and her body riddled with bullets and left exposed to view! O my God! can such things be and no justice for it? The only evidence being that the stomach of the dead woman contained arsenic and a box of "Rough on Rats" was found in this woman's house, who was a cook for the white woman. It may be unwise to express myself so strongly but I cannot help it and I know not if capital may not be made of it against me but I trust in God.[20]

In the face of this growing onslaught against the humanity of African-Americans, Wells rejoiced at the growing unity she perceived forming among Blacks of that period. In 1887, she wrote that Blacks were beginning to think and realize that only in unity can there be strength. She also revealed her penchant for action, noting that "the men of the race who do think are endeavoring to put their thoughts in action to inspire those who do not think."[21] For her, Black people had to unite if they were to survive. The most effective spokespersons for Black people were those Blacks who evaluated what needed to be done and then drew a blueprint for action.

WOMANHOOD

Wells was a true spokesperson of the women of her period. She adhered to the ideal of the cult of true womanhood and its emphasis on virtue for women. She recorded a defense made by the editor of one of the local Memphis papers, *The Scimitar*, on behalf of "respectable" Black people and added that his defense included Black womanhood:

> it was not now as it had been that colored women were harlots etc., whose virtue could be bought, that there were as decent among them as among their own race; that there were some who were disgraces to their race, but that the white race had no room to talk, the same was true of them.[22]

Although she was intolerant of immorality, Wells defended the reputation of a "silly woman" who engaged in an extramarital affair with an "equally scatterbrained boy" who boasted about their relationship. The young man was killed by the brother of the woman and Wells wrote:

> It seems awful to take human life but hardly more so than to take a woman's reputation and make it the jest and byword of the street; in view of these things, if he really did them, one is strongly tempted to say his killing was justified.[23]

Wells equated murder with the sullying of a woman's reputation. She hedged somewhat on vindicating the actions of the outraged brother. Her general tone was sympathetic toward the woman, but less so for her unfortunate lover.

Like many women of her day, Wells utilized her strong sense of Christian duty in the public realm. She did so from the understanding that women must be in the world of thought and action. When she was called to respond to the theme of women and journalism at a newspaper convention, she lamented over what she did not say because she was surprised at the request.

> I offered no word of thanks on behalf of my sex for the flattering encomiums bestowed on them by our editors and the hearty welcome accorded our entrance into this field. I wished and may never have a more favorable opportunity to urge the young women to study and think with a view to taking place in the world of thought and action. The suddenness of the thing drove everything out of my head but I will remember next time.[24]

Wells developed and expanded these themes found in her early diary in her later adult professional public and private writings. These early concerns and attitudes matured and set the tone for her perceptions of the growing industrial order surrounding her. This emerging order with its understanding of religion, work, class, and roles was complex. However, Wells held to her early ideals. They became her guides as she faced change and resistance to change. Her perception of justice and duty, evidenced so early in her diary, never wavered in adulthood. Throughout her life, she responded to lynching and violence, Christian duty and responsibility, leadership, and the role of religion out of the stance of her early years.

Mature Years: Social Critic and Activist

In her mature writings, Wells amplified the themes of her younger years. Throughout her later articles and autobiography she continued to stress Christian duty and the role of the church. Her anti-lynching stance evolved into a crusade of national and international scope. She held high her ideals for womanhood and was outspoken in her view of leadership.

Wells combined penetrating social analysis with decisive action. The high moral code she set for herself and others was a motivating force in her crusade for justice. Through the Black religious and social protest tradition, Wells combined a deep spirituality with a strong sense of social responsibility and witness.

CHRISTIAN DUTY

Wells expanded her early views of Christian duty to address social responsibility. In reference to lynching, she refused any attempt to paint it as a problem distinctive to the African-American community:

> Lynching is no longer "Our Problem," it is the problem of the civilized world, and Tennessee could not afford to refuse the legal measures which Christianity demands shall be used for the punishment of crime.[25]

While acknowledging that Blacks are capable of committing crimes, she refused to accept that the thousands who were hanged, shot, and burned alive were guilty in each case.

For her, Blacks as well as whites, had to take responsibility for eradicating lynching and mob rule from the American scene. Wells believed in the power of truth. For her, facts wore well in the face of misrepresentation and deception.

> "What can I do to help the cause?" The answer is always this, "Tell the world the facts." When the Christian world knows the alarming growth and extent of outlawry in our land, some means will be found to stop it.[26]

She assumed the moral rectitude of the representatives of Christianity:

> When I present our cause to a minister, editor, lecturer, or representative of any moral agency, the first demand is for facts and figures....The preachers, teachers, editors and humanitarians

of the white race, at home and abroad, must have facts laid before them, and it is our duty to supply these facts.[27]

In *A Red Record*, Wells offered five lines of responsible action.[28] First, the reader should make known the facts of lynching which Wells-Barnett presented in the pamphlet itself.

Second, the reader should be active in getting "churches, missionary societies, Y.M.C.A.'s, W.C.T.U's and all Christian and moral forces in connection with your religious and social life" to pass resolutions of condemnation and protest every time a lynching takes place. Further, such resolutions must be sent to the places where lynchings occur.[29] She was clear about the duty of the church and other religious institutions regarding lynching. These organizations were to take the lead in agitating for an end to mob rule and violence. Wells assumed the moral agency of religious institutions as voices of protest in the face of injustice.

Third, Wells used an economic argument. She suggested that the reader protest the loss of capital in any given area where lynch law and mob violence occur.[30]

Fourth, she urged the reader to think and act for "it is the white man's civilization and the white man's government which are on trial."[31] She maintained that the eradication of lynching was key to whether civilization or anarchy would prevail in the United States. Wells was sharp in her estimate of Christianity and:

> ...whether the precepts and theories of Christianity are professed and practiced by American white people as Golden Rules of thought and action, or adopted as a system of morals to be preached to heathen until they attain to the intelligence which needs the system of Lynch Law.[32]

Finally, she urged agitation on behalf of a bill in Congress that would create a commission to study the charges of rape and the cases of lynching. She ended with a strong statement of the responsibility of the people and the government to maintain law and order and reminded the reader:

The colored people of this country who have been loyal to the flag believe the same, and strong in that belief have begun this crusade.[33]

ROLE OF INSTITUTIONAL RELIGION

Wells maintained a living faith. Christianity was not a concept for her, it was her faith. She could not suffer in silence as the religion that gave her strength and comfort was abused and mocked. She wrote:

> Civilization cannot burn human beings alive or justify others who do so; neigh can it refuse a trial by jury for black men accused of crime, without making a mockery of the respect for law which is the safeguard of the liberties of white men. The nation cannot profess Christianity, which makes the golden rule its foundation stone, and continue to deny equal opportunity for life, liberty and the pursuit of happiness to the black race.[34]

Wells' estimate of the church was as stringent as her standards for its clergy. In an article in the *Daily Inter Ocean*, Wells was scathing in her estimate of white Christianity in the face of unbridled and rampant lynchings. She wrote with an impassioned pen:

> they are too busy saving the souls of white Christians from future burning in hell-fire to save the lives of black ones from present burning in the flames kindled by the white Christians. The feelings of the people who do these acts must not be hurt by protesting against this sort of thing, and so the bodies of the victims of mob hate must be sacrificed, and the country disgraced, because of that fear to speak out.[35]

With incredulity, she attacked segregated worship by relating the story of a young mulatto man who was dragged from "one of the leading churches in Memphis, Tenn., by a policeman and shut up in the station-house all day Sunday for taking a seat in the church..."[36]

Her *Daily Inter Ocean* articles did not allow Wells' British audience to succumb to the false belief that this behavior was confined to the South. She related similar cases in the North and the

North's tacit approval of southern behavior. She remarked, "as far as I knew the principle has always yielded to prejudice in the hope of gaining the good will of the south."[37] Wells extended her judgment to the YMCA and the WCTU and noted that these organizations bent to the rule of expediency as well:

> He [a clergy from England attending a national YMCA convention in the United States] was told that there had been a few [Blacks] in previous meetings, but this particular year (I forget which one) special effort had been made to get Southern delegates to be present , so no colored ones had been invited. These were the only terms upon which the YMCA and WCTU had obtained a foothold in the South, and they had consented to the arrangement which shut the negro out. They continually declared the negro degraded, intemperate, and wicked and yet shut him out from all influences in which he might become better.[38]

Convinced that religion must be put into action if it is to have any impact on the social fabric of society, she again voiced the theme of a living faith:

> When our Christian and moral influences not only concede these principles theoretically but work for them practically, lynching will become a thing of the past, and no governor will again make a mockery of all the nation holds dear in defense of lynching for any cause.[39]

Arguments grounded in the rationale of expediency held no force or persuasion for Wells. Her religious faith remained simple, plain and natural. She had no use of, or belief in, a God or a faith that was distant. The God she knew, felt, experienced, and sought to embody "came to earth to seek and save that which was lost."[40] Wells viewed lynching and the toleration, if not justification, of it as supreme social evil.

ANTI-LYNCHING CRUSADE

Wells did not tolerate apathy or indifference by African-Americans any more than the apathy of the religious institutions of her day. In 1893, as the toll for lynching mounted, Wells did not disguise her outrage and anger with the lack of unity or protest by Blacks.

> Our race still sits and does nothing about it and says little except to doubt the expediency of or find fault with the remedy proposed, no plan of raising money by which the things can be investigated, the country aroused and the temple of justice, the pulpit and the press besieged until public opinion shall demand a cessation of the reign of barbarism, lynch law and stake burning.[41]

The proposed remedy was the creation of a federal commission to study the lynch law and to make recommendations for its eradication. Wells was a supporter of this plan and used her column to give it a national voice among the Negro press of her day. Wells criticized the nascent Black accommodationist movement with its call to

> sacrifice its [the race] political rights for the sake of peace. They honestly believed the Negro should fit himself for government and when he should do so, the objection to his participation in politics would be removed. This sacrifice did not remove the trouble nor move the South to do justice. One by one the Southern states have legally disfranchised the Negro.[42]

Her estimate of the effectiveness of the accommodationist stance is clear from the passage. Wells saw no benefit resulting from the forfeiture of rights or dignity. She was unwilling to deem the position as resulting from lack of thought, but wished to point out the bankruptcy of such an approach.

Unequivocal in her judgment of the motives of white lynchers, Wells noted that "white men down there [the South] do not think any more of killing a negro than they do of slaying a mad dog." The lynching she referred to in the article involved the lynching of Black men charged with burning barns. The incident proved that Blacks were lynched for crimes other than rape or alleged rape of white women. She closed the article with "An excuse is made by the whites for the purpose of shielding themselves and leaving them free to murder all the negroes they wish."[43]

Further Wells-Barnett saw lynching as representing

> the cool, calculating deliberation of intelligent people who openly
> vow that there is an "unwritten law" that justifies them in putting
> human beings to death without complaint under oath, without
> trial by jury, without opportunity to make defense, and without
> right of appeal.[44]

In this, her most systematic and thorough article on lynching, Wells-Barnett was eloquent in her outrage as she recounted the rationale for lynching. She attributed its beginning to Reconstruction and gains made by Black people during the period. Wells noted that "one Southern State after another raised the cry against 'negro domination' and proclaimed there was an 'unwritten law' that justified any means to resist it."[45] She went on to equate the horrors of lynching with that of the Spanish Inquisition and the barbarism of the Middle Ages.

Wells rejected the notion that Blacks were naturally immoral and incapable of civilized behavior. Rather, she developed an interesting twist on the ability of whites to model proper conduct or misconduct by noting that "the negro has been too long associated with the white man not to have copied his vices as well as his virtues."[46] Wells further noted that Black women have long been the victim of rape at the hands of white men. She ends with the piercing observation that "what becomes a crime deserving capital punishment when the tables are turned is a matter of small moment when the negro woman is the accusing party."[47] In short, what Blacks asked for was equal justice.

Four viewpoints in regard to lynching were proposed by Wells. The first centered on consistency.[48] She appealed to the national record of speaking out on behalf of "the Armenian Christian, the Russian Jew, the Irish Home Ruler, the native women of India, the Siberian exile, and the Cuban patriot."[49]

Second, Wells appealed to economy. She noted that the United States must pay compensation to other countries for any of their citizens who are lynched because the government was unable to protect the populace or serve justice.[50]

Third, she regarded the country's honor. She abhorred the government's acceptance that it cannot protect "its women save by hanging, shooting, and burning alleged offenders."[51]

Finally, she appealed to love of country:

> With all the powers of government in control; with all laws made by white men, administered by white judges, jurors, prosecuting attorneys, and sheriffs; with every office of the executive department filled by white men—no excuse can be offered for exchanging the orderly administration of justice for barbarous lynchings and "unwritten laws." Our country should be placed speedily above the plan of confessing herself a failure at self-government.[52]

Ultimately, Wells rested her argument on moral agency. In response to Jane Addams' article, which condemned lynching but accepted the argument that Black men were guilty of rape, Wells called for Christian and moral forces to insist that "truth, swift-winged and courageous, summon this nation to do its duty to exalt justice and preserve inviolate the sacredness of human life."[53]

Again, she did not allow the North to escape its moral responsibility. She accused the North of surrendering its position of moral rectitude. She condemned the North's

> lethargic attitude toward the lynching evil. The belief is often expressed that if the North would stand as firmly for principle as the South does for prejudice, lynching and many other evils would be checked.[54]

Wells believed in the country's ideals and considered them to be one with Christian belief and doctrine.

> In the celebration of the fiftieth year of the Negro's freedom, does it seem too much to ask white civilization, Christianity and Democracy to be true to themselves on this as all other questions? They can not then be false to any man or race of men. Our democracy asserted that the people are fighting for the time when all men shall be brothers and the liberty of each shall be the concern of all. If this is true, the struggle is about to take in the Negro.[55]

Throughout her writings, Wells was clear to note the responsibilities of the United States as a Christian nation. Wells wrote during a period in which the nation was considered the political expression of Christianity, nationally and internationally. There was no real separation between public religion and the government. Wells drew no such distinction in her writings.

Her strong sense of moral conduct grew not only from her early experiences in the church and her religious upbringing, but was a product of the national, religious, and political consciousness of her era. She sought justice and the equal application of the law for Blacks and whites alike. She did not doubt that some African-Americans committed crimes which demanded punishment. However, she held firmly to the principle of due process. The guilty must be punished, the innocent must be set free. The courts of this nation must be allowed to carry out justice.

A 1891 article in *The Free Speech* showed yet another facet of her moral code. The article defended the use of retaliatory violence by Blacks to the crime of lynching. It is not certain that Wells was the writer, but it is most certain that such an article would not appear in the paper without her knowledge or approval. In part, the article noted:

> The whites control all the machinery of government of the South. It is systematically used against the blacks. As if this were not enough, irresponsible parties lynch black men for and without provocation, a party of Alabamians recently lynched a black man for the fun of the thing. The way to prevent retaliation is to prevent lynching. Human nature is human nature.[56]

Hence, in the absence of law and order and an effective judicial system, retaliatory violence may be the only solution to lynching. Wells noted in her autobiography that she bought a pistol after the lynching of a close family friend, Tom Moss, because of the threat to her when she refused to stop calling attention to the lynching and the need to bring the lynchers to justice.[57]

Although her preference was to work through the established systems of government and due process, Wells was pragmatic in the face of social evil. When faced with a complete rejection of her rights, she prepared to defend herself. She was not so caught up in the United States ideal that she could not intuit the personal danger to herself and to others who sought justice in "the land of the free and the home of the brave."

WOMANHOOD

As strong of character as Wells was, she remained wedded to the ideal of the cult of true womanhood. She believed, as did countless Black and white women of her day, that women were the repositories of moral integrity and virtue. Writing in *The New York Age*, she painted the picture of the ideal southern Black woman:

> As a miser hoards and guards his gold, so does she guard her virtue and good name. For the sake of the noble womanhood to which she aspires, and the race whose name bears the stigma of immorality—her soul scorns each temptation to sin and guilt. She knows that our people, as a whole, are charged with immorality and vice; that it depends largely on the woman of today to refute such charges by her stainless life....She strives to encourage them [men] all things honest, noble and manly...[58]

The themes of the cult are captured in these few phrases: a woman's virtue and good name, a woman's responsibility to be the paragon of moral conduct, her duty to encourage men to a higher moral life. Over thirty years later, Well-Barnett had not lost these standards. She passed them on to her two young daughters, Ida and Alfreda:

> I know my girls are true to me, to themselves and their God wherever they are, and my heart is content. I have had many troubles and much disappointment in life, but I felt that in you I have an abiding joy. I feel that whatever others may do, my girls are now and will be shining examples of noble true womanhood. And so mother's heart is glad and happy when she thinks of her daughters, for she knows that wherever they are and whatever they are doing they are striving to please her and reach the ideal of true womanhood.[59]

Wells-Barnett blended the strong influence of the cult of true womanhood with an equally strong sense of Christian duty. Her views on motherhood reveal the strong influence of its ideals. Writing after the birth of her children, Wells stated:

> ...I had to become a mother before I realized what a wonderful place in the scheme of things the Creator has given woman. She it is upon whom rests the joint share of the work of creation, and I wonder if women who shirk their duties in that respect truly realize that they have not only deprived humanity of their contribution to perpetuity, but that they have robbed themselves of one of the most glorious advantages in the development of their own womanhood.[60]

Later, she wrote with pride of Madame C.J. Walker who amassed a fortune selling Black hair care products. Wells-Barnett was among Walker's doubters when she predicted her success in the hair care industry. Wells-Barnett noted Walker's meager education, but also that Walker "was never ashamed of having been a washer-woman earning a dollar and a half a day. To see her phenomenal rise made me take pride anew in Negro womanhood."[61]

As late as March of 1930, she spent time "reviewing [her] campaign and urging women voters to do their Christian duty and vote for race women on Primary Day April 8th."[62] Christian duty and womanhood were tied to justice and moral agency. True womanhood meant virtue and right action both in the private and public realms. Wells did not believe that woman's moral influence could be limited. A woman must never content herself with her own salvation. She was responsible for her race as well.

LEADERSHIP

Wells was moving in her appeals to the conscience of the leaders of the land. She held "men who stand high in the esteem of the public for christian character, for moral and physical courage, for devotion to the principles of equal and exact justice to all, and for great sagacity,"[63] accountable for the continued lawlessness in the land as the death toll from lynching mounted.

[They] stand as cowards who fear to open their mouths before this great outrage....their tacit encouragement, their silent acquiescence, the black shadow of lawlessness in the form of lynch law is spreading its wings over the whole country.[64]

Wells held African-American leadership responsible. She believed that if Blacks possessed self-respect, the friction between the races would be reduced.[65] She disapproved of Black compromise in the face of lawlessness and lynching. Referring to the Tom Moss lynching, she believed that "the Afo-American ministers, newspapers, and leaders counselled obedience to the law which did not protect them. Their counsel was heeded and not a hand was uplifted to resent the outrage."[66]

She had no patience for cowardice and believed that part of racial pride and leadership was tied to defending life and limb against racist hostility. Expanding on this theme, Wells wrote:

...a Winchester rifle should have a place of honor in every black home, and it should be used for that protection which the law refuses to give. When the white man who is always the aggressor knows he runs as great a risk of biting the dust every time his Afro-American victim does, he will have greater respect for Afro-American life. The more the Afro-American yield and cringes and begs, the more he has to do so, the more he is insulted, outraged and lynched.[67]

Writing in May of 1893, Wells held the ideal that the United States had a distinct place within civilization as a Christian nation. She referred to the United States as "this Christian nation, the flower of the nineteenth century civilization " that could not stop the slaughter of Blacks.[68] Wells saw the irony of a federal government that maintained it was powerless, but state troops could shoot Blacks "like cattle, when in desperation the black men attempt to defend themselves, and then tell the world that it was necessary to put down a 'race war.'"[69]

Wells was making a moral appeal based upon the ideals of the country. By referring to the United States as both a Christian nation and the flower of civilization, she addressed the conscience of the country and its duty to provide moral leadership. She was certain that when the people and the government of the land lived up to the established social mores "a sentiment against lynch law as strong, deep and mighty as that roused against slavery prevails." She concluded "I have no fear of the result."[70]

Later, in 1900, Wells again appealed to the national character and the Christian and moral forces of the nation. She pointed out that Blacks were denied access to newspapers, religious periodicals, and magazines to refute the slander that appeared on their pages from white authorities from the South. She even noted that the "leading pulpits of the country are open to stories of the negro's degradation and ignorance but not to his defense from slander."[71]

Wells was clear about the locus of leadership in the African-American community. She commissioned Black preachers, editors and teachers to "charge themselves with the responsibility" of agitating for a restoration of the peace and due process along with their white counterparts.[72] She placed responsibility squarely in the hands of white leaders, as they worked within their spheres of influence, just as Black leadership worked within its domain.

> Not until the white editors, preachers and teachers of the country join with him [the Negro] in his fight for justice and protection by law can there be any hope of success.[73]

Wells-Barnett could not tolerate Booker T. Washington's model of leadership. She decried his proclivity for telling "chicken jokes" which she, and other Black leaders, felt were detrimental to Black social uplift. When Julius Rosenwald asked Wells-Barnett if African-Americans had accepted Washington as their leader, she responded that although he was respected, not everyone agreed with Washington's accomodationist position. She likened Washington's remarks to Rabbi Hirsch, who was a leading Jew in the city of Chicago, telling Gentile audiences stories about Jews burning down their stores to collect the insurance. She ended their exchange:

> I am sure you would not, and a great many of us cannot approve Mr. Washington's plan of telling chicken-stealing stories on his own people in order to amuse his audiences and get money for Tuskegee.[74]

School teachers, press, and pulpit provided the key leadership positions in United States society. Wells earnestly believed that persons in these areas of leadership must be united in a "vigorous denunciation of all forms of lawlessness and earnest, constant demand for the rigid enforcement of the law of the land."[75] Wells clearly saw moral agency and justice as the responsibility of leadership. Anyone or any group which did not have the dignity of the person and respect for the law as part of its agenda could not provide valid leadership.

NOTES

[1] Ida B. Wells, Diary, 8 February 1885, Special Collections, Joseph Regenstein Library, University of Chicago, Chicago.

[2] Ibid., 1 January 1886.

[3] William John Faulkner, ed., "How The Slaves Worshipped" in *The Days When the Animals Talked: Black American Folktales and How they Came to Be* (Chicago: Follett Publishing, 1977), 54.

[4] Wells, Diary, 14 September 1886.

[5] Ibid., 3 January 1887.

[6] Ibid., 18 January 1887.

[7] Ibid., 14 February 1887

[8] Ibid., 20 February 1887.

[9] Ibid., 28 March 1887.

[10] Ibid., 16 July 1887.

[11] Dwight Lyman Moody (1837-99) was one of the greatest revivalists of the nineteenth century. His theology was a blend of optimism and a strong evangelical impulse.

[12] Ibid., 8 February 1885.

[13] Faulkner, 52.

[14] Wells, Diary, 28 November 1886.

[15] Ibid., 1 February 1886.

[16] Ibid.

[17] Ibid.

[18] Ibid., 24 April 1887.

[19] Ibid., 18 March 1885.

[20] Ibid., 4 September 1886.

[21] Ibid., 18 April 1887.

22 Ibid., 4 December 1886.

23 Ibid., 8 February 1887.

24 Ibid., 12 August 1887. This convention was composed of writers, editors, and publishers of Negro papers. It was held in Louisville, Kentucky. In her autobiography, Wells writes "I went to Louisville to the first press convention I had ever attended and was tickled pink over the attention I received from those veterans of the press." *Crusade*, 32. She also notes that she was the first woman representative at the convention. In 1889, Wells was elected secretary to the National Press Association.

25 Wells, *A Red Record: Tabulated Statistics and Alleged Causes of Lynching in the United States, 1892-1893-1894* (Chicago: Donohue and Henneberry, Printers, Binders and Publishers, 1894; reprint, New York: Arno Press, *On Lynching: Southern Horrors, A Red Record, Mob Rule in New Orleans*, 1969), 73.

26 Ibid., 101.

27 Ibid. A strong argument can be made that Wells placed extremely high expectations on the role of religion and Christianity in shaping public opinion. However, when viewed within her context, her heavy reliance on the "Christian and moral forces" of society to shape, change, and motivate public moral agency is in consonance with the impact of evangelical religion in her era.

28 Ibid., 97-99.

29 Ibid., 97.

30 Ibid.

31 Ibid., 98.

32 Ibid.

33 Ibid., 99.

34 Ida B. Wells-Barnett, "Our Country's Lynching Record," *Survey*, 1 February 1913, 574.

35 Wells, *Daily Inter Ocean*, 19 May 1894.

36 Ibid.

37 Ibid.

38 Ibid.

39 Wells, "Our Country's Lynching Record," 574.

40 Wells, Diary, 8 February 1885. Wells makes these observations after hearing Dwight Moody preach at a revival in Memphis.

41 Wells, "The Reign of Mob Law, Iola's Opinion of Doings in the Southern Field," *New York Age*, 18 February 1893. TMs, Special Collections, Joseph Regenstein Library, University of Chicago, Chicago.

42 Wells, *The Weekly Call* (Topeka, Kansas), 22 April 1893.

43 Wells, "Ida B. Wells Speaks" handwritten draft dated 2 September. No year given, no paper cited. Special Collections, Joseph Regenstein Library, University of Chicago, Chicago.

44 Wells, "Lynch Law in America," *The Arena*, January 1900, 15.

[45] Ibid., 17.

[46] Ibid., 21.

[47] Ibid.

[48] Ibid., 22.

[49] Ibid.

[50] Ibid., 23.

[51] Ibid.

[52] Ibid., 24.

[53] Wells-Barnett, "Lynching and the Excuse For It," *The Independent*, 16 May 1901, 1136.

[54] Wells-Barnett, "Our Country's Lynching Record," 574.

[55] Ibid.

[56] *The New York Age*, 19 September 1891 and *Weekly Avalanche* (Memphis), 6 September 1891.

[57] Wells, *Crusade*, 62. "I felt that one had better die fighting against injustice than to die like a dog or a rat in a trap. I had already determined to sell my life as dearly as possible if attacked. I felt if I could take one lyncher with me, this would even up the score a little bit."

[58] Wells, *New York Age*, 18 February 1888.

[59] Wells, Handwritten letter to her daughters regretting her inability to be with them to help celebrate Halloween, 30 October 1920, Special Collections, Joseph Regenstein Library, University of Chicago, Chicago.

[60] Wells, *Crusade*, 251.

[61] Ibid., 378.

[62] Wells, Diary, 25 March 1930.

[63] Wells, *Southern Horrors*, 14.

[64] Ibid.

[65] Ibid., 18.

[66] Ibid., 19.

[67] Ibid., 23.

[68] Wells, "Lynch Law in All Its Phases," *Our Day*, 11, no. 65. (May 1893): 344.

[69] Ibid.

[70] Ibid., 346.

[71] Wells, "The Negro's Case in Equity," *The Independent* 26 (April 1900): 1010.

[72] Ibid., 1011.

[73] Ibid.

[74] Wells, *Crusade*, 331.

[75] Wells-Barnett, "How Enfranchisement Stops Lynchings," *Original Rights Magazine*, June 1910, 46.

VI

IDA B. WELLS-BARNETT:
THE ANTI-LYNCHING CRUSADE

Ida B. Wells-Barnett held a deep and abiding respect for the laws of the nation and the dignity of each person. Her early diary as well as her early years in journalism bear testimony to her powerful sense of justice in the public realm and the moral responsibility of the individual in his or her private and public life. Wells-Barnett believed strong, moral leadership was key to any hope of social uplift for African-Americans and social change on a national level.

Her own style of leadership focused on writing and speaking. She led with a stalwart pen, a keen sense of social analysis, and an incisive tongue. Wells-Barnett's leadership of the anti-lynching crusade of the 1890's led to her clash with Frances Willard, president of the Women's Christian Temperance Union. Both women sought a more humane, inclusive, and moral nation. However, their inability to hear fully each other's agenda and appreciate sufficiently each other's peculiar political and social circumstances is an excellent case study of the dynamics between white and African-American women social reformers and the difficulties they had in working together on shared issues.

The clash between Wells-Barnett and Willard also provides insight into the character and passion of Wells-Barnett. Throughout her life, Wells-Barnett was congruous in her understanding of Christian duty, womanhood, and the moral obligation to speak and model the truth as she understood it. This high moral code gave Wells-Barnett a leadership style marked with integrity. Her clash with Willard had its roots in this moral code as she held Willard, other social reformers, and the nation to measure of this code.

Background to a National Disgrace: Lynching

Three factors contributed to the rise of the lynch law in the United States and the resulting anti-lynching campaign. Racial segregation, which had been a primarily northern social phenomenon, moved to the South in the years following the Civil War. This racial segregation was then joined by the emergence of legalized disenfranchisement. Further, the clash between the Victorian family model, which undergirded southern gender relationships, and the number of interracial relationships, spawned an ideology which justified mob violence and lynching. The chronology of lynching combined with these three phenomena of the period to provide the context for Wells-Barnett's entry into anti-lynching protest.

LEGALIZED SEGREGATION
AND DISENFRANCHISEMENT: 1830-1900

Racial segregation had it roots in the North, where it matured before moving to the South. Although slavery was near nonexistent in the North by 1830, a strict color line was in place. Free Blacks enjoyed limited freedom. They could not be bought or sold, they could not be separated from their families, they had to be paid for any work performed. The Negro Convention Movement and such figures as Henry Highland Garnet and David Walker illustrated that free Blacks of the North could agitate and organize for racial justice.[1]

However, northern Blacks did not mistake their limited freedom as an absence of racism. Whether pro-slavery or anti-slavery, the major political parties and their respective constituents believed Blacks to be inferior. Few whites believed that Blacks had any other place in society than that of subservient. The methods used to assure this place for Blacks in northern society were both legal and extra-legal.

By 1860, nearly every phase of Black life in the North was segregated from whites. All railroad cars, stagecoaches, steamboats had special Jim Crow sections designated for Blacks alone. This segregation extended to theaters, lecture halls, hotels, restaurants, resorts, schools, prisons, hospitals, and cemeteries. In white churches, Blacks sat in "Negro pews" or in "nigger heaven" and had to wait to receive communion after the whites.[2] Until Massachusetts permitted Black jurors in 1855, Blacks could not serve on juries throughout the North.[3]

The North was clear in its attitude of white racial superiority and Black inferiority. Abraham Lincoln was a lucid spokesperson for the views of many whites regarding Blacks. In 1858, five years before he issued the Emancipation Proclamation, Lincoln stated:

> I will say then that I am not, nor ever have been in favor of bringing about in any way the social and political equality of white and black races—that I am not, nor ever have been in favor of making voters or jurors of negroes, not of qualifying them to hold office, not to intermarry with white people,...there is a physical difference between black and white races which I believe will for ever forbid the two races living together on terms of social and political equality.[4]

The North was not the paragon of virtue and justice it sought to portray in relation to the South and slavocracy. Northerners contented themselves with a virtually slave-free society, however they failed to recognize that the presumptions and stereotypes undergirding the attitude of white supremacy and Black inferiority would make the North a poor teacher for the South during Reconstruction and beyond.

In the South, the social disorganization of the initial year of Reconstruction engendered white fear of Black insurrection. Provisional state legislatures adopted the Black Codes designed to relegate Blacks to their presumed inferior place in the southern social, political and economic structure. The states of Mississippi, Florida, and Texas adopted racial segregation laws for the railroads within their boundaries. The 1866 Texas law was the most far-reaching. All railroad companies were required "to attach to passenger trains one car for the special accommodation of freedmen."[5] The segregation of public schools, colleges, jails, hospitals were all features of Reconstruction and sanctioned by Reconstruction governments.

At the same time as segregation became more institutionalized in the South, Blacks began to appear as jurors, judges, legislators, voters, and merchants. *The Standard* of Raleigh, North Carolina noted "the two races now eat together at the same table, sit together in the same room, work together, visit and hold debating societies together."[6] Although the observations of the newspaper were not the norm for the South, there was some movement to mix the races.

The Reconstruction Act of 1867 with its incipient Jim Crowism, drew heated protest from Blacks. Demonstrations in New Orleans, Richmond, Virginia, and Charleston, South Carolina focused on segregated street cars. The 1868 state legislatures of South Carolina and Mississippi received demands from free Blacks that the civil laws protect their rights on common carriers and public accommodations.[7]

These acts of radical protest were not the norm for the majority of Blacks. Blacks rarely entered public accommodations that were clearly inhospitable. Black leaders drew a distinction between social equality and public equality. They sought the latter. Public equality meant civil and political rights in the mind of these leaders.[8] The early writings of W.E.B. DuBois reveal the logic behind this ideology.

> Let us then, recognizing our common interests...work for each other's interest, casting behind us unreasonable demands on the one hand, and unreasonable prejudice on the other. We are not foolish enough to demand social equality or amalgamation, knowing full well that inexorable laws of nature regulate and control such movements. What we demand is to be recognized as men, and to be given those civil rights which pertain to our manhood.[9]

C. Vann Woodward credits the South's embrace of extreme racism to the relaxation of significant opposition to racism by the liberal North, the decline in power and influence of the southern conservatives, and a collorary decline of the influence of the idealism of the southern radicals.[10] When the liberal North agreed to the Compromise of 1877, this signaled the beginning of the North's retrenchment on race. Eventually the North and South differed little on their race policies. Northern liberals and abolitionists began to voice the "shibboleths of white supremacy regarding the Negro's innate inferiority, shiftlessness, and hopeless unfitness for full participation in the white man's civilization."[11]

Discontent and disappointment led to the decline of the southern conservatives. The 1880s saw a series of financial scandals in the Redeemer governments set up by the conservatives.[12] These scandals, which began to turn the tide of public opinion, combined with an even more powerful dissatisfaction with the conservative economic policies that caused agrarian depression in the 1880s and 1890s. Turning to one vain policy after another, the conservatives eventually raised the cry of "Negro domination" and "white supremacy" as a last attempt to regain social and political control and crush the rival Populist movement.[13] The conservatives resorted to fraud, intimidation, bribery, and violence, eventually undermining their moral position on race previously based on moderation and equity.

The Populist position suffered from its very beginning, arousing suspicion and prejudice. Their success was the seed of their failure, for Populists were able to achieve a fair amount of racial harmony and cooperation. This harmony and cooperation threatened the social order of the South and the relentless attempts by their opponents to drive the movement apart finally led to its demise.[14]

By the beginning of the 1890s, the door was wide open for untempered racism in the South. Economic, social, and political encumbrances combined to create a social and economic depression. Social and political reforms did not materialize in the manner hoped for, leading to further frustration. In this climate, the South sought a scapegoat. With the sanctions against racism lifted, Blacks became the target of white frustrations.[15]

The 1896 Supreme Court decision in *Plessy versus Ferguson*, which held that racial segregation did not violate the Fourteenth Amendment if the facilities provided were equal, supplied the backdrop for the disenfranchisement of the Black male vote. The new suffrage laws also affected poor or illiterate whites.[16] By 1906, the laws of every southern state excluded Blacks from primary elections. This state of affairs did not extend to poor or illiterate whites.

Disenfranchisement also united with partisan politics. The bulk of legislation legalizing disenfranchisement came during the

time the Democrats were facing stiff opposition from other parties.[17] George Fredrickson conjectures that maintaining white
supremacy was the one thing that held the post-Reconstruction
Democratic Party together. He suggests that limiting or eliminating
Black suffrage was a way of re-emphasizing the party's central issues,
as well as reducing any political opposition, particularly from Black
Republicans.[18]

In 1898, during the period of northern retreat, the United
States expanded into the Pacific and the Caribbean. This expansion
brought eight million people of color under United States rule and
dictate.[19] The attendant attitude of imperialism is found in the
pages of *The Nation* which responded matter-of-factly, "of course,
[they] could not be allowed to vote."[20] The ideology of racism
extended beyond African-Americans in the continental United States
to include Hispanic, Asian, and Caribbean peoples.

THE RISE OF THE LYNCH LAW
AND MOB VIOLENCE: 1877-1900

The lynch law emerged on the national scene in the late
eighteenth century in an area on the south side of the James River in
Virginia.[21] The form of punishment consisted of thirty-nine lashes
which were inflicted without trial or law, but on the suspicion of guilt
which could not be "regularly proven."[22] This form of punishment
took its name from a gentlemen named Lynch who set the first
example of it.

By the nineteenth century, especially after the Civil War,
murder became associated with lynching. Lynching ultimately
became defined as

> a formal extra-legal trial—the lynchers professing to represent for
> a time society itself, freed from artificial restraint which hampers
> its proper action—on the alleged ground of offenses recognized
> as felonies by the very law which they supplant, though not
> perhaps chargeable with the same penalties.[23]

The reasons given for lynching ranged from rape and murder
to mistaken identity. Crawford notes that in one case from Washing-

ton state, the reason was one of economy—to save the taxpayers' money.[24] The victim was a prisoner who had cost Whitman County $30,000.[25] In the antebellum South, vigilance committees carried out the lynch law to suppress both white dissidence and slave rebellion.[26] These early nineteenth century vigilance committees with their mock-trials, confessions extracted through torture, and staged public executions set the stage for racially motivated lynching to follow after the Civil War.[27]

Racially motivated lynching reached its height between 1877, when the federal troops withdrew from the South, and 1890, when the new caste system of the South reified.[28] In 1892, the year of Thomas Moss' lynching, 255 people died at the hands of lynch mobs.[29] Hall suggests that lynching increased with deadly regularity "when the dominant image of blacks in the white mind shifted from inferior child to aggressive and dangerous animal."[30]

Writings by southern intellectuals like Philip A. Bruce helped to fan the flames of murderous rhetoric which turned to physical violence. Bruce coined the phrase "black peril" in his *The Plantation Negro as Freeman*.[31] He was a trained historian, the son of a large plantation owner, who owned 500 slaves, the brother-in-law of writer Thomas Nelson Page, the nephew of the Confederacy's secretary of war, and a Harvard graduate. His work carried influence and respect in the South and in the North. His thesis was clear and to the point: when slavery ended Blacks no longer had the civilizing influence of white society. Blacks regressed to their primitive and criminal state, without the masters' influence and grew closer to the "African type" than slaves had been.[32] For Bruce, this was true equally for the Black legislator, the teacher who had graduated from college, the common laborer, and the preacher.

Radical racists believed there was no place for African-Americans in the South or North. Joel Williamson observes that the advocates of radical racism believed the end might come in a race war which the superior whites would win.[33] The bottom line for the adherents of radical segregation and racism was that whites and Black could not live side by side on United States soil.

According to records dating from 1889 to 1918, in *The Chicago Tribune*, Tuskegee Institute, *The Crisis* magazine (since 1912), and the National Association for the Advancement of Colored

People (NAACP), 3,224 persons were killed by lynching.[34] Of this
group, 703 were white and 2,522 were Black. In a gender breakdown
between the two racial ethnic groups, among the whites, 691 men and
eleven women were victims of the lynch law. Among the Blacks,
2,472 men and fifty women were victimized.

The NAACP study showed lynching decreasing by 61.3% from
1889 to 1919. However lynching among whites (77.6%) declined at
a higher proportion than Blacks (54.4%). Since 1903, the number of
whites who were lynched decreased steadily.

The breakdown of the alleged offenses which prompted
lynching between Blacks and whites reveal the charge of rape as
second in percentage, with murder being first among both groups.

	WHITE	BLACK
1. accused of murder	46.0%	35.5%
2. rape and attacks on women	8.4	28.4
3. crimes against person and property	17.8	
4. crimes against property	17.4	see 3
5. crimes against person	8.7	see 3
6. miscellaneous crimes	18.0	12.0
7. no crimes charged	0	5.6[35]

One of the striking features of these statistics is "no crimes
charged." Only African-Americans appear in this category. White
people, on the other hand, were charged with particular crimes which
sparked the lynchings. The NAACP report makes note of the fact
that when rape was the charge against Blacks, it rested on such
evidence as "entering the room of a woman" or "brushing against
her."[36] Although the victims and their friends often asserted that
there was no intention on the part of the victim to attack a white
woman or commit rape, the lynch law was carried out.

Rumors of rape became a "folk pornography" in the South.[37]
Hall notes that the fear of lynching served to hold both Blacks and
women in their respective places as subordinate to southern white
men. She states it is "no accident that the vision of the Negro as
threatening beast flourished during the first organizational phase of
the women's rights movement in the South."[38] Lynch law served as
severe sanction against voluntary sexual relations between African-
American men and white women.

Southern whites followed a Victorian model for sex and family roles.[39] Men viewed themselves as providers and protectors and women were the moral guardians of the home. In the Reconstruction and Redemption, eras this model evolved such that white women and Black women, like male and female slaves before them, were viewed as the property of white men.[40] White men could not tolerate the image or the reality of Black men crossing the color and caste barrier to have intimate relationships with white women. However, the prevalence of miscegenation before, during, and after slavery indicates it was permissible for white men to have such relations with Black women.

Lynch law was not an activity carried out by a small group of people avenging the rape of white womanhood. It involved large segments of the populace. Jacquelyn Dowd Hall notes that it was often the presence of "men of property" leading the lynch mob that caused sheriffs to demure from upholding their legal responsibility to keep the peace.[41] In rural areas, planters sometimes used lynching as a means of coercion and increased profit given that the incidence of lynching rose in the summer months after planting when all that remained was the profitable harvest season.[42]

Mob violence was the instrument to maintain segregation and solidify a rigid caste division between racial groups which were bound to the same society, legal system, and economy. In addition, lynching served to reinforce the hierarchical power relationships based on gender. The drive to maintain white superiority is tied to what Hall attributes to a siege mentality. She writes, "whites felt themselves continually under siege. Lynching persisted as much to reaffirm solidarity and demonstrate power *to whites themselves* (her emphasis) as to punish and intimidate blacks."[43] Continuing this line of insight, Fredrickson notes that the prime agent of white-supremacist terror in the South was the mob.[44] He posits that the white power structure of the South was "relatively fragile" because it did not have within it systematic control over Black social location, movement, and labor.[45]

Lynching was an effective means for maintaining white superiority and Black inferiority until African-Americans like Ida B. Wells-Barnett began to speak out as individuals and organize Black and white resistance to lynching. Ida B. Wells-Barnett plunged into this mix of caste, color, and gender. Her refusal to accept the rationale of rape as an excuse for the lynch law gave public voice to the sexual double standards of the South and revealed lynching in its true form—a means of social control.

The Anti-Lynching Campaign Begins

The March 9, 1892 lynching of Thomas Moss, a close friend of Ida B. Wells, marked the beginning of her anti-lynching crusade.[46] Moss' lynching was not due to the charge of rape. As one of the growing number of Blacks who began to make economic gains in the South, Moss and his business partners opened a grocery store and sold at prices competitive to the white store owner across the street. Their crime was that they were successful, Black, and chose to defend their store against attack by whites rather than allow it to be ransacked and destroyed. The lynching of these three men who were leading citizens in the city of Memphis, was not carried out by a few lower class whites. Members of the respectable white establishment of Memphis comprised the lynch mob. Wells wrote, "The more I studied the situation, the more I was convinced that the Southerner had never gotten over his resentment that the Negro is no longer his plaything, his servant, and his source of income."[47]

The Black community of Memphis was devastated. They had believed that lynching would never become part of their lives. Wells saw their only recourse to be boycott and exodus. No attempt was made to punish the murderers, whose identities were known. She echoed Tom Moss' last words and urged the Blacks of Memphis to leave that city for the West.[48]

Lynching was an act of political and economic repression in Wells' eyes. She did not believe that the problem of lynching was due to poor education. Her study of 728 lynchings revealed that only a third of those cases contained any charge of rape. However, the charge of rape against Black men was leveled so consistently that the whole nation took it to be true at some point.[49] Wells' attack on the rape myth was an attack against southern sexual mores. The South contented itself with the illusion that any liaison between an African-American man and a white woman must be an involuntary one for the woman. Wells was quite clear that such liaisons were ill advised, but she was candid about the willingness of white women.

> I also had the sworn statement of a mother whose son had been lynched that he had left the place where he worked because of the advances made by the beautiful daughter of the house. The boy had fallen under her spell, and met her often until they were discovered and the cry of rape was raised.[50]

Meanwhile, white men seduced and raped Black women and girls with impunity.

When Wells suggested in an editorial that women were responsible agents in interracial liaisons, it created a firestorm in Memphis among the whites.[51] Luckily, she was attending an African Methodist Episcopal Church General Conference in Philadelphia and went on to New York. The office of *The Free Speech* was broken into, vandalized, and destroyed. Her co-owners fled Memphis and she was threatened with lynching. T. Thomas Fortune met her at the ferry landing in Jersey City with a dispatch from *The Daily Commercial.*

> The fact that a black scoundrel is allowed to live and utter such loathsome and repulsive calumnies is a volume of evidence as to the wonderful patience of Southern whites. But we have had enough of it. There are some things that the Southern white man will not tolerate and the obscene intimations of the foregoing have brought the writer to the very outermost limit of public patience. We hope we have said enough.[52]

On June 5, 1892, *The Age* carried a seven-column article on Negro lynching written by Wells in exile. It contained names, dates, places, and circumstances of hundreds of lynchings for alleged rape. The response was overwhelming with 10,000 copies of the issue sold, 1,000 in Memphis alone.

In one of her columns for *The Age,* Wells gave another detail of that fateful night when Moss, McDowell, Stewart, and other Black men defended the People's Grocery.[53] One of the men escaped in spite of his wounds. He was found three days later some twenty miles from the scene of the grocery store. He told his captors that Dr. Elbert, a Black physician, had taken him away in his buggy, tended his wounds, and given him money. This transpired the day before the lynching. A Black woman heard a group of white men declare they were going after Dr. Elbert late on Tuesday night. She warned him and he left on the ten o'clock train. Wells concluded "It is currently believed that this is the only thing which prevented his being the fourth man lynched on March 9, in Memphis, Tenn."[54]

Wells was aware that her message was not reaching the white newspapers. This was anathema for her. She believed that ruling class whites were the key to social change and her desire was to manipulate their self interest to effect that change. Wells' appeals focused on the powerful groups outside of the South, which she believed had moral and economic authority, but who were not listening. Her dilemma was how to reach those key leaders. Non-southern whites, both in this country and in England, were the key Wells saw to halt lynching.

The British Anti-Lynching Campaign:
The Clash With Frances Willard

Ida B. Wells carried this knowledge and strategy with her to England in 1893. Wells believed that England's role as a leading importer of American cotton gave British views additional weight in American affairs. Her analysis of lynching and her demystification of the political motivations behind the manipulation of both Black male and female and white female sexuality led to confrontations with women like Frances Willard. Willard considered herself progressive, but she was unable to see lynching as an institutionalized practice. Willard's inability to see this led to their clash in England and in the United States.

Frances Willard was the heart and soul of the Women's Christian Temperance Union (WCTU). When she traveled to Britain as the guest of Lady Somerset in 1894, the English press heralded her as the "Uncrowned Queen of American Democracy." At this point, the WCTU had become the most formidable women's organizations in the country. There was a branch in every state with a total membership of over 200,000 women. Willard saw temperance as a means of politicizing women who considered a direct demand

for suffrage too radical.[55] Her appeal to followers was that suffrage
was needed for women if women were to protect their homes from
vice. Hence, under her prodding, the WCTU endorsed suffrage at
the early date of 1887.[56]

The events at the October, 1890, WCTU national convention
helped to set the stage for the confrontation between Wells and
Willard. This was the first time that the WCTU held a national
convention in the South. In *The Red Record*, Wells writes that the
southerners set out to win over the northerners, without troubling to
hear the Negro side of the question. These temperance people
accepted the white man's story of the problem with which he had to
deal. "It is only after Negroes are in prison for crimes that efforts of
these temperance women are exerted without regard to race, color,
or previous condition."[57]

Willard's position against the Federal Election Bill that would
give national government control over national elections was
troubling to Wells.[58] Willard's hesitant and equivocal stand on
lynching and her defense of the southern record fueled her response
to the bill. She defended the South as being wronged in Northern
public opinion and noted the number of "alien illiterates" and
drinkers who vote in the North with what she believed to be less than
desirable results. She concluded:

> It is not fair that they [alien illiterates and drinkers] should vote,
> nor is it fair that a plantation Negro, who can neither read nor
> write, whose ideas are bounded by the fence of his own field and
> the price of his own mule, should be entrusted with the ballot...[59]

Wells' reply to this was

> in all the ten terrible years of shooting, hanging, and burning of
> men, women and children in America, the Women's Christian
> Temperance Union never suggested one plan or made one move
> to prevent those awful crimes.[60]

Wells looked at temperance from a racial and economic standpoint. As a participant in a symposium on temperance for *The
A.M.E. Church Review*,[61] she took a tough and uncompromising
stance on drinking. Writing in 1891, Wells criticized African-

American inability to stand up and throw the effects of alcohol from their doors. For her, it was poor economics and bad business when farmers received their year-end pay and spent it on liquor each. One of the most useful factors in race progress—the farmer—was kept at a dead level, without money, without ambition, and consequently at the mercy of the landholder.[62]

Wells went on to suggest in the article that a course of instruction on the issues of alcohol, from an economic standpoint, be taught in the schools as part of teaching temperance. She called on the press with their ability to

> revolutionize public sentiment by showing how intemperance is sapping our physical and financial resources. The writer knows one secular journal which has lost many dollars by refusing to advertise saloons.[63]

Finally, ministers had to preach temperance if any affect was going to be made. Her closing lines echoed the self-help theory dominant in the late nineteenth century:

> The Negro's greatest lack is his seeming incapacity for organization for his own protection and elevation. Yet every reader of these lines, who loves his race and feels the force of these statements, can make himself a committee of one to influence some one else.[64]

Willard and Wells did not argue on the issue of temperance. The argument was one of race.

Wells' first trip to England, sponsored by the Society for the Brotherhood of Man, set the stage for the confrontation in 1894 during her second trip there. Her first trip met with limited success as she began the long education process of alerting the British populace to the horrors of the South and lynching. In a May 16, 1893 letter to the editor of *The Daily Post*, Wells replied to a city councillor's letter stating the people of Britain had no effect on the affairs of United States. She argued that the pulpit and press of the United States refused to comment on lynching or allow any voice of an alternative opinion. Wells saw no other recourse than to turn to religious and moral sentiments in Britain.

The moral agencies at work in Great Britain did much for the
final overthrow of chattel slavery. They can in like manner pray,
write, preach, talk and act against civil and industrial slavery;
against the hanging, shooting and burning alive of a powerless
race....If the moral reforms of the age have been brought about by
Christianity here is one which calls loudly for Christian moral
offort...I believe that the silent indifference which she [Great
Britain] has received the charge that human beings are burned
alive in Christian (?) Anglo-Saxon communities is born of
ignorance of the true situation;...[65]

Wells was repeatedly asked about the feelings of great
Christian moral leaders like Dwight Moody and Frances Willard. In
honesty she had to say that neither of these leaders had spoken out
against lynching. Indeed Willard seemed to condone it. When asked
for proof, Wells could offer none for she had not come prepared to
address this part of the effects of Jim Crow and lynching. Her trip
was cut short by a dispute between the members of the society, but
she returned a year later in 1894 to spend March through July
speaking out against the injustices heaped against her people.

In a *Daily Inter Ocean* dispatch Wells was pointed in her
criticism of Willard and Bishops Fitzgerald and Haygood and the
picture painted by white Americans of the southern Black, of "great
hordes of ignorant and dangerous negroes" who rape white women:

Unfortunately for the negro race and for themselves, Miss
Frances E. Willard and Bishops Fitzgerald and Haygood have
published utterances in confirmation of this slander, and the
magazines of my country have printed this libel on an entire race
to the four corners of the earth.[66]

She set forth her task clearly to show:

1. that all the machinery of law and politics is in the hands of
those who commit the lynchings; they, therefore, have the
amending of the laws in their own hands; and that it is only
wealthy white men whom the law fails to reach, in every case of
criminal procedure the negro is punished. 2. Hundreds of negroes,
including women and children, are lynched for trivial offenses, on
suspicion, and in many cases when known to be guiltless of any
crime, and the law refuses to punish the murderers because it is

not considered a crime to kill a negro. 3. Many of the cases of
"assault" are simple adultery between white women and colored
men.[67]

In her first trip, Wells told the British press that Willard
blamed Blacks for the defeat of temperance legislation in the United
States and cast aspersions on Black people. The second time she
came prepared with newspaper clippings to substantiate her charges.
Wells brought personal letters from the South, statistics showing the
increase in lynching, and photographs of some of the victims. She
described men burned alive, women hanged, children shot, and the
carnival atmosphere accompanying many lynchings. The lurid
details of the lynch law shocked the British public. Their questions
about Willard's position on the subject grew.

Frances Willard had made her first trip south in 1881. In each
of her trips, upper-class whites entertained her. Willard was able to
make an opening and receive recognition for the WCTU in a way
that had not been possible previously. Charmed by the culture and
hospitality of those who entertained her, after her first trip in 1881,
she wrote:

> Everywhere the Southern white people desired me to speak to the
> colored. In Charleston I had an immense audience of them in the
> M.E. Church, North; in New Orleans, Mrs. Judge Merrick, a
> native of Louisiana, whose husband was Chief Justice in that state
> under the Confederacy, invited the Northern teachers to her
> home, and wrote me with joy that the WCTU would yet solve the
> problem of good understanding between sections. I was present
> repeatedly in the gallery when legislatures of the Gulf States voted
> money for negro education, and for schools founded by North-
> erners.[68]

Willard's visit was at a time before the retrenchment process
was fully institutionalized. Her optimism was fueled by belief in
those who entertained her and shared with her their vision of the
South. Willard went on to speak of the suppressed vote of Blacks
and offered her analysis of how to free that vote once again:

> ...nothing would liberate the suppressed colored vote so soon as
> to divide the white vote on the issues, "wet" and "dry"; that the

South "Solid" for prohibition of the liquor traffic might be exchanged for the South Solid against the North, by such a realignment of those moving armies of civilization popularly called "parties," as would put the temperance men of North and South in the same camp.[69]

In 1890, she held another view of the southern Negro as a "great dark faced mob." She gave an interview to *The New York Voice*, a temperance paper, which generated angry protests from Blacks.

> The colored race multiplies like locust of Egypt. The grog-shop is its center of power....The safety of women, of children, of the home is menaced in a thousand localities so that men dare not go beyond the sight of their own roof-tree.[70]

In her autobiography, Wells described the Black response:

> Every Negro newspaper in the South quoted and criticized the interview. Marked copies of their journals were sent to her, my own among the number. But so far as anyone knew, Miss Willard never retracted or explained the interview.[71]

Wells' dispatch to *The Daily Inter Ocean* pierced to the heart of the matter:

> Miss Willard has gone even further in that she has put herself on record as approving the Southerner's methods of defying the constitution and suppressing the negro vote; has promised that "when I go North there will be no word wafted to you from pen or voice that is not loyal to what we are saying here and now"; has unhesitatingly sown a slander against the entire negro race in order to gain favor with those who are hanging, shooting, and burning negroes alive. Because of such utterances the South is encouraged and justified in its work of disgracing the Nation, and the world is confirmed in the belief that the negro race is the most degraded on the face of the earth. Those who read and accept this last-quoted statement forget that these same white men were not afraid to go beyond the sights of their rooftrees during the civil war and leave the safety and honor of their homes, their wives, daughters, and sisters only in the protection of the negro race.[72]

When Wells was questioned and challenged again by the press and British temperance workers, she gave a copy of Willard's interview to the editor of *Fraternity* to publish. After Wells showed the finished copy of her article to Florence Balgarnie, her hostess, Balgarnie noted that Lady Somerset, who was Willard's hostess in England, would resent the article and take it as a personal attack. Balgarnie was sure that Lady Somerset would buy up the entire edition rather than have the article circulated. Balgarnie appealed to the editor of *Fraternity* to stop the May edition distribution until she could talk with Lady Somerset.

The events that followed highlight the dynamics of race and class between Black and white women of the era.[73] Wells' challenge to the sexual ethics, or lack of them, of white and African-American America dominate the exchange. Lady Somerset's response to Belgarnie's overture was that if the interview appeared in print, she would make sure Wells never had any other speaking opportunities in Great Britain. Lady Somerset asked for the name of the editor and the address of the journal and terminated the conversation. Wells accused Balgarnie of setting her up for insult by giving Lady Somerset the necessary information to stop the distribution of the paper. Balgarnie insisted that Wells write Lady Somerset to give her the whole story of how the interview came to be published. Wells did so, but heard nothing and considered the matter closed. Unknown to Wells, a cable was sent to Frederick Douglass by Lady Somerset asking him to disavow his protege.[74]

Two weeks after the May edition of *Fraternity* carrying Willard's 1890 interview appeared, *The Westminster Gazette*, a leading London afternoon daily, carried an interview with Miss Willard conducted by Lady Somerset. In part, Willard stated:

> I was interviewed as to the colored vote, and I frankly stated that I thought we had irreparably wronged ourselves by putting no safeguard on the ballot box in the North that would sift out alien illiterates, who rule our cities today with the saloon as their palace, and the toddy stick as their scepter. It is not fair that they should vote, nor is it fair that a plantation Negro who can neither read nor write whose ideas are bounded by the fence of his own field and the price of his own mule should be entrusted with the ballot.[75]

In the last line of interview she told Lady Somerset

> I should be sorry to have my words thus construed but I think
> that British justice may be trusted to guard my reputation in that
> particular and in all others.[76]

Wells' response to the interview was swift and incisive:

> [the] concluding sentence of the interview shows the object is not
> to determine how best they may help the Negro who is being
> hanged, shot, and burned, but to guard Miss Willard's reputa-
> tion.[77]

She also included a fact of which no one in England was aware,
"There is not a single colored woman admitted to Southern WCTU,
but still Miss Willard blames the Negro for the defeat of prohibition
in the South!" Frances Ellen Watkins Harper was the only Black to
serve on the WCTU's executive committee and board of superin-
tendents—and she often criticized the racism of its members. Willard
did not denounce lynching, for fear that it would antagonize the
WCTU's southern branches, which excluded Black women. Wells
concluded her response to the interview:

> Miss Willard is no better or worse than the great bulk of white
> Americans on the Negro question, they are afraid to speak out,
> and it is only British public opinion which will move them.[78]

When asked about Wells' charges that the church makes no
response to lynching, Willard wondered why Wells made no mention
of the fact that the Methodist Church passed a resolution expressing
the "strong horror which everybody must feel in the presence of such
cruelty." Wells responded:

> ...in every case the Northern churches, which do not practice these
> things themselves, tacitly agreed to them by the southern church-
> es; and that so far as I knew principle has always yielded to
> prejudice in the hope of gaining the good will of the South.[79]

Lady Somerset's campaign would have fared better if it hadn't
coincided with a racist barrage from the United States against Wells.

The Memphis *Scimitar* recommended Wells be tied to a stake on Main Street and branded with a hot iron. The *New York Times* declared Black men were prone to rape and that Wells was "a slanderous and nasty-minded mulatress."[80] A Black clubwoman, Josephine Silone Yates, defended Willard and the WCTU saying Wells' statements were misleading and unjust. A letter supporting this view was signed by Frederick Douglass and others. *The Woman's Era* took Wells' side.

> Doubtless Miss Willard is a good friend to colored people, but we have failed to hear from her and the WCTU any flat-footed denunciation of lynching and lynchers.... *The Woman's Era* is not satisfied with Miss Willard's rather mild treatment of the lynching outrages in the South,...[81]

The British sense of fair play was offended and one editor wrote:

> It is idle for men to say that the conditions which Miss Wells describe do not exist...Whites of America may not think so; British Christianity does and all the scurrility of the American press won't alter the facts.[82]

Before she left in July, the British Anti-Lynching Committee formed, with British notables among its members. Wells now had access to white groups in United States previously closed to her. British opinion broke the silence of many United States leaders such as Richard Gilder, editor of *Century* magazine, Samuel Gompers, the labor leader, and ultimately Frances Willard.

The Campaign Returns to the United States

The reaction to Wells in the United States was far from neutral. The southern press, Black and white, chose sides on the issue. The northern press remained at an elegant, if not condescending, distance from the debate—choosing to ignore the racism and lynchings taking place in the North, content to see lynch law as a southern problem.

THE WHITE RESPONSE TO WELLS
AND HER CAMPAIGN

The Press

The Memphis Appeal-Avalanche was not unusual among the southern press in its rhetoric regarding lynching and its refusal to allow the northern press to dictate southern moral conduct.

> The self-respecting, law-abiding negro in the South is far more safe from molestation than the millionaires of Chicago and New York are from anarchist assassins. The negro property owners in Memphis are numerous. We doubt if there are any negro property owners in Chicago. But reverting to the lynchings, how comes it that the *Inter-Ocean* has no word of sympathy for the women who have suffered from the villains?...But it is false and wicked to make it appear to the Northern mind, as the *Inter-Ocean* strives to do, that the lynchings of the South are without cause, and that the hanging of negroes is due merely to a spirit of malevolence on the part of the whites toward the blacks. When an unprotected woman is assaulted whether the crime take place in New Hampshire, Oregon or Texas, chivalrous men in the neighborhood forget there are such things as courts, and they at once seize a rope. This is human nature, and it is quite the same the world over.[83]

And then in the next day's edition:

> *The Appeal-Avalanche* has time and again recorded itself as against lynch law, no matter where the lynchings occurred, but so long as negroes or whites either, commit rape, there will be lynchings. But we would like to call the attention of *The Boston Herald* to a face and we would respectfully invite the usually fair and impartial journal to comment upon it editorially. The World Almanac for 1892 gives the number of lynchings in the United States for 1892....From these figures we learn that outside of the Southern states there were 30 lynchings and only 20 legal executions in 1891. We would like to ask the *Herald* what right the Northern section of the country has to lecture the Southern section on lawlessness when the lynchings in the North almost equal the legal executions?[84]

The Memphis Commercial Appeal responded to a Black newspaper convention's endorsement of Wells. The *Appeal* suggested the proper response on the part of the Black press. The paper denounced lynching, as did most of the southern press, but also noted that its denunciation was seen as extreme by its peers. Then, in amazing candor, it expressed the opinion that only "representative white men of the South" can turn the tide of public opinion against lynching and not those who support Wells' attack on white womanhood.

> Almost every newspaper in the South has been constant and untiring in its efforts to suppress lynchings, but it is impossible to do anything so long as negroes themselves persist in feeding the fire with incendiary writings and speeches. The Commercial has been called extreme and intemperate in its denunciation of lynchers and lynching. It has never failed to demand that negroes accused of crime shall have a fair trial in the courts.... Ida Wells and those who act with her are encouraging assaults upon white women by disseminating such atrocious slanders. The only way in which such methods can act upon public opinion is to infuriate it.[85]

The white press response to Wells' campaign continued in this vein:

> Miss Wells does not represent all the colored people of the Union. It is stated in reliable papers that the better class of negroes in the South acknowledge that Miss Wells exaggerates and makes wholesale charges that are not justified by the facts.[86]

The Register of Mobile, Alabama stated its opinion on lynching as well.

> ...there are some kinds of crimes which, if not punished instantly, will not be adequately punished—that is to say, neither the criminal nor his sympathizers will feel the strong arm of the Nemesis which the crime has brought into play.[87]

Also joining the chorus of newspapers attacking Wells and supporting the myth of the Black rapist and Black illicit behavior were *The*

Constitution of Atlanta and *The Commercial Appeal* of Memphis respectively. *The Appeal* also commented on her British campaign and British anti-lynching sentiment.

> All good citizens admit that lynch-law is wrong, but they are rapidly coming to the conclusion that the negroes themselves are the only people who can suppress the evil, and the way for them to get rid of it is to cease committing the peculiar and shocking crimes which provoke it....every colored preacher, teacher, writer, and leader should endeavor to convince his race that an upright and law-abiding life will lead to happiness and prosperity...[88]

And later in the same editorial:

> As to the force of English public opinion—bah! The so-called public opinion that is manifesting itself by adopting resolutions endorsing the slanders of this woman, receives very little respect in England and none at all in this country. Negroes are novelties in England, and therefore interesting, but we know something of the tender mercies of English conduct in dealing with negroes away from home. With a long record of bloodshed, rapine, and cruelty, it is a most amusing exhibit of impudence for Englishmen to become critics of other people.[89]

There were a few white presses that supported Wells' work. *The Iowa State Register* of Des Moines responded to Bishop Hugh Miller Thompson of Mississippi and his defense of lynching. In its response, one can see the qualifications placed on the lynch law.

> The bishop's reasoning is not bad, but it is dangerous. There are certain crimes and certain conditions under which *The Register* would not hesitate to uphold lynch-law, but the giving of such advice from such a high source in the South, where lynchings are drawn along the color-line generally, is very dangerous. The people are not always able to decide who is worthy of hanging.[90]

However the tone of *The Commercial Appeal* and *The Mobile Register* were more representative of the response of the white press of the South.[91]

Southern Governors

An amazing open letter signed by a judge, the sheriff, the mayor, editors, teachers, ministers, lawyers, bankers, and tradesmen of the city of Santa Cruz was sent to Wells and circulated in the white and Black presses of the United States.

> We, the undersigned citizens of Santa Cruz, having our attention called to your mission in England, and to the terrible cruelties resulting from the prevalence of lynch-law in many of our States, which falls both upon black and white, and which is a shame and a disgrace to our religion and our civilization, hereby invite you on your return from England to lay your case before the citizens of Santa Cruz. In favor of the enforcement of just and impartial laws for all, without regard to color or creed, we are yours sincerely, etc.[92]

This letter is amazing given the initial response of the majority of the southern governors. Note the bitter response of Governor Fishback of Arkansas to a letter from the London Anti-Lynching Committee concerning a triple lynching in his state.

> ...Precisely because I sympathize with your benevolent purpose do I deplore the criminal folly of your officious meddling in a matter for the rectification of which you are prepared by neither national training, national habit, nor national character....[93]

Fishback was joined by Governor Charles T. O'Ferral of Virginia saying that it "is a pretty pass" when English moralists "stick their noses into our internal affairs...It is the quintessence of brass and impudence...."[94]

However Governor Tillman of South Carolina held sheriffs responsible for doing their job and keeping the mobs at bay:

> It may well be understood once and for all in South Carolina that the law must be enforced and that Sheriffs, instead of dodging real or imaginary mobs, must defend their prisoners with their lives, if necessary. If an officer of the law cannot protect a prisoner then he has no business to arrest him; and the prisoner once arrested must be safe from molestation of any authority except that of the court.[95]

Bishop Atticus G. Haygood

Atticus G. Haygood wrote one of the most thorough apologies
for lynch law from the church perspective in an article for *The
Forum*. Haygood was a southern Methodist Episcopal Church
bishop and an agent for the John Slater Fund. He was seen as an
advocate for Black progress,[96] but he succumbed to the rhetoric and
rationale of lynching. He, like others, believed that Black men were
guilty of the crime of rape. Although he did not agree with the lynch
law as the solution to this alleged crime, he did use its "existence" as
the basis for his response to why lynching was so pervasive in the
South.

Haygood was clear as to the motives of the lynchers and the
motives for their actions.

> If one private citizen has no moral or civil right to put a man to
> death, a hundred banded together have not the right. And why
> not the hundred banded together? Because their object is to
> overawe and overpower the law. Lynchers are conscious of their
> lawlessness, and seek protection in masks or numbers.[97]

Yet his next statement was a call for a halt of assaults by negroes on
"white women and little white girls" or "there will most probably be
still further displays of vengeance that will shock the world."[98] He
then moved to a defense of the actions of lynchers by noting that
superstition, ignorance, and low human development are not the
factors.

> These tortures do not belong to that dark time when women were
> hanged in New England for witchcraft; there is no superstition in
> Texas or Kentucky about witches, or other supernatural pow-
> ers—at least among white people. These burnings are not to be
> accounted for by any theory of superstition, or ignorance, or low
> human development, but by what we know of the elemental forces
> that control human nature throughout all time and the world
> over.[99]

Haygood saw the unconditional enfranchisement of Blacks as
a "deadlier crime against republican government and civilization
than the extremist Federalist believed secession to be..."[100]

Haygood appealed to the rhetoric of radical segregationists and disenfranchisement advocates when he stated:

> This particular crime was practically unknown before Emancipation....An ignorant race, that in and through the ministry of slavery had grown into all that made it better than naked Africans, were suddenly turned loose, without knowledge of civil law, into a freedom they did not understand, mistaking most naturally license for liberty. The recoil was tremendous. It is a wonder that the negro did not do worse. Presently came enfranchisement and complete citizenship without fitness of any sort....the gift of the ballot to him meant two things: first, the peculiar love the North had for him; second, that it was given to him to keep the old masters and rebels down.[101]

He also noted the wrong-headedness of missionaries whom Haygood believed emphasized Black rights over the responsibilities of citizenship. This only produced Black insubordination rather than enhance the social order.[102]

Haygood had clear reasons for calling attention to what he believed to be the effects of emancipation on younger Blacks.

> ...for the reason that the older negroes were less affected by the evils of that period. Nearly all crimes of violence by the negroes are committed by those who were children in 1865 or who have been born since that time. Nearly all the negroes in Southern penitentiaries are under thirty-five;...The older negroes, as a class, are the best citizens as well as the best laborers to-day, as all Southern people know.[103]

He also defended southern behavior toward Blacks. Although he admitted that this behavior was not perfect, he was sure

> ...that Southern white people have borne themselves, under trials never known before in history, as well as any people in the world could have borne themselves....The Southern white people are not cruel and never were. They are kind-hearted people; good to one another and to all men. They are kind to dumb brutes....They were kind to the negroes when they were slaves; they are kind to them now.[104]

Haygood explained the burning of Blacks and lynching as products of temporary insanity: "I give frankly my opinion: the people who burned them were for the time insane."[105] This was a truly unique explanation and carried much weight given Haygood's position in the church and his record as an advocate for Black progress. He added,

> No race, not the most savage, tolerates the rape of women, but it may be said without reflection upon any other people that Southern people are now and always have been most sensitive concerning the honor of their women—their mothers, wives, sisters, daughters. A single word questioning the purity of Southern women has cost many a man his life.[106]

He concluded the article with a plea for the continued education of Blacks, for he believed that the uneducated were guilty of rape and other crimes. Haygood placed the responsibility in the hands of Black ministers and school teachers.

> If the negro preachers and negro school-teachers can be awakened in their duty as to this particular matter, they can do more than all others put together....All primary schools for negro children are taught by negro men and women; all negro pulpits, with exceptions too few to count, are occupied by negro preachers. If these teachers and preachers are brought to understand that upon them, at this time, is the exigent duty of teaching their people that the assaulting of white women must cease;...[107]

Despite virulent protest from white southerners, Wells' campaign did have an effect on southern opinion and actions. Businessmen, governors, and newspapers alike realized the declining investment of British dollars into the southern economy. When six alleged barn burners were shot while being brought to the Shelby County jail, white business leaders condemned the crime publicly. They went so far as to call a public meeting in the Merchants' Exchange where they adopted resolutions censuring the "wicked, fiendish, and inexcusable massacre," demanded the arrest and conviction of the murderers, and raised two funds: the first for apprehending the criminals and the second for the benefit of the widows and orphans of the slain men.[108]

The Shelby County grand jury indicted thirteen white men for the murder and went on record as being appalled, announcing hope for a conviction followed by the death penalty.

> We cannot close this report without expressing our horror of the cold-blooded, brutal, butchery of these six defenseless men, the cruelty of which would cause even a savage to hang his head in shame.[109]

The next day, *The Commercial Appeal* editorialized:

> if this crime goes unpunished, every friend of Memphis must be dumb before the accusations of its enemies, for silence will be our only refute from the pitiless fire of denunciation that will be heaped upon us.[110]

THE AFRICAN-AMERICAN RESPONSE TO WELLS AND HER CAMPAIGN

African-Americans had a mixed response to Wells. In an 1894 resolution, the Women's Mite Missionary Society of the Third Episcopal District of the African Methodist Episcopal (AME) Church in Cleveland commended Wells and her crusade.

> Resolved. That we, the Mite Missionary convention assembled, do hereby extend our heartfelt sympathy to Miss Ida B. Wells, who is laboring in England to create a healthy sentiment in regard to the unjust treatment, the lynchings and floggings of our people in the south.
> Resolved. That we especially commend her for the fearless manner in which she has entered the campaign against the wholesale slaughter of Negroes in the south;...[111]

However, her former business partner at *The Free Speech*, J.L. Fleming, wrote that her "fire eating speeches nowhere on the globe will help the situation."[112] The majority of the Colored School Teachers Association of Georgia voted down a resolution commending Wells. *The Memphis Appeal-Avalanche* published an interview with the former Congressman John M. Langston who thought Wells leaned toward "notoriety and revenue" rather than patriotism and added his belief that the evils of the South were being remedied quickly.[113]

The AME Church's Bishop Henry McNeal Turner wrote a defense of Wells' character and her crusade. He condemned Blacks who would not defend their own rights:

> I know of editors of our colored papers who are in profound sympathy with Miss Wells, but will not say a word through their papers. The bulk of our school teachers are scullions. They sympathize with Miss Wells, commend her labors, spirit and motives, yet when they meet in convention they will adopt no commendatory resolutions; nor will they make a speech favorable to her, and why? Because they are afraid they will lose their positions. They sacrifice their man and womanhood to the will of those who traduce and degrade them and thereby become scullions. Whenever a people are so abnormalized by their environment that they are afraid to lift up their voices in protest against their murderers and exterminators, it is time to leave there or ask for enslavement.[114]

African-American ministers were divided in their support of Wells. The Reverend Benjamin Imes pastored a congregation in the city of Memphis during the period of the Thomas Moss lynching. As a major voice in the African-American community of Memphis, Imes believed that race and color were no longer handicaps and that white prejudice motivated Blacks to excel. He was known for his moderate stances on social issues and his desire to work through the system to effect legal recourse and social rights for Blacks. When the courts prevented legal redress for Blacks who were denied equal access to hotels, restaurants, first class railroad cars, and theaters, Imes joined other Black leaders in calling the Tennessee legislature to repeal local discrimination. This group proposed a new constitutional amendment on a national level to overrule the 1883 Supreme Court defense of segregation.[115]

Like the early position of W.E.B. DuBois, Imes saw social equality and political rights as two distinct issues. He sought political rights, the equality of public privilege, not social equality which Imes felt "was something which could never be legislated and would best be left alone to work itself out....segregation laws which denied Blacks civil equality were grossly unfair and unchristian."[116]

Imes and Wells were all too familiar with a Memphis in which Blacks voted, held public office, served on the police force. They, like countless other Blacks, were shocked and angered at the radical segregationist and racist campaign launched by the younger generation of whites. The Memphis *Weekly Avalanche* was representative of this new spirit among whites.

> The older men have been contemplating the situation, lo these many years. They're saying "If the North will let us alone, we'll work this out in time." The time for that sort of talk has gone by. The young men of today say, "We are going to work this out, and do it right now...and the North can do all the howling it wants to."[117]

The Reverend Taylor Nightingale, along with J.L. Fleming and Wells, led the Black protest of this racist ideology in *The Free Speech* newspaper.

> The old Southern voice that was once heard and made the Negroes jump and run like rats to their holes is "shut up," or might well be, for the Negro of today is not the same as Negroes thirty years ago, and it can't be expected that the Negro of today will take what was forced upon him thirty years back. So it is no use to be talking now about Negroes ought to be kept at the bottom where God intended them to stay; the Negro is not expected to stay at the bottom.[118]

After the Tom Moss lynching, several Black clergy played an active role in the Black exodus from Memphis to the West. However, Imes was less extreme in his response. He issued a public statement expressing the terror and hopelessness felt by the Black community of Memphis. But he refused to emigrate and instead tried to reason with Blacks and whites alike. He deplored retaliatory violence. After Wells published her famous editorial which resulted in her being forced into exile from Memphis, Imes proposed an interracial meeting to discuss racial conflict and restore harmony in Memphis.

Although he criticized the tendency of whites to blame the entire Black community for the offenses of a few, Imes also stated that most Blacks were appalled by Wells' rashness. He joined a dozen community leaders who sought calm and cessation or lessening of hostilities by censuring Wells for slandering southern white womanhood:

> Therefore speaking for ourselves and that large portion of our people who are capable of exercising a sober judgment and forethought, as we trust, we desire to put on record a most positive disapproval of the course pursued by Miss Ida Wells, through the medium of the New York Age, in stirring up from week to week, this community and wherever that paper goes, the spirit of strife over the unhappy question at issue. We see no good to come from this method of journalism on either side;...an ordinary prudence at least is demanded. Virtue cannot be encouraged by sowing scandal and broadcast, polluting the minds of the innocent and pure. The sad tending toward crime is deplorable wherever the fault may be found and it is a common duty to improve and elevate the moral tone of social life among all classes, and that, too, by methods worthy of a civilized and professedly Christian people.[119]

However by the end of 1892, Imes had grown weary of his futile attempts at reconciliation and left the city for a pulpit in Knoxville, Tennessee.

Mrs. N.F. Mossell captured the spirit of Wells' supporters. She noted with her characteristic elegance:

> Who shall say that such a work accomplished by one woman, exiled and maligned by that community among whom she had so long and valiantly labored, bending every effort to the upbuilding of the manhood and womanhood of all races, shall not place her in the front ranks of philanthropists, not only of the womanhood of this race, but among those laborers of all ages and all climes?[120]

The Clash Between Willard and Wells Continues

The confrontation continued between Wells and Willard into the fall of 1894 and the WCTU convention in Cleveland, Ohio in November. Some convention delegates made an effort to secure the adoption of a resolution to protest lynching. Willard gave them assurance that such a resolution would be adopted, but then attacked Wells in her annual address.

> It is my firm belief that in the statements made by Miss Wells concerning white women having taken the initiative in nameless acts between the races she has put an imputation upon half the white race in this country that is unjust, and save in the rarest exceptional instances, wholly without foundation....unanimous opinion of the most disinterested and observant leaders of opinion whom I have consulted on the subject.[121]

Wells' response to the charges was swift:

> At no time nor in any place, have I made statements "concerning white women having taken the initiative in nameless acts between the races."...at no time, or place nor under any circumstance have I directly or inferentially "put an imputation upon half the white race in this country."...when the facts were plain that the relationship between the victim lynched and the alleged victim of his assault was voluntary, clandestine and illicit.[122]

In a *Cleveland Gazette* article Wells wrote in a similar vein:

> We did not expect this from one who has stood so long for humanity. We have to give the facts. In giving them no imputation is cast upon the white women of America and it is unjust and untruthful for any one to so assert.[123]

The Reverend R.C. Ransom, an influential local pastor in Cleveland, revealed to a gathering to honor Wells that "a few misguided Afro-Americans" in the city of Cleveland wanted to present Willard with a bouquet on behalf of the African-American women of Cleveland. The report in *The Gazette* gave the audience response:

The audience showed in an unmistakable manner that it knew
that such action would have been not only a back handed "blow
in the face" for Miss Wells and the race movement she leads, but
a rank insult to every Afro-American lady in the city.[124]

When the committee on resolutions reported their work, no
protest was made concerning lynching. When a resolution against
lynching was introduced from the floor and read,

> then that great Christian body, which in its resolutions had
> expressed itself in opposition to the social amusement of card
> playing, athletic sports and promiscuous dancing; had protested
> against the licensing of saloons, inveighed against tobacco,
> pledged its allegiance to the Prohibition party, and thanked the
> Populist party in California and the Democratic party in the
> South, wholly ignored the seven millions of colored people of this
> country whose plea was for a word of sympathy and support for
> the movement in their behalf. The resolution was not adopted,
> and the convention adjourned.[125]

The Gazette gave yet another side of events of that convention when
it described the

> peculiar conduct and actions of the two "colored" delegates (from
> Michigan)—Madams Preston and Thurman. Strange to say,
> these women sided with Miss Willard as against Miss Wells and
> the race, and therefore in no sense were they representatives of
> our people. Madam Preston is a well known elocutionist. Afro-
> Americans should remember her and Mrs. Thurman as women
> who forsook Miss Wells, their race and its greatest cause at
> present to cling to a woman, Miss Willard, portions of whose
> annual address is an insult to the race.[126]

However, the December 6, 1894 Union Signal contained the
following resolution:

> The National WCTU...is utterly opposed to all lawless acts in any
> and all parts of our common lands and it urges these principles
> upon the public,...when no human being shall be condemned
> without due process of law; and when the unspeakable outrages
> which have so often provoked such lawlessness shall be banished
> from the world...[127]

This was not the resolution offered originally. Wells challenged
Willard on her negative statements concerning Wells in a private
talk. Willard's response was that someone in England told her it was
a pity that Wells attacked the white women of America.[128] Wells'
response was measured, but to the point:

> ' Oh, then you went out of your way to prejudice me and my cause
> in your annual address, not upon what you had heard me say, but
> what somebody had told you I said?[129]

Willard's reply was less than satisfactory to Wells, saying that Wells
"must not blame her for her rhetorical expressions—that I had my
way of expressing things and she had hers."[130]

The editorial notes of *Union Signal*, December 6, 1894 contained Willard's explanation as well:

> But as this expression has been misunderstood she desires to
> declare that she did not intend a literal interpretation to be given
> to the language used, but employed it to express a tendency that
> might ensue in public thought as a result of utterances so sweep-
> ing as some that have been made by Miss Wells.[131]

Wells response to this was

> When the lives of men, women and children are at stake, when the
> inhuman butchers of innocents attempt to justify their barbarism
> by fastening upon a whole race the oblique of the most infamous
> of crimes. It is little less than criminal to apologize for the butch-
> ers today and tomorrow to repudiate the apology by declaring it
> a figure of speech.[132]

Of the many biographies of Willard, only one contains any
mention of the conflict between Willard and Wells. Mary Earhart's
account of the conflict between Wells and the anti-lynching campaign encompasses three pages. It begins,

> At the national convention of 1894 Miss Willard tried to make
> her position quite clear by stating in her address that both the
> World's WCTU and the national Union made no distinctions of

color. The South under the freedom of state's rights maintained separate organizations for whites and blacks while the North and West had mixed ones; but in either case the colored people were represented in the national Union. ...It is inconceivable that the WCTU will ever condone lynching, no matter what the provocation.[133]

Earhart thought this made Willard's position clear, but she notes "the Negroes felt that she had not been definite enough in her stand and made some rather trenchant criticism of her."[134]   She noted that Willard was defended by a February 6, 1895 statement to the press signed by Frederick Douglass, William Lloyd Garrison, Lyman Abbot, Julia Ward Howe, and others, but the criticisms of Willard's position never stopped. At the National Conference of Colored Women months later, she was again condemned for her indefinite stand on lynching. Earhart's evaluation of the whole affair is quite telling, "The matter in itself was not serious, but it is significant of the opposing sentiment which seemed to spread during the late nineties."[135]

Neither Willard nor Earhart were able to understand the criticism of Wells and other anti-lynching advocates. The issue was not one of temperance or illiteracy but the effects of radical racism and disenfranchisement. Blacks died due to the charge of rape that was actually a subterfuge for white southern and northern hegemony.

Wells challenged not only this hegemonic ideal, but its underlying sexual mores and double standards. Willard, and other white women social reformers such as Jane Addams, could not comprehend that the charges lodged against Black men were largely false. Even more shattering to the status quo was the truth that white women willingly entered into sexual relationships with Black men. Wells saw her mission in clear terms. She researched her subject thoroughly, gathered the statistics needed, and provided her own trenchant social analysis to lay bare southern society and morality. Above all, the truth had to be and was—told.

NOTES

[1] C. Vann Woodward, *The Strange Career of Jim Crow*, 3d ed., rev. (New York: Oxford University Press, 1974), 18.

[2] Leon F. Litwack, *North of Slavery: The Negro in the Free States, 1790-1860* (Chicago: University of Chicago Press, 1961), 97.

[3] Woodward, 20.

[4] Abraham Lincoln quoted in Woodward, 21.

[5] Quoted in Woodward, 24. No source given.

[6] Quoted in Woodward, 26. No source given.

[7] Woodward, 27.

[8] Ibid., 28.

[9] W.E.B. DuBois, "An Open Letter to the Southern People (1887)," in *Against Racism: Unpublished Essays, Papers, Addresses, 1887-1961*, ed. Herbert Aptheker, (Amherst: University of Massachusetts Press, 1985), 4. In later years, DuBois moved from this position.

[10] Woodward, 69. The southern conservatives believed Blacks to be inferior, but did not conclude that an inferior race should be segregated or humiliated. Conservatives practiced paternalism vis-a-vis free Blacks. The southern radicals were Populists. They were vigorously anti-lynching and sought to bring an end to the color line and grant full rights to Blacks.

[11] Ibid., 70.

[12] Ibid., 75.

[13] Ibid., 79.

[14] Ibid., 80.

[15] Ibid., 81.

[16] George M. Fredrickson, *White Supremacy: A Comparative Study in American and South African History* (New York: Oxford University Press, 1981), 277.

[17] Ibid.

[18] Ibid., 278.

[19] Woodward, 72-73.

[20] Quoted in Woodward, 72. No source given.

[21] Floyd W. Crawford, "Ida B. Wells: Her Anti-Lynching Crusades in Britain and Repercussions From Them in the United States, 1958" TMs, Special Collections, Joseph Regenstein Library, University of Chicago, Chicago.

[22] Ibid.

[23] Floyd W. Crawford, "Ida B. Wells: Some American Reactions to Her Anti-Lynching Crusades in Britain, 1963" TMs, Special Collections, Joseph Regenstein Library, University of Chicago, Chicago.

[24] Ibid.

[25] *New York Times*, 5 June 1894.

[26] Jacquelyn Dowd Hall, *Revolt Against Chivalry: Jessie Daniel Ames and the Women's Campaign Against Lynching* (New York: Columbia University Press, 1979), 131.

[27] Ibid.

[28] Ibid.

[29] Ibid., 132.

[30] Ibid., 133.

[31] Philip A. Bruce, *The Plantation Negro as Freeman* (New York, n.p. 1889).

[32] George M. Fredrickson, *The Black Image in the White Mind: The Debate on Afro-American Character and Destiny, 1817-1914* (New York: Harper and Row, Publishers, 1971), 244-45; 258-62.

[33] Joel Williamson, *The Crucible of Race: Black-White Relations in the American South Since Emancipation* (New York: Oxford University Press, 1984), 111.

[34] National Association for the Advancement of Colored People, *Thirty Years of Lynching in the United States, 1889-1918* (National Association for the Advancement of Colored People, 1919; reprint, New York: Negro Universities Press, 1969), 7. The geographic breakdown was: North—219, South—2,834, West—156, and Alaska and unknown localities—15.

[35] Ibid., 9.

[36] Ibid., 10.

[37] Hall, 150. Williamson, 111-19.

[38] Hall, 153.

[39] Williamson, 115. Hall, 148-49.

[40] Hall, 156.

[41] Ibid., 140.

[42] Ibid.

[43] Ibid., 144.

[44] Fredrickson, *White Supremacy*, 252.

[45] Ibid.

[46] Also lynched with Moss were Calvin McDowell and Henry Stewart. These three men were business partners in the People's Grocery Company.

[47] Ida B. Wells, *Crusade for Justice*, ed. Alfreda Duster (Chicago: University of Chicago Press, 1970), 70.

[48] Moss' last words were "tell my people to go West—there is no justice for them here." Wells, *Crusade*, 51.

[49] Wells was among those who initially accepted the rape charge against black men. In *Crusade for Justice* she writes "I had accepted the idea meant to be conveyed—that although lynching was irregular and contrary to law and order, unreasoning anger over the terrible crime of rape led to the lynching; that perhaps the brute deserved death anyhow and the mob was justified in taking his life.", 64. Later in the same work, Wells comments on Frederick Douglass' initial acceptance as well: "He had been troubled by the increasing number of

lynchings, and had begun to believe it true that there was increasing lasciviousness on the part of Negroes.", 72.

[50] Ibid., 65.

[51] Wells, "Lynch Law in All Its Phases" *Our Day.* 11, no. 64. (May, 1893): 338.

[52] Dorothy Sterling, *Black Foremother: Three Lives* (Old Westbury, New York: The Feminist Press, 1979), 82-83.

[53] Undated column in *The Age,* "Marriage Bells" Special Collections, Joseph Regenstein Library, University of Chicago, Chicago.

[54] Ibid.

[55] Paula Giddings, *When and Where I Enter: The Impact of Black Women on Race and Sex in America* (New York: William Morrow and Company, 1984), 91.

[56] Ibid.

[57] Wells, *A Red Record: Tabulated Statistics and Alleged Causes of Lynching in the United States, 1892-1893-1894* (Chicago: Donohue and Henneberry, Printers, Binders and Publishers, 1894; reprint, New York: Arno Press, *On Lynching: Southern Horrors, A Red Record, Mob Rule in New Orleans,* 1969), 82.

[58] Ibid., 82-83. This bill gave the federal government control over the national elections in several states. The Black vote had been systematically suppressed since 1875 in the southern states. Many believed, along with Wells, that the bill would have given Blacks the protection of the federal government and assured Blacks access to the ballot box.

[59] Ibid., 83.

[60] Ibid., 86.

[61] Frances Ellen Watkins Harper and others, "Symposium—Temperance" *The A.M.E. Church Review* 7, no. 4 (April 1891): 372-81.

[62] Ibid., 380.

[63] Ibid.

[64] Ibid., 381.

[65] Wells, *Crusade,* 100-01.

[66] Wells, "Ida B. Wells Abroad," *Daily Inter Ocean,* 9 April 1894.

[67] Ibid.

[68] Frances Willard, *Glimpses of Fifty Years: The Autobiography of an American Woman* (Chicago: Woman's Temperance Publication Association, 1889), 373.

[69] Ibid., 373-74.

[70] Sterling, 91-92.

[71] Wells, *Crusade,* 112.

[72] Wells, *Daily Inter Ocean,* 28 April 1894.

[73] Ibid., 202-11.

[74] Wells began her friendship with Frederick Douglass early in her exile to

New York City. Douglass wrote an introductory letter of support and thanks to Wells' anti-lynching pamphlets *Red Record* and *Southern Horrors: Lynch Law in All Its Phases* (New York: The New York Age Print, 1892; reprint, New York: Arno Press,. *On Lynching: Southern Horrors, A Red Record, Mob Rule in New Orleans*, 1969). Arna Bontemps and Jack Conroy, *They Seek A City* (Garden City, NY: Doubleday, Doran and Co., Inc., 1945), 76.

[75] Wells, *Crusade*, 204.

[76] Ibid., 208.

[77] Ibid.

[78] Wells, *Crusade*, 209.

[79] Ibid., 155.

[80] Sterling, 91.

[81] Giddings, 91-92 n. and Maude T. Jenkins, "The History of the Black Woman's Club Movement in America" (PhD diss., Teachers College, Columbia University, 1984), 91.

[82] Giddings, 92.

[83] *Memphis Appeal-Avalanche*, 30 May 1892.

[84] Ibid., 31 May 1892.

[85] *Memphis Commercial Appeal*, 9 June 1894.

[86] "How Miss Wells' Crusade is Regarded in America," *Literary Digest*, 28.

[87] Ibid.

[88] Ibid.

[89] Ibid.

[90] Ibid.

[91] Ibid. One editorial from *The Commercial Appeal* stated: "It is only when she had put an ocean between herself and the fact that she could get a patient audience." *The Mobile Register* provided a unique view of the United States judicial process: "There are two things about the South that English people cannot understand: the relationship between the whites and blacks in the counties where blacks are in the majority; the second is the dilatory character of our legal processes."

[92] Ibid.

[93] *New York Times*, 23 November 1894.

[94] Crawford, "Ida B. Wells: Her Anti-Lynching Crusades in Britain and Repercussions From Them in the United States, 1958."

[95] *The New York Age*, 17 October 1891.

[96] Atticus G. Haygood, "The Black Shadow in the South," *The Forum*, October 1893: 167-75. In the article his only regret "in looking back at those years of consecration to the negro's cause, is that he could not do more to help his 'brother in black' to worthier conceptions of his relations to the government, to society, to the church, and so into better and nobler manhood and womanhood.", 170.

[97] Ibid., 167-68.

[98] Ibid., 168.

[99] Ibid., 168-69.

[100] Ibid., 170.

[101] Ibid., 172.

[102] Ibid., 173.

[103] Ibid., 173-74.

[104] Ibid., 170.

[105] Ibid., 171. Mrs. N.F. Mossell also picked up the insanity theme in her *The Work of the Afro-American Woman*, 2d ed. (Philadelphia: Geo. S. Ferguson Company, 1908; reprint, New York: Oxford University Press, 1988), 40. She describes the mobs as "these poor people were generally drunk and half insane and always bestial. The church must not keep silent while the press spoke out..."

[106] Haygood, 171.

[107] Ibid., 174.

[108] David M. Tucker, "Miss Ida B. Wells and Memphis Lynching," *Phylon: The Atlanta University Review of Race and Culture* 32, no. 2 (Summer 1971): 121.

[109] *New York Times*, 16 September 1894.

[110] Memphis *Commercial Appeal*, 17 September 1894.

[111] *The Cleveland Gazette*, 14 July 1894.

[112] Mildred Thompson, "Ida B. Wells-Barnett: An Exploratory Study of an American Black Woman, 1893-1930," (MPh diss., George Washington University, 1979), 104.

[113] Ibid.

[114] *Topeka Weekly Call*, 4 August 1894.

[115] David M. Tucker, *Black Pastors and Leaders: Memphis 1819-1972* (Memphis: Memphis State University Press, 1975), 42. The 1893 Supreme Court decision declared Charles Sumner's Civil Rights Law unconstitutional.

[116] Ibid., 43.

[117] *Weekly Avalanche*, 11 July 1889.

[118] Ibid., 13 June 1889.

[119] Memphis *Appeal Avalanche*, 30 June 1892. This letter was signed by Imes along with such leaders as B.T. Fields and M.H. Barker.

[120] Mossell, 46.

[121] Wells, *Red Record*, 80 and *Cleveland Gazette*, 24 November 1894.

[122] Wells, *Red Record*, 81.

[123] *Cleveland Gazette*, 24 November.1894.

[124] Ibid.

[125] Wells, *Red Record*, 87.

[126] *Cleveland Gazette*, 24 November 1894.

[127] Wells, *Red Record*, 87-88.

[128] Ibid., 89.

[129] Ibid.

[130] Ibid.

[131] Ibid.

[132] Ibid., 89-90.

[133] Mary Earhart, *Frances Willard: From Prayers to Politics* (Chicago: University of Chicago Press, 1944), 360.

[134] Ibid., 361.

[135] Ibid., 362.

VII

TOWARD A CONTEMPORARY
WOMANIST CHRISTIAN SOCIAL ETHIC

Womanist 1. From *womanish.* (Opp. of "girlish," i.e. frivolous,
irresponsible, not serious.) A black feminist or feminist of color.
From the black folk expression of mothers to female children,
"You acting womanish," i.e., like a woman. Usually referring to
outrageous, audacious, courageous or *willful* behavior. Wanting
to know more and in greater depth than is considered "good" for
one. Interested in grown-up doings. Acting grown up. Being
grown up. Interchangeable with another black folk expression:
"You trying to be grown." Responsible. In charge. *Serious.*[1]

In her life and work, Wells-Barnett sought the truth and
centered herself in a strong understanding of Christian duty. Her
understanding of her personal authority as well as that of Christians
in relation to justice shaped her and created her understanding of
liberation and reconciliation, suffering and obedience. Using Wells-
Barnett's strong sense of social and moral rectitude, an outline of a
contemporary womanist Christian social ethic emerges from these
themes. Liberation, reconciliation, suffering, and obedience surface
from Wells-Barnett and from the communities she shaped.

Her peculiar perspective of leadership and its difficulties is a
final theme that arises from this study. Wells-Barnett was not
unusual in her inability to work in coalitions. Many who are on the
cutting edge of leadership are unable to work in partnership. Her life
and witness help provide resources for a prophetic voice as well as
pastoral witness.

The Role of African-American Women in Women's and African-American Social Analysis

Ida B. Wells-Barnett was a strong, determined, and proud African-American woman whose life and witness were one. However, she and other women of her time lived in the public/private realm dichotomy which began in the late nineteenth century when work became largely male-identified and located away from the home. Women were to be feminine, domestic, modest, and delicate. They were exalted as moral guardians of the home and radiant sources of purity in the new industrial order.

> She sits, she walks, she speaks, she looks—unutterable things! Inspiration springs up in her very paths—it follows her footsteps. A halo of glory encircles her, and illuminates her whole orbit. With her, man not only feels safe, but actually renovated. For he approaches her with an awe, a reverence, and an affection which before he knew not he possessed.[2]

Men dominated, and continue to be the dominant sex in society, due to their participation in public life and the relegation of women to the private or domestic sphere. This relegation gave rise to universal male authority over women and a higher valuation of male roles over those of females.[3] The public realm contains the institutionalized rules and practices which define the appropriate modes of action. It provides the political, economic, legal, cultural and social institutions in which human beings live as a society. In addition, the wide range of actions and practices covered by law are the purview of the public sector. The private realm is that place of individual actions and interpersonal relations.

African-American women live within this split between the private/public realms. Compared to their white counterparts, Black women were and continue in a somewhat different social position within the Black community, whether it is rural or urban. Black males are excluded from the public sphere of the dominant white culture in large measure.[4] This dynamic suggests that the sex-role relationships between Black men and women cannot be adequately explained by a notion of structural oppression between the private and public spheres or the differential participation of men and women in the public sphere.[5] The public life of the dominant must be differentiated from that of the dominated society. The public life of the dominated society is always subject to the stresses put upon it by the dominant society. The private life of the dominated society suffers even more than that of the dominant society's.

Along with the peculiar nature of the public/private realm split for Black women, the women's suffrage movement played a role in the lives of working class, African-American, and immigrant women. In the 1890s, the rhetoric of the suffrage movement shifted to one of expediency.[6] The claim made by middle class white women was that exclusion from a political right granted to immigrant, African-American, and working class men was an insult to native-born, white, middle class women. By 1910, these arguments softened against immigrants and working class people. However this was not true in relation to African-Americans.

Traditional African-American cultural analysis and criticism have characterized the turn of the century as the age of Booker T. Washington and W.E.B. DuBois. The effect has been to limit the conceptual framework of historical interpretation to theories of exceptional male intellectual genius.[7] Such works as Washington's *Up From Slavery* (1901) and DuBois' *Souls of Black Folk* (1903) are presented as the best and brightest contributions from Black Americans of the period. Their representation as such comes at the expense of foundational works by African-American women. Frances Ellen Watkins Harper's *Iola LeRoy, Shadows Uplifted* (1892) and Wells' *Southern Horror* (1892), *A Red Record* (1895) and *Mob Rule in New Orleans* (1900) have received scant attention.

Feminist theory and investigations of the nineteenth and early twentieth century women writers, theorists, and activists habitually omit or obfuscate the role and contributions of women of color. The essay by Ellen DuBois and Linda Gordon, "Seeking Ecstasy on the Battlefield: Danger and Pleasure in Nineteenth-Century Feminist Sexual Thought" is an example of this. In the essay they write, "the black woman's movement conducted a particularly militant campaign for respectability, often making black feminists spokespeople for prudery in their communities."[8]   This is an extraordinarily narrow view of the complicated role of the African-American woman's movement within the Black community and within the larger social context of United States social relations and economics. Like their white sisters, African-American women had a range of reactions to the social, cultural, political, and religious milieu which constituted the United States and the international scene at the turn of the century.

Womanist Ethical Analysis

Womanist ethics begins with the realization of the traditional role and place to which Black women have been assigned and relegated. Katie G. Cannon points out that the assumption of what she terms the "dominant ethical systems" implies that the doing of ethics in the Black community is either immoral or amoral.[9] This traditional reflection is predicated on the existence of freedom and a wide range of choices for the moral agent.[10] This freedom is not available to white women and women and men of color, as well as poor people and representatives of marginal groups in United States society.

Cannon goes on to note that dominant ethics makes a virtue of qualities that lead to economic success: self-reliance, frugality, industry.[11] Further, dominant ethics assumes that the moral agent is free and self-directing and can make suffering a desirable norm. In Cannon's view, this understanding of moral agency is not true for African-Americans. The reality of white supremacy and male superiority force Blacks and whites, women and men, to live in different ranges of freedom.[12] In situations of oppression, freedom is not a choice nor is self-reliance. Frugality is enforced and suffering is present, but neither is chosen. Cannon believes that Black ethical values cannot be identical with the obligations and duties which white society requires of its members.[13]

An African-American woman as a moral agent must contend with race, sex, class, and other sources of fragmentation. The challenge for the Black woman as moral agent is to create and then articulate a positive moral standard which critiques the elitism of dominant ethics at its oppressive core and is relevant for the African-American community and the larger society.

A Paradigm of Authority

The emerging social order of the late nineteenth century and early twentieth century of the United States featured change. The rise of radical segregation and racism as national phenomena, the political and economic effects of the Civil War, the changing nature of roles within the family, and the role of the family transformed individuals and social groups. The emerging industrial base, evangelical Christianity, and the suffrage movement for women and African-American men affected the nation.

Change can be viewed as developmental or as radical.[14] Developmental change involves variations within the social order. Society is seen as in transition with various events influencing the social order.[15] Change within the boundaries of the social order is seen as a natural consequence of progress. The alternative model of change is radical. Radical change involves significant turning points with society in which a marked change in direction or a new social structure emerges.[16]

Luther Gerlach and Virginia Hine suggest that a key marker of radical change is raised when "those who occupy positions of power in the existing social structures resist that change."[17] This means that those individuals and groups who seek to change the order of things must "mobilize for collective power to oppose the power vested in existing structures."[18]

Wells-Barnett certainly falls within the framework suggested by Gerlach and Hine. Her anti-lynching and social agitation were direct responses to the social disruption of African-Americans and women in United States society. Her mission was designed to enhance the quality of life for two groups suffering discrimination as she constantly appealed to the utopian ideal of America as the "land of the free and the home of the brave."

Wells-Barnett began her public career with a brief "write up" of her refusal to leave the ladies' car for the smoking car of a train. Subsequently, she was physically thrown off the train by three men. She went on to sue the railroad company. The lower court ruled in her favor. The Supreme Court of Tennessee overturned the lower court ruling in favor of the railroad. Writing in her diary, Wells was devastated.

> The Supreme Court reversed the decision of the lower court in my behalf, last week. Went to see Judge G. this afternoon and he tells me four of them cast their personal prejudice in the scale of justice and decided in face of all the evidence to the contrary that the smoking car was a first class couch for colored people as provided for by that statute that calls for separate coaches but first class, for the races. I had hoped such great things from my suit for my people generally. I have firmly believed all along that the law as on our side and would, when we appealed to it, give us justice. I feel shorn of that belief and utterly discouraged, and just now if it were possible would gather my race in my arms and fly far away with them. O God is there no redress, no peace, no justice in this land for us? Thou hast always fought the battles of the weak and oppressed. Come to my aid at this moment and teach me what to do, for I am sorely, bitterly disappointed. Show us the way, even as Thou led the children of Israel out of bondage into the promised land.[19]

To her detractors, Wells-Barnett sought to transform the social order. In her own view, she only sought to reform society and to open the social order so that women and African-Americans could be active participants. Wells-Barnett did not tolerate any form of domination or authoritarian construct which was not life-enhancing and modeled her understanding of Christian values and action. Although she often took unilateral action, Wells-Barnett did not model an authority of domination. She dedicated her work in the public realm to breaking down authoritarian structures which constrained people rather than fostered human freedom and achievement.

Two paradigms of authority[20] emerge from a consideration of the social and moral perspectives of Ida B. Wells-Barnett: authority as domination and authority as partnership.[21] The latter is the paradigm which reflects community, partnership, and justice. The former is primarily a means of subjugation.

The traditional concept of power is a natural consequence of an authoritarian model of obedience based on submission. The world is separated into entities with little or no interrelationship.[22] Power becomes the property of these separated entities and is identified with domination: power over.[23] This concept of power involves the notion of invulnerability.

Wells-Barnett did not shy away from challenging authoritarian power although she was impatient when working with groups. When her local Equal Rights League was slow to organize a protest against the Elaine, Arkansas riot,[24] she pushed them to appoint a committee to send resolutions of protest to the president, a senator and congressmen from Arkansas, and the governor of Arkansas. She was made the chairperson of the committee.

Wells-Barnett penned a letter signed by the president of the Equal Rights League, Oscar DePriest of the People's Movement, and herself as president of the Negro Fellowship League. DePriest received a wire from Congressmen Madden asking for the names of those who were lynched. DePriest asked Wells-Barnett to reply to the congressman and invited her to the next meeting of the People's Movement to present a strong resolution for them to act on. Wells-Barnett neglected to take the matter back to the League before responding to the request for information and the resolution. Her reply, in letter form, appeared in the *Chicago Defender*. This letter galvanized financial support to help with legal fees for the twelve imprisoned men.

The governor of Arkansas decided that the prisoners deserved a new trial and issued a stay of execution. Wells-Barnett's effective, though unilateral actions on behalf of the League, were not appreciated. When she arrived at the meeting of the local Equal Rights League after the swirl of events, chapter members were denouncing her for failing to bring the work of her committee back to the League before networking with other organizations and effecting the stay of execution.

> "But...action had to be taken at once. It would be two weeks before I could accept Mr. DePriest's invitation if I had waited to come to the league meeting before doing so. Those men are under sentence of death and there was no time to be lost."[25]

A bylaw was adopted in this meeting which suspended any member of the League who took any work the League was engaged in to another body. Wells-Barnett's reply and subsequent action are models of ornery resistance to authoritarian models of power. She reminded the League that when she first broached the subject, their response was that nothing could be done. However, "not only had we sent protests to national and state officials but our leading newspapers and one of our largest organization had acted as the result of our work; that circumstances alter cases, and I thought that they would be glad that so much had been done in such a short while." The League stood fast in the bylaw. Wells-Barnett left the meeting and never worked with the Equal Rights League again.

The concept of power which comes from decision and responsibility effects change and is able to work with others: power with.[26] This power requires openness, vulnerability, and readiness to change. It is dynamic and concerned with the responsibility human beings have as moral agents for personal and social transformation.

"Power over" is dysfunctional to society because it inhibits diversity and growth. It restricts vision and movement and reduces flexibility and responsiveness. "Power with" is power that emerges out of the life of the people, not that which is imposed upon them. Persons experience it when they engage in interactions that produce value. "Power with" summons persons to develop their capacities for nurturance and empathy as well as interconnectedness. Its project is justice.

The concept of authority which arises out of this understanding of power is shared authority. The key here is partnership which begets coalitions. Shared authority is a dynamic process in which the openness to the future evident in "power with" is manifest in the actual living out of movements for change and transformation.[27] Shared authority recognizes the plurality in United States culture and is attentive to the various leadership styles and structures intrinsic to this diversity.

Wells-Barnett chafed in organizational structures and coalitions. She made honest and full attempts to be a part of the work of the group. However, her penchant for reasoned and strategic action often superseded debate and long meetings. Her work with Celia Barker Wooley, a Unitarian minister, to establish a center to foster better interracial cooperation and understanding is a case in point. Wooley, in Wells-Barnett's mind, controlled the enterprise. Little happened without Wooley's approval. When Wells-Barnett was asked, by the president of the women's club which was a part of the center, to organize a program at the last minute, Wells-Barnett did so. Her program, "What It Means to Be a Mother" was an apparent success until Wooley decried the importance of motherhood. For Wells-Barnett, this "seemed like a dash of cold water on the enthusiasm I has succeeded in arousing."[28]

Wooley later engaged in what Wells-Barnett termed "double-dealing" by trying to prevent Wells-Barnett's election to the presidency of the club. Wells-Barnett was mindful of her reputation of being difficult to work with in a group. Her work with the club was an honest attempt to work within the structures of an organization *and* the autocratic control of Wooley. Wooley's attempt to block Wells-Barnett was the final straw. In anger, but with complete resolution, she informed Wooley that "I say to you that I have finished with trying to help you carry on the center and that if in the future I ever lift a finger, you yourself will have to come and beg me to do so."[29]

The Center struggled for two more years, but attendance declined. Wells-Barnett was clear of the outcome—"those who had so illy advised her were not themselves active in making up for the loss of the woman who had labored so hard to make it a success."[30] When Wooley did ask her to come back to the Center, Wells-Barnett declined citing other work in which she was now engaged.

Wells-Barnett's life and social justice work modelled authority as a contextualized commitment based on accountability to God through the risen Christ. This commitment is also grounded in a mutual accountability to those in the immediate communities of people as well as those representative of the diversity in which persons live and must be in coalition. The individual's particular context informs him or her of a segment of the world. He or she must be in dialogue with others who are not members of that specific context.

The irony of Wells-Barnett's life was that as strong as she was in following through in her Christian duty, she was unable to work effectively or for long periods with others. Her obituary in the *Chicago Defender* captures her abilities and personality well: "elegant, striking, and always well groomed,...regal though somewhat intolerant and impulsive."[31] Time and again, Wells-Barnett was unable to understand why others found different pathways to effect social change once she had blazed the trail. Her penchant for unilateral action and impulsive confrontation was an anathema for many of her peers such as Mary Washington, Mary McLeod Bethune, and Mary Church Terrell.

The events surrounding the admittance of the Ida B. Wells Club as a charter member of the League of Cook County Clubs, an association of Chicago women's clubs, is a case in point. Although Wells-Barnett was no longer the president of the club, she agreed to represent the club with another member of the club at the inaugural event of the new association. Her rationale for such action was that the Ida B. Wells Club did not have a meeting before the inaugural event and she did not want to loose this important moment. The new president of the Wells Club, Mrs. Agnes Moody, was not pleased. She charged Wells-Barnett with usurping her prerogatives. Further, she planned to inform the League that Wells-Barnett's actions had not been authorized by the club. Wells-Barnett regretted her actions, but the damage had been done.

She had to spend the next few days lobbying members of the club to endorse her actions on behalf of the club. The resolution to endorse passed, but Moody stepped down from the chair "declaring that the club had two presidents and that that action ignored her."[32] Wells-Barnett implored the members to refuse the resignation, which they did. Moody blocked the secretary from sending a letter to the League stating that the club had ratified Wells-Barnett's action. When Wells-Barnett learned of this, she described it as "mischief" and went to the home of the corresponding secretary to engage her support to write the needed letter. She explained the circumstance to the corresponding secretary who agreed with her and wrote the letter.

As Wells-Barnett recounts the episode in her autobiography, she is unaware of the impact of her actions on the elected leadership of the club. Her concern was to take advantage of a moment to effect justice. Her desire to respond favorably to the invitation extended by her white sisters blinded her to protocol and true action in coalition. Rather than consult with Mrs. Moody, she took matters into her own hands. As she challenged authoritarian models of power, she neglected the key feature of effective coalition work—dialogue.

Her relentless challenge to unjust social structures and the illegitimate use of authority spilled over into her work with those groups with a similar social justice agenda. Shared authority, a concept which often eluded Wells-Barnett, is a tool for dialogue within partnership. Each participant is recognized and valued as a co-creator of God's Kingdom on earth. The views, the experience, the analysis of each person is given full weight as strategies of transformation and community are constructed and enacted.

OBEDIENCE

Wells-Barnett was an effective public speaker. Early in her public career in 1894, she had an opportunity to make a considerable amount as a contract speaker for the Slayton Lyceum Bureau. The sole stipulation was that she must not talk about lynching. When she explained to Mr. Slayton that her only "excuse" for public speech was to tell others about the outrage of lynching, he replied that the American people did not want to hear it.

> He said that if I felt that I could not make a speech on any other except lynching he would have a speech written for me in his office which I could commit to memory. He thus intimated that it did not matter much what I said so long as they could book me to appear on that circuit.[33]

She refused the offer because she was "dedicated to the cause" and felt it "sacrilegious to turn aside in a money-making effort for myself."[34]

Wells-Barnett's understanding of Christian duty is grounded in an evangelical understanding of obedience. However she and other social activists of her day shaped the traditional perception of obedience to address concerns for social justice and moral rectitude. There are two models of obedience to which Wells-Barnett could appeal. The first model, the authoritarian, depicts obedience as a self/other relationship exclusively. The relationship consists of an imbalance of power.[35] There is a fear of the strength of the person who is asserting superiority.

Obedience in this model is not a standard, but a behavioral technique. One never asks the question "Why?". The worldview of the authoritarian model is more Greek than Hebraic. Greek thought stressed order and did not tolerate continual change. The biblical worldview is that of movement toward a goal. The authoritarian model cannot adequately express the will of God for the world because this model is interested in the preservation of order and has a hostility toward the future.

Obedience concentrated completely on a higher and guiding other becomes blind to the world.[36] Obedience that is blind to the world and only follows directions has divested itself of all responsibility. Responsibility implies willingness to engage in freedom. This kind of "world blindness" formalized conception of Christian obedience leads to volunteered obedience as an end in itself. This in turn leads to easy manipulation by the authority figure(s) for its own purposes. The Bible, tradition, and experience are used as tools of repression rather than growth and guidance. The individual or group does no independent interpretation or reflection.

In the Hebrew Bible, there is always a relationship between obedience and justice. People directly concerned with shaping the world entrusted to humans must obey the will of God. Obedience implies responsibility: a decision which first discovers God's will and then decides the appropriate response. An advance determination of the situation or the will of God is not appropriate. The person can make the decision in the now. Jesus requires an obedience that has its eyes wide open as the individual accepts responsibility for the order of the world and engages in transforming that order.

The second model of obedience, discerning, is the model from which Wells-Barnett operated. Discerning obedience is power with others or power in process. It is found in interactions that produce value and summon the agent to develop his or her capacity for empathy and interconnectedness. The agent operates through an understanding of God's will for justice and truth.

> The old Southern voice that was once heard and made the Negroes jump and run like rats to their holes is 'shut up' or might well be, for the Negro of today is not the same as Negroes were thirty years ago, and it can't be expected that the Negro of today will take what was forced upon him thirty years back. So it is no use to be talking about Negroes ought to be kept at the bottom where God intended for them to stay; the Negro is not expected to stay at the bottom.[37]

AUTHORITATIVE USE OF SCRIPTURE

> I think I shall ask for a class of youths and see if I can not
> influence them in a small degree to think on better things. The
> bible and its truths are dealt with too flippantly to suit me.[38]

These reflections from her early diary indicate the central place
of the Bible in her life. Over twenty years later, Wells-Barnett was
still teaching Sunday school classes. She taught a class of young men
at Grace Presbyterian Church for ten year. In this class, Wells-
Barnett sought to discuss the Bible lessons "in a plain common-sense
way and tried to make application to their truths to our daily
lives."[39]

The Bible is also focal to the life of the Christian community
and vital for the very breath of the Black Church and African-
American religious experience. However it is only one of the sources
used to make moral judgments.[40] Scripture, alone, is not sufficient
to make any particular judgment authoritative. Scripture, human
experience, tradition, insights gained from the social sciences, the
humanities, and the physical sciences conjoin.

Wells-Barnett began with her experience and commitments.
She sought to understand the linkages between living and all the
dimensions of Christian life. Perhaps unwittingly for Wells-Barnett,
but intentionally for womanists, this is done from the perspective of
gender, culture, race, and ecclesial context. The Bible, liturgies,
church doctrines, and creeds mean little if womanists do not seek to
make them come alive, or if they bear no significance to Black
women's experience.

Womanists seeking to develop a contemporary Christian social
ethic begin with the experiences of disappointment and triumph. The
stories of the Bible come alive and are useful as the faithful seek to
make faith-filled decisions and actions. Experience is in dialogue
with scripture. From such a rich history of lived experience and
biblical witness, womanists must be open to God's ongoing revelation in the world.

The tradition of the historic Black Church is also a part of this
dialogue with scripture. The songs, prayers, and sermons of Black
folk, as well as the actions they undertook through their understanding of the gospel, shape an approach to scripture. African-American

women must hold in tension the images of themselves provided by scripture and their community.

Wells-Barnett was in constant dialogue with her tradition, her experience, and scripture as she sought to understand the particular path to justice she must follow. As evidenced in her early diary, she took seriously the need for proper Bible study and moral leadership. She began to teach Sunday school with the hope of influencing young men's minds. When she realized the power of her position as role model, she resolved to always live out that position. As a Sunday school teacher in her later years, Wells-Barnett wrote of a class she taught for ten years: "every Sunday we discussed the Bible lesson in a plain and common-sense way and tried to make application of their truths to our daily lives."[41]

For Wells-Barnett, the Christian tradition was one of duty, responsive witness to God's word, and spotless moral conduct. When, in 1894, a group of A.M.E. ministers debated the efficacy of endorsing her work, Wells-Barnett's strong sense of God's presence and aid as she did the work God called her to, led her to respond with indignation:

> I cannot see why I need your endorsement. Under God I have done work without any assistance from my own people. And when I think that I have been able to do the work with his assistance that you could not do, if you would, and you would not do if you could, I think I have a right to a feeling of strong indignation.[42]

Her reliance on scripture to inform and guide her in her social reform work and her understanding of duty are evidenced when she wavered in going to investigate the lynching of "Frog" James in Cairo, Illinois in 1909. After her initial refusal, some gentle persuasion applied by her ten year old son caused Wells-Barnett to relent.

> I looked at my child standing there by the bed reminding me of my duty, and I thought of that passage of Scripture which tells of the wisdom from the mouths of babes and sucklings.[43]

The social and physical sciences and the humanities have valuable contributions to make as women and men seek to discern whom they are called to be. The world is increasingly complex and bears little resemblance to the world of the Bible. There may be parallels as well as analogies, but the fact remains that the world is filled with artificial intelligence and toys and cartoons that proclaim that they are the "masters of the universe." The tools of sociology, political science, history, psychology, communication, biology help uncover the structures of domination in the world. This does not mean a disregard for the specifically theological insights from Christian tradition. Rather, it is a recognition that theological insights must be grounded in reality. This reality must be as accurate as possible rather than a skewed perception of truth.

Wells-Barnett provides an excellent model for this understanding. Her early functionalist insistence on objective knowledge, through her constant search for the truth and the facts of any given issue, evidence this.[44] She followed a method of collecting the facts and then publishing them to get at the truth of the American dilemma of injustice as she sought God's will for the country and her people. Wells-Barnett relied not only on a strong and living faith. She used reliable statistics and interviewed those involved in a given social problem. Her search for truth was relentless and thorough. She was never satisfied with simple explanation, rumor, or innuendo. She sought to be "a better Christian with more of the strength to overcome, the wisdom to avoid and have the meekness and humility that becometh a follower of Thee [God]."[45]

Wells-Barnett's approach helps to inform the agenda of a womanist Christian social ethic. The tools from the sciences and humanities can foster an understanding of scripture which elicits a broadened worldview. The faithful are held accountable for their actions because actions are not done in a vacuum, but are done in the midst of community and partnership.

Scripture employs a variety of ways to provide identity and to supply a vision and guidelines for the person as a responsible moral agent. Wells-Barnett stood in a strong African-American tradition as she sought to appropriate the biblical heritage of faith and community through Bible study and in her living. She kept this tradition a vital part of a womanist social ethic, in which scripture informs humanity of how God works with people, as well as nations, in grace *and* judgment. Scripture guides faith journeys and helps persons share their journeys with others. Scripture provides some of the pieces to the puzzle of how to live faithfully as a person of God. Human beings live in the tension of the written revelation of God found in scripture and the revelation of God in the world today. The Bible points to the presence and power of God in our midst.

Authority in Community

Authority in community is grounded in a realistic assessment of the present as people seek to live out of a vision of the future. This future vision gives the responsible moral agent what Letty Russell so aptly names "advent shock."[46]   Wells-Barnett was not content with her world, for it contained injustice. She provides an example for contemporary womanists that keeps them from being content with the present because of a shared vision of a coming just society.

The world of Wells-Barnett and the contemporary scene are both full of competing interests and agendas. Wells-Barnett lived during the struggle between Booker T. Washington's accommodationist stance and W.E.B. DuBois' representation of the Black protest tradition. Each man and those who adhered to either philosophy struggled against the pinnacle complex in which authority is a tool for domination.[47]

The task of a womanist social ethic promotes the recognition that an effective justice stance recognizes shifting roles and tasks among the justice-seekers. Women and men move from the role of nurturer to that of woundedness and all points in between. It is crucial that humans learn to allow one another to shift into other roles. This is particularly difficult in that women are socialized as "natural" nurturers and must be reminded that they are called to learn how to allow others to care for them as well.

Occasionally, the multiracial and gender inclusive nature of a womanist social ethic means strained dialogue. The difficulty of shared authority in diversity is evident, but the commitment to justice keeps the participants committed to group struggle. A womanist social ethic recognizes the necessity of somewhat different routes to understanding ourselves and ways in which each person as a responsible moral agent functions in a multiracial context and as women and men.

PAIN AND SUFFERING

The words of Marcia Ann Gillespie,

> It would seem that in order to qualify as heroine or leader, a Black woman's life must be one of personal loss, denial and sacrifice,[48]

provide the context for a womanist interpretation which considers the areas explored by white feminists, but also take a hard look at how Black women theorists have described Black womanhood. They also address the call by Gillespie to the Black church.

> [Churches must] provide aid, succor and practical support to our afflicted, our unemployed, our homeless and those who are striving to keep it all together. They must help us love our children by opening their doors after school so that our children don't wander the streets with keys around their necks and risk a repeat of Atlanta.[49]

Black women theorists have moved from Wells-Barnett's embrace of the ideology of the cult of true womanhood and a later romantic notion of how the Black woman has survived under adversity to one that is more realistic. The analyses of Joyce Ladner and Bell Hooks are representative of this shift. Joyce Ladner notes that much of the current focus on being liberated from the constraints of society being proposed by white women liberationists in the late 1960s and early 1970s never applied to Black women.[50] She posits that Black women have always been "free" and able to develop as individuals under the harshest of circumstances. She believes that this accounts for a female personality rarely described in scholarly journals.

Ladner's image of the Black woman is one of obstinate strength and survival. This is not the epitome of the U.S. model of femininity. Ladner's view of the strong Black woman contains elements of truth, but is overly optimistic in its assessment. She is equating survival and perseverance in the face of oppression with health.

> Usually, when people talk about the "strength" of black women they are usually referring to the way in which they perceive black women coping with oppression. They ignore the reality that to be strong in the face of oppression is not the same as overcoming oppression, that endurance is not to be confused with transformation.[51]

The reality is that most Black women work outside the home out of necessity and the majority do not control the source of their income. More than forty percent are heading single parent households and nearly thirty-six percent are below the poverty line. The Black woman joins her people in suffering as a state of being.

The punitive nature of suffering is reinforced by biblical tradition. Wisdom teaching focused on the concept that wickedness led to disaster while righteousness led to prosperity.[52] The roots of this understanding are in the older demonic conceptions of Yahweh's dangerous power as well as the pre-exilic prophetic warning that national disaster would be the outcome of God's judgment on faithlessness.[53] In the New Testament, Jesus repudiated suffering as an implication of guilt but reserved some cases when this could hold. The healing of the paralytic is closely related to the forgiveness of sins.

The question "Is suffering the will of God?" needs to be considered. This is a question which emerges from African-American experience and its interaction with other racial ethnic groups and oppressed communities. The answer takes two paths, acceptance or rejection. Those who accept suffering as God's will see it as a disciplinary measure from God and the highest way to follow Christ.[54] The proponents of this view posit that there would be no courage without suffering or the possibility of it, therefore, suffering ennobles. Pain is seen as good; it serves to warn the individual or group so that preventive action can be taken before any real damage is done. The overcoming of obstacles produces free, mature persons and stimulates love and compassion.

Wells-Barnett joins those who reject suffering as God's will and believe that it is an outrage that suffering exists at all. Although the details of analyses may differ, a womanist ethic must be dedicated to eliminating suffering on the grounds that its removal is God's redeeming purpose.

Wells-Barnett was clear that the founding of the Negro Fellowship League was designed to uplift the race. The League was the result of a discussion in her Sunday school class centering on how to respond to the 1908 Springfield riot and the lynching of three Black men, in what Wells-Barnett described, "the shadow of Abraham Lincoln's tomb."[55] The League met to discuss issues of importance to the Black folk of Chicago. Eventually the League persuaded the young men who gathered to debate the issues of the day that some practical course needed to be found. This led to the establishment of a settlement house on State Street in Chicago to combat the crime and vice of that neighborhood.

> ...I did not think that our Christian forces should leave State Street to the devil. If we could have a modern, up-to-date reading room set down there in the midst of all those temptations, and a consecrated young man in charge of it, whose duty it would be to visit the saloons and poolrooms several times a day distributing cards to the young men he found therein, inviting them to this reading room, it would be a splendid beginning in the way of having something that would help the young men who came to the city.[56]

Theologians Dorothee Soelle and James Cone provide a helpful foundation. While the bulk of their reflections are descriptive and/or do not deal directly with the experience of Black women, they do offer some words to conder in looking at Wells-Barnett's understanding of suffering.

Soelle gives three essential dimensions of suffering: physical, psychological, and social.[57] She believes that powerlessness signals that the individual does not believe that her or his behavior can influence or have an impact. This point is crucial in understanding how Soelle views suffering, for she believes that the more a person perceives that suffering is a natural part of life, the lower the self-esteem of that person.[58] Every attempt to humanize suffering must begin with powerlessness and move into activating the forces that can free persons to overcome their feeling of powerlessness.[59]

Soelle posits that the majority of Christian literature on suffering suppresses the three dimensions of suffering, particularly the social dimension.[60] She uses the term "Christian masochism" to describe the traditional Christian view. This is the belief that God allows suffering to break human pride, demonstrate human power-lessness, and exploit human dependency.[61] Submission becomes a source of pleasure in Christian masochism and suffering is a test for people to pass sent by God.

Soelle believes that Christian masochism places a low value on human strength and calls for the veneration of a God who is extremely powerful, but lacks a sense of the good.[62] Hence, suffering becomes an endurance test that makes it easy to be insensitive to the suffering of others because the focus is me-centered.

> The God who produced suffering and causes affliction becomes the glorious theme of a theology that directs our attention to the God who demands the impossible and tortures people—although this theology can, of course, show no devotion to such a God.[63]

Soelle points to the sadistic nature of the traditional under-standing that suffering is punishment for sin and that humans *must* suffer as a result of their sin, because God acts justly and not capriciously.[64] These masochistic presuppositions are based on the belief that God draws humans near in this manner to win souls. Soelle notes that at best, this is a qualified love that is neither radical nor fundamental.[65] She believes that any attempt to look upon suffering as caused by God in any fashion is in danger of regarding God as sadistic.

Soelle notes that the picture of the suffering Christ is not the traditional notion of God who does not suffer.[66] For Soelle, a God who does not suffer is an apathetic God, one who is physically beyond the reach of eternal influences and is psychologically moribund. The Gospels do not reflect this God in the life and ministry of Jesus. She suggests that worshipping a being or presence that is free from suffering is inviting ourselves to be apathetic to suffering. A possible result is that being free from suffering is only possible on a personal rather than corporate level.

For Soelle, Jesus' dignity lies in his fear of death, for she believes that a person without fear despises her or himself too much to be able to fear for the self. Soelle does not believe it helpful or appropriate to isolate Jesus' suffering so that it outweighs other forms of suffering or the suffering of others.[67] She believes that Jesus' experience can happen to anyone. The threat of death calls one's certainty of God's love and redemption into question. She does not believe that distinguishing Jesus' suffering is any different from any suffering in which there is the experience of being forsaken by God.

Hence, suffering is experienced as a threat to the relationship of humans with God. Yet the paradigm that Jesus presents for Soelle is a *chosen* suffering. Jesus willingly went to the cross to effect the resurrection. For her to say that human beings are created in the image of God without accepting the same cross as Jesus, is what she terms a "suffering-free Christianity." This Christianity is one in which others suffer.[68] For Soelle, to seek the image of Christ is to live in revolt against oppression and to remain with the oppressed and disadvantaged.[69] The redemptive suffering of Christ on the cross becomes an attainable paradigm, rather than a symbol, for Soelle.

James Cone does not question the reality of suffering, he questions its location.[70] Cone believes that the weight of the biblical view of suffering is not the origin of evil, but what God in Christ has done about evil.[71] Cone notes that within philosophical discourse human suffering is an aspect of the problem of evil. The problem then becomes how to rationally reconcile a God of unlimited power and goodness with the presence of evil.[72] From these two foundations, Cone proceeds to develop his understanding of suffering in the Black religious tradition.

Cone sees the reality of God's presence in the earthly ministry of Jesus and Jesus' death on the cross. The oppressed are set free to struggle politically against the imposed injustice of the rulers. The resurrection is God breaking into history and liberating the oppressed from their present suffering. Cone believes that Christians are called to suffer with God in their fight against evil.[73] Therefore suffering must be reinterpreted in light of the cross and the resurrection and the call for the faithful to become liberated sufferers with

God. Cone posits that the main reason theologians have said little that can be used in the struggle of the oppressed is because they have been spectators and not victims of suffering.[74] He believes that the God-encounter happens only in the fight for justice.

Cone admits that there is no historical evidence that proves God actually liberates Black people from oppression.[75] Instead, African-American Christians turn to Jesus as God's active presence in their lives. This Jesus helps them know that they were not created for bondage but for freedom. He believes that humanity's meaning is found in the fight of the oppressed for freedom, for it is in this fight that God joins humanity and grants vision to see beyond the present to the future.[76] The Black view of suffering is based on the claim of scripture and Black Christian experience that the God of Jesus is a liberator of the oppressed.

Most African-Americans are well aware of the inordinate location of suffering in African-American life. Cone's view of suffering differs from the traditional view of suffering, yet remains conservative in that he embraces the concept of suffering while questioning its location. Like Soelle, he calls for decisive action in the elimination of suffering in the lives of the dispossessed. But the question remains: why this suffering?

The Black Church in this country has paid serious attention to the Old Testament. The suffering of the children of Israel is likened to the suffering of Black people. It identifies heavily with the Exodus and the journey through the wilderness. Most Black folk in the church grew up with stories of Moses, Abraham, Ezekiel, and Esther. Suffering becomes the entry key to the Kingdom. The notion of the inevitably and desirability of suffering needs to be questioned.

Also helpful here is the distinction between pain and suffering made by Audre Lorde. Further, this distinction can be expanded upon in theological and ethical discourse.[77] For Lorde, suffering is unscrutinized and unmetabolized pain. It is a static process which usually ends in oppression. Pain is an experience that must be recognized, named, and then used for transformation. It is a dynamic process pointing toward transformation. Suffering is the inescapable cycle of reliving pain over and over and over when something close triggers it.

For Lorde, suffering is sinful because people do not choose to act through their finite freedom on behalf of their liberation from sin to justice, If, as most Black women in the church do, people take the resurrection event seriously, then true suffering has been removed through the redemptive event of the resurrection. Through the Suffering Servant, God has spoken against evil and injustice. The empty cross and tomb are symbols of the victory. The oppressed are set free to struggle against injustice, not out of their suffering, but out of their pain that can be recognized and named as injustice and brokenness. The resurrection moves humanity past suffering to pain and struggle. Another way to view this movement is through the resurrection. This event can be understood as God's breaking into history to transform suffering into wholeness—to move the person from victim to change agent. The gospel message's call is transformation: good news, liberation, sight, action.

Lorde's distinction is extremely helpful when considering the life and work of Wells-Barnett. Black women have historically taken the opportunity to redefine suffering for other women, the Black Church, and society. Wells-Barnett did so in a radical and exciting way for her time. She was unwilling to accept the world as interpreted through the eyes of others—those who would not challenge the power structure or who chose to acquiesce to the socio-political circumstances of her time.

The Fellowship Herald newspaper later echoed her refusal to accept the living conditions of African-Americans in the early twentieth century. Again expressing concern about the vagrancy rates in Chicago among young African-American men, Wells-Barnett offers through the pages of *The Herald*:

> What is to be done? This is the question every law-abiding citizen should ask himself. "What can I do to make conditions better" should be the next question he should ask himself. The ministers, professional men, leaders of organizations should ask themselves: "what have we done to help this situation?" Surely with all the forces that make for good citizenship at work, some solution of this grave problem can be formed.[78]

She saw the challenge for the African-American community to work in partnership with the intention of moving from suffering to pain. Within the framework of Lorde's model, Wells-Barnett understood suffering as a way of being that prevented effective action and denied the individual or the group the ability and right to say "No" to their oppression. Black women have suffered with death-dealing images designed to keep African-American women and men in a reactive stance. This reactive stance is the ground of being for suffering. The reactive stance does not allow for creative change or challenge the present conditions. Wells-Barnett was never content to merely react to the situation, she always moved to change it.

Within any oppressed group, the members of that group are prevented from acknowledging anger and frustration at the system and at the tensions under which they must live. If God is a just God and a loving God, oppressed people must allow themselves to search for the roots of their suffering, the unmetabolized and unscrutinized pain, which exists in their lives and threatens their existence.

Wells-Barnett pursued this search her entire adult life. She could not accept the lynch law, conditional suffrage, rioting, or vagrancy. Wells-Barnett's relentless crusade for justice models learning to trust and value anger and indignation rather than be victimized by injustice. Her response to the chairman of the new board, who would take over her work at the Negro Fellowship League, is particularly telling. When he expressed his amazement that there were "no leading people of the race" active in the League, Wells-Barnett replied that although she had tried, she had not been able to interest anyone:

> But then...neither did Jesus Christ have any of the leading people with him in his day when he was trying to establish Christianity. If I remember correctly, his twelve disciples were made up of fishermen, tax collectors, publicans, and sinners. It was the leading people who refused to believe on him and finally crucified him.[79]

To live and work through pain acknowledges the human ability to effect change in individual lives and in the lives of others. However Wells-Barnett's stance illustrates that one must learn to move from the reactive position of suffering to that of the transforming power of pain. Wells-Barnett lived her life through the critical stance of pain. She refused to accept the "facts" handed to her. She investigated the conditions and circumstances surrounding various lynchings and the truth she discovered freed her from the misconceptions which promoted the injustice of lynching and its use as a tool for social and political control. Suffering leaves one without the critical tools necessary to examine the oppressive conditions that a Black woman or any oppressed individual or group must live.

The roots of this stance are grounded in the liberating message of the empty cross and the resurrection. God has taken suffering out of the world through the resurrection of Jesus. Because God loves humanity, God gives all peoples the opportunity to embrace the victory of the resurrection. The resurrection moves the oppressed past suffering to pain and struggle. The resurrection is God's breaking into history to transform suffering into wholeness. Suffering is evil and not representative of God's will or the justice God's love portrays for us.

Suffering, and any discussion that accepts suffering as good, is a tool of oppression. Pain allows the victim to examine her or his situation and make a plan for a healthy future. A position of pain encourages an examination of the past and the recovery of the truth. Pain promotes self-knowledge which is a tool for liberation and wholeness. The pain of late nineteenth century African-American life gave Wells-Barnett the power to question what was written about Black womanhood and Black people in light of the truth she found in the lives of African-Americans.

Pain assumes that the individual is a loved and cared for child of God and that she or he is blessed with the ability to survive and struggle regardless of the circumstance and oppression. A womanist social ethic cannot dodge the question of God's goodness. The womanist ethic is drawn to question continually the inordinate amount of suffering that is the lot of the oppressed. Like Wells-Barnett, this ethic is challenged to a new awareness of God's presence within humanity as a liberating event. Situations of oppression do not reveal the mystery of God's love. The revelation of God's love manifests itself in work to end oppression.

To embrace suffering is to loose the richness of the liberating love of God. Pain names suffering as sin and plots a strategy to defeat sin. Wells-Barnett was not always successful in her agitation for social change, but she was well aware that every strategy to defeat sin may not be successful but this was not a sign of God's judgment. It was a sign of incomplete praxis on her part or on the part of others.

A contemporary womanist social ethic would understand this as a signal for the need to reevaluate and try different strategies to bring in the just Kingdom. Her words to twelve African-American men jailed unjustly in Elaine, Arkansas reveal the depth of her belief in God's liberating love.

> I have been listening to you for nearly two hours. You have talked and sung and prayed about dying, and forgiving your enemies, and of feeling sure you are going to be received in the New Jerusalem....But why don't you pray to live and ask to be freed?...let all of your songs and prayers hereafter be songs of faith and hope that God will set you free;....Quit talking about dying; if you believe your God is all powerful, believe he is powerful enough to open these prison doors, and say so....Pray to live and believe you are going to get out.[80]

The critical skills evident in pain are crucial for all victims of oppression. Pain is used by the person who is coming to wholeness *and* concerned about the oppressive conditions of those she or he joins in partnership. Pain allows the person to critique her or his individual circumstance and that of her or his community of partnership. Womanists cannot be content with a liberation that addresses only a particular person or group's wholeness. Like Wells-Barnett's social analysis, a womanist social ethic must embrace all segments of society if it is to be thorough and rigorous.

LIBERATION AND RECONCILIATION

A womanist social ethic is rooted in liberation and reconciliation. These concepts are the components of transformation for the individual and society.

Liberation has spiritual and social dimensions. The aim of liberation is to restore a sense of self to the oppressed as free people and as spiritual beings. This search for self was exhibited consistently by Wells-Barnett. Her aim was steady and relentless in declaring the dignity and worth of African-Americans. She took this farther and called all of United States society to truly live up to its claim of being the land of the free and the home of the brave. This call is most poignant in the closing lines of her most systematic essay on lynching:

> The voice of the people is the voice of God, and I long with all the intensity of my soul for the Garrison, Douglas, Sumner, Whittier and Phillips who shall rouse this nation to a demand that from Greenland's icy mountains to the coral reefs of the Southern seas, mob rule shall be put down and equal and exact justice be accorded to every citizen of whatever race, who finds a home within the borders of the land of the free and the home of the brave.
>
> Then no longer will our national hymn be sounding brass and a tinkling cymbal, but every member of this great composite nation will be living, harmonious illustrations of the words...[81]

She ends the passage with the lines from the United States national anthem.

Wells-Barnett included Black society in that call. In reaction to the governmental hanging of twelve Black soldiers implicated in a 1917 riot in Houston, Texas, as they awaited overseas orders, She resolved to hold a memorial service to protest their deaths. These twelve men were thrown into nameless graves to placate southern hatred.[82] She could not hide her disappointment that none of the churches of Chicago would donate space for the memorial service. She resolved to sell buttons made for the occasion, doing so because she did not "want white people to know that we were so spineless as to not realize our duty to make a protest in the name of the Black boys who had been sacrificed to race hatred."[83]

Wells-Barnett had a strong sense of the power of African-American self-affirmation and dignity. She sought to place a representative Black woman on an Illinois state committee to develop an appropriate celebration for the fiftieth anniversary of Black freedom.[84] In response to the question of whether she wished to be the Black woman named to the committee:

> I do not care who is appointed so long as it is a woman of character and ability; but I do not see how colored women can be

true to themselves unless they demand recognition for themselves
and those they represent.[85]

This strong sense of pride and self-worth is the spiritual
dimension of liberation. This dimension concentrates on the
acquisition and possession of power that enables the individual to be
her or himself fully. It fosters the security to give the self to others
in a love that requires no response in kind. This does not mean that
a person participates in self-abnegation. Giving of oneself does not
mean an automatic forfeiture of dignity or worth.

Spiritual liberation requires a delicate balancing act. The
balance is between wholeness and destruction. Womanists can learn
from Wells-Barnett. Although she gave all of herself for the race, she
pondered why her people did not repay her service with thanks and
with their own efforts at racial uplift and social agitation.[86] Wells-
Barnett sought validation of her work in her people as well from
God. She yearned for a reciprocal love from African-American
society that matched the love she extended on behalf of her relentless
battle to attain African-American civil rights.

Social liberation is participation in the world. It is a concern
for others through the human witness to faith. Liberation, as a
whole, requires that each person acquire an attitudinal mind set that
refuses to accept any external restraint which would deny her or him
the right of being. Implicit in this is a strong self-affirmation that
cannot be challenged successfully by external force. Wells-Barnett
clearly modeled social liberation.

Wells-Barnett visited the twelve African-American men who
were jailed, found guilty of murder in the first degree, and sentenced
to death for their alleged leadership role in the Elaine, Arkansas riot
which was the result of Black tenant farmers and sharecroppers
attempting to organize a labor union.[87] After listening to the men
sing, pray, give testimony, and cry Wells-Barnett spoke of the need
to pray for freedom.

Liberation combats the doubleconsciousness the oppressed live
in this society. This doubleconsciousness involves seeing oneself
through the revelation of others. This tragic twist of self-perception
was spelled out by W.E.B. DuBois in his discussion of doubleconsciousness:

After the Egyptian and the Indian, the Greek and Roman, the Teuton and Mongolian, the Negro is a sort of seventh son, born with a veil, and gifted with second-sight in this American world,—a world which yields him no true self-consciousness, but only lets him see himself through the revelation of the other world. It is a peculiar sensation, this double-consciousness, this sense of always looking at one's self through the eyes of others, of measuring one's soul by the tape of a world that looks on in amused contempt and pity.[88]

Liberation lights the path to being bicultural.[89] It is more than external conditions that impinge on living, it is also the terror from within which is the mutilation of the spirit and the body. The challenge is to refuse dehumanization and affirm the value and gifts all peoples bring to society and to the church.

An important distinction must be made: liberation and freedom are not the same. Liberation is a process, freedom is a state of being.[90] Liberation is God's work of salvation in Jesus who died for humanity and lives yet again within human beings. Liberation is the process of struggle with ourselves and with each other which begets the transformation of all to   full humanity. Liberation establishes freedom, yet it must go on to explore greater dimensions of personhood.

Wells-Barnett modelled a liberation ethic. She, like the process of liberation, could not be content with the situation, regardless of the health produced for some people. She always saw the possibility of being transformed anew. Through liberation, freedom may be made manifest. When a person is made whole, she or he must give of that wholeness. Like many women of her day, Wells-Barnett saw her responsibility as a woman to be one in which she gave of her abilities and talents. Although the act of giving may fragment, this fragmentation opens a person for the possibility of new and greater transformation. Liberation is dynamic, it never ends.

Reconciliation has both an objective realm and a subjective realm.[91] The objective realm is God's activity in humanity in which God creates a new relationship with people.[92] This new relationship is the gift of freedom. This freedom is the new being whom God creates in the person through her or his faith and the faith of others. The objective realm also holds the freedom which is God's activity of love and grace in life. Wells-Barnett's early diary provides a sense of the power of this dynamic.

> ...a clean page, a new book is before me in this New Year; only God knows what is to be recorded here. Oh! may the record be to Thy glory and honor! I go forth on the pilgrimage of this New Yers (sic) with renewed hope, vigor, a remembrance of the glorious beginnins (sic) and humbly pray for wisdom, humility, success in my undertakings if it be my Father's good pleasure, and a stronger Christianity that will make itself felt.[93]

The subjective realm of reconciliation is the realm of human interaction.[94] This realm is the restoration of harmony with others and within individuals. In this realm, humans acknowledge a respect for the world shared with others as well as the need for others and their experience. The subjective realm of reconciliation is what people do in partnership with others to remain faithful to God's gift of freedom.

Wells-Barnett's entire adult life was spent in search of the subjective realm of reconciliation. She believed in the American ideal of a land for all peoples. Wells-Barnett worked in whatever field she felt necessary to bring about a just society for African-Americans and women through her pursuit and publishing of the truth. She was a devout believer in the law of the land and believed that humans needed to embody the high founding ideals of the United States. Writing in 1901, Wells-Barnett states:

> The Christian moral forces of the nation should insist that misrepresentation should have no place in the discussion of this important question [lynching], that the figures of the lynching record should be allowed to plead, trumpet tongued, in defense of the slandered dead, that the silence of concession be broken, and that truth, swift-winged and courageous, summon this nation to do its duty to exalt justice and preserve inviolate the sacredness of human life.[95]

Wells-Barnett's life is an example of arguing that a womanist social ethic must refuse to order liberation and reconciliation—both must be present and operating in order for transformation to take place. A non-reconciled people cannot be a liberating people and a non-liberated people cannot be reconciling. The object of transformation is to name and eradicate oppressive structures. The twin commitment to liberation and reconciliation is crucial.

Leadership

A discussion of leadership which stems from the social and moral perspectives of Ida B. Wells-Barnett entails prophetic voice and pastoral voice. Both concepts are central to understanding Wells-Barnett—both her strengths and weaknesses as a leader *and* her relationship to other African-Americans and the wider community of people concerned with social justice and social change in the closing years of the nineteenth century and the early twentieth century. A critique of Wells-Barnett and her leadership style frames this final section.

PASTORAL VOICE

The pastoral voice[96] entails the ability to be self-critical, to provide comfort, to accept others, and to encourage growth and change. Unfortunately, Wells-Barnett was unable to do this to a satisfactory degree. As an extremely proud woman, Wells-Barnett kept herself from allowing for the humanness in herself, let alone in others. She could not readily admit her miscues and failings.

When the pastor of the church she attended committed a scandal, Bishop Abraham Grant, who was in charge of the district in which Bethel A.M.E.Church belonged, assured her that the minister would be moved at conference time. Wells-Barnett attended the conference on the day the appointments were to be read. The Bishop drew her aside and informed her that the congregation would withdraw from connection if the minister was moved. The Bishop chose to leave him in the appointment rather than risk the loss of the congregation. Bishop Grant hoped that she would continue her work at the church. But her moral standards would not allow such a thing.

...it was a shock to be told by one of the heads of the church that he was compelled to condone such immoral conduct;...I was sorry but that there was nothing left for me to do but withdraw; I had a family of growing children and all my teaching would be null and void if I continued in a church with a man who had become so notoriously immoral.[97]

With African-American and white women social reformers, she consistently either could not see or found it difficult to accept compromise as integral to working in groups. She placed herself in dubious positions such as her first trip to England in 1893 sponsored by the Society for the Brotherhood of Man. In that trip Wells-Barnett unwittingly placed herself in the middle of a delicate situation in which her hostess for the trip admitted her love for a man of color. Although the Society for the Brotherhood of Man was progressive, they were not ready for such a volatile case. When Wells-Barnett ignored her better judgment and sided with her hostess, her trip came to an early end due to the internal politics of the Society. Wells-Barnett's somewhat halting loyalty cost her a year of anti-lynching work in Britain. Her rigid moral code did not permit her to consider the alternative arguments of other Society members or to entertain a compromise position.

The pastoral voice, the voice of leadership in community, must always be prepared to consider all of the information, the varying social contexts that groups and individuals bring to bear, the various means of social analysis. No one element in the world or in the society contains all of the truth—all of what social reformers need in discerning God's will. Wells-Barnett's leadership in community was not as effective as it could have been because she could not accept the humanness of being human. She could understand structures, but because the pastoral voice within her was not developed, she could not fully consider the need to care for the people behind the institutions. She was not able to accept and recognize the diversity that can occur around any social justice issue.

In short, Wells-Barnett lacked the ability to combine the prophetic with the pastoral. Her passion for social change was deep and abiding. She could not always make her passion flesh, because she was unable to accept the reality of human failing, human wavering. It is imperative that a leader struggling for social change hold in tension personal and social transformation. If only one form of transformation is addressed, the person advocating change will not be able to be a full participant in community or mobilize that community for change.

Wells-Barnett could not work effectively with other Black leaders or groups. She consistently put forth her own agenda and often took unilateral actions which destroyed any notion of coalition and dialogue. As she described these events in her autobiography, one is able to see her inability to grasp how her unilateral actions could hurt or anger others. Her reactions were puzzlement and even indignation. As she tried to work in the various women's groups in Chicago, she was often marginalized and sometimes completely cut off from the decision-making process. Her response was embitteredness rather than self-examination as to why her experience with groups was a pattern rather than an occasional misunderstanding.

Wells-Barnett was on the cutting edge because that was the only way she could express her concern for social justice in the lives of Black people in the United States. As a cutting edge person, she performed the invaluable service of debunking myths and stereotypes about Black and white southern men and women. She was a strong and passionate voice for justice, but she could not work in community and with groups because she could not relax her own rigid moral standards to allow for human failings and weaknesses. In clinging to a fiercely high moral code of conduct for herself as well as others, Wells-Barnett often alienated people with her attitude of disdain and disapproval.

Wells-Barnett could not understand that the personal side of transformation in which people are being changed and renewed requires an entirely different set of critical and analytical skills to effect change. She *was* an excellent agent for agitation and through this allowed others with the skills of prophetic voice and pastoral voice to mobilize Black folk for social change.

PROPHETIC VOICE

Cutting edge, or being a cutting edge as an advocate for social justice, suggests the notion of prophetic voice. As an active churchwoman her entire adult life, Wells-Barnett was exposed to the Bible and took seriously the life and ministry of Jesus. Although her social analysis was not overt in her religious impulse, her passion for justice and social change make evident her concern for right relationships among peoples. As a cutting edge person, she had a strong and willful prophetic voice on behalf of the injustices she saw heaped on Black folk in the United States. Her religious impulse was embedded deeply in her social analysis.

Prophetic voice contains five key threads.[98] The first is the resolution and ability to discern the will of God. God is on the side of oppressed peoples. Hence, the primary task of the Christian is to transform the present unjust structures into just ones. As is evident from discussion in preceding chapters, Wells-Barnett modelled this concern and commitment. For her, "the voice of the people is the voice of God."[99]

Interestingly, her agitation had both manifest and latent functions.[100] Concerning manifest function, her conscious motivation was to stop lynching and to speak out against injustice wherever she perceived it. The larger social recognition of her analysis reveals the latent function of her work. The consequences of her actions led to an analysis that revealed the use of lynching as a means of social control and white supremacy and the beginning of an organized Black woman's club movement in the city of Chicago.

Wells-Barnett's refusal to bend to the rape myth provided another lens to view the accommodationist-protest division within African-American society. Also it unmasked the sexual dynamics of southern society and led to an increase in African-American participation in the social and political affairs of the nation. Her work fostered Black pride and an early impulse for Black self-determination.

Second, in discerning the will of God, the prophetic voice also exposes the oppressive nature of society. The committed Christian must stand for justice and transformation. Again, Wells-Barnett is an excellent example of this concern. Wells-Barnett believed the only recourse open to the Black folk of Memphis after the lynching of Thomas Moss was an economic one—boycott and exodus. Moss was a Black man whose "crime" was opening a successful grocery store that took business away from a white grocer across the street.

No attempt was made to punish the murderers, whose identities were widely known. Wells-Barnett urged the Blacks of Memphis to leave:

> Memphis has demonstrated that neither character nor standing avails the Negro if he dares to protect himself against the white man or become his rival. We are outnumbered and without arms. There is only one thing left that we can do—leave a town which will neither protect our lives and property, not give us a fair trial, but takes us out and murders us in cold blood.[101]

Entire congregations left the city. Over 2,000 Blacks left in two months' time. Businesses that depended on Black patronage began to fail. The superintendent of the railway company called on Wells-Barnett at her newspaper, *The Free Speech*, to ask to urge her readers to ride the streetcars again. White homemakers complained about the shortage of domestic workers. When a white real estate agent remarked, "You got off light. We first intended to kill every one of those thirty-one niggers in jail, but concluded to let all go but the leaders,"[102] he revealed the true power dynamics behind lynching—it was not a series of isolated phenomena, but a broad-based movement to intimidate Blacks.

Wells-Barnett saw lynching as a new tool for repressing emancipated Blacks. Whites resented African-Americans who were able to compete with them economically and move ahead in the social structure. She knew Blacks could be enormously influential in electoral politics. This fact did not elude white southerners who knew African-Americans had the potential to upset the South's longstanding political and economic white power base.

Third, the prophetic voice must be an agent of admonition—pointing out the wrongdoing in society and stressing the need to have human action (and inaction) conform to God's will. Wells-Barnett was strong in her warnings of the consequences of continued disharmony with divine intentions. Her unwavering attack on the rape myth/fiction meant that she unmasked the entire southern sexual mores mythology and reality.

The charge of rape made against Black men appeared so consistently that the whole nation (including Wells-Barnett and other Blacks like Frederick Douglass at first) believed it to be true at some point. In 1904, *Harper's Weekly* carried an article stating that middle class Blacks were a greater threat than lower class Blacks. This was because the Black middle class was more likely to aim at social equality and lose the awe which during slavery caused Blacks to respect the woman of the superior race. *Harper's* called rape "The New Negro Crime."

Wells-Barnett's attack on the rape myth was an attack against southern sexual mores. Southern white men believed that any liaison between an African-American man and a white woman was involuntary on the part of the woman. Wells-Barnett was quite clear that Black men might be weak if not stupid in contracting such alliances, but she was equally clear that white women sometimes were willing participants. Meanwhile, white men seduced and raped Black women and girls with impunity.

Miscegenation laws were to protect white women, but left Black women the victims of rape by white men. Simultaneously, these laws granted to these same men the power to terrorize Black men as a potential threat to the virtue of white womanhood.[103] She was incensed that the same lynch mob that killed a Nashville Black man accused of *visiting* a white woman left unharmed a white man *convicted* of raping an eight-year old Black girl. She refused to back down from publishing the facts behind lynchings even when a delegation of Blacks asked her to in 1894. For Wells-Barnett, this was an issue of justice.

Lynching was an act of political and economic repression in Wells-Barnett's eyes. She did not believe, as did Booker T. Washington and W.E.B. DuBois, that the problems of lynching were due to education.

> Even to the better class of Afro-Americans the crime of rape is so revolting that they have too often taken the white man's word and have not given the lynch law neither,... the investigation nor condemnation it deserved...They have gone on hoping and believing that general education and financial strength would solve the difficulty, and are devoting their energies to the accumulation of both.[104]

She drew an analysis between political terrorism, economic oppression, and conventional codes of sexuality and morality which rocked the foundations of southern (as well as northern) patriarchal manipulation of race and gender.[105] In *Southern Horrors* she drew the connections between rape and lynching as a contemporary phenomenon and argued there was no historical foundation for that association: "The crime of rape was unknown during four years of civil war, when the white women of the South were at the mercy of the race which is all at once charged with being a bestial one."[106]

Wells-Barnett's studied the lynching of 728 Black men, women, and children in the ten-year period preceding the Moss lynching. In only a third of those cases were Blacks accused of rape, much less guilty of the crime. Most died for crimes like incendiarism, race prejudice, quarreling with whites, and making threats. Thirteen-year old Mildrey Brown was hung on the circumstantial evidence that she poisoned a white infant. During Wells-Barnett's investigations she discovered a large number of interracial liaisons which she spoke of in print. She took the matter further by stating that white women had taken the initiative in some of these liaisons.

Two months after the Moss lynching Wells-Barnett wrote in *The Free Speech* the article that would banish her from Memphis.

> Eight Negroes lynched since last issue of the *Free Speech*, three for killing a white man, and five on the same old racket—the alarm about raping white women. The same program of hanging, then shooting bullets into the lifeless bodies. Nobody in this section of the country believes the old threadbare lie that negro men rape white women. If Southern white men are not careful they will overreach themselves, and public sentiment will have a reaction. A conclusion will then be reached which will be very damaging to the moral reputation of their women.[107]

Fourth, the prophetic voice must confront. The root meaning of confront is "to face together." Implicit in this is a relationship between equals. There must be mutual respect for the dignity of others, a willingness to engage in dialogue, and an awareness and acceptance of diversity. If one thrives in a power dynamic which place one over and against rather than with, all prophetic voice is lost.

Wells-Barnett was not afraid of confrontation. In exposing or even suggesting that white women were willing sexual partners of Black men Wells-Barnett told the truth, but created a firestorm. In exposing the number of rapes white men committed on Black women

and girls, she laid bare the tremendous double standards of accept-
able moral and Christian behavior whites operated with. She refused
to remain silent even when a delegation of Black men asked her to in
August of 1894.

> I indignantly refused to do so. I explained to them that wherever
> I had gone in England I found the firmly accepted belief that
> lynchings took place in this country only because black men were
> wild beasts after white women; the hardest part of my work had
> been to convince the British people that this was a false charge
> against negro manhood and that to forsake that position now,
> because I was back in my own country, would be to tacitly admit
> the charge was true, and I could not promise to do that.[108]

Finally, the prophetic voice seeks to create a community of
faith, partnership, justice, and unity. This speaks of the need to
engage in pastoral relationship as well as prophetic. To omit the very
human need for affirmation, respect, and acknowledgment makes
empty and incomplete any move to be prophetic. Wells-Barnett took
seriously the promise of a just world and devoted her life to attaining
that for her people.

In reviewing the prophetic in the individual, two key elements
aid in understanding why Wells-Barnett's leadership style was such
that she was unable to work successfully with others for significant
periods. The first is that the prophetic voice is an agent of admonition. Wells-Barnett provided an invaluable gift to African-American
society when she began to unmask the double standards of southern
society.

She held fast to her stand on the power of economics in
shaping and changing United States social opinion. She gave new
vision and provided new possibilities for Black interactions with a
racist culture. She also provided an alternative model from the
stereotype of Black women as the mammy or the slut. The danger in
being an agent of admonition is that one can fall into believing that
he or she is the only one who has the ability to accurately discern
God's will for the liberation of the oppressed. This is certainly true
of Wells-Barnett.

Repeatedly, she forged ahead with her own agenda and
methods. Often times this was at the expense of relationships with

her peers. She alienated herself among Black clubwomen and with Black and white leaders of her day.[109] Her clash with Frederick Douglass concerning the Colored Jubilee Day and with Frances Willard were not unusual for her.

In her autobiography, Wells-Barnett details defeat after disappointment with the ascendence of Booker T. Washington. She does not seem fully aware of the long shadow cast by Washington and his representatives and the effect they had on her organizing and agitation for social change on the behalf of African-Americans. Wells-Barnett went to various organizations with her proposals already formulated and then asked for their endorsement. In the cases in which she did receive endorsement, her proposals were often sidetracked or derailed by Washington representatives who were members of the various women's clubs and church associations and favored a more gradualist approach.

The prophetic voice must be confrontive. Wells-Barnett was excellent at addressing unjust structures, but she did not always remember that people are the ones who help create, maintain, and even tear down those structures. In confronting, the prophetic voice must always keep in mind that a root meaning of confrontation is to face together. The emphasis must be on together. If one thrives in a power dynamic which places one over and against rather than with, all prophetic voice is lost. For all her ability to discern and analyze, she could not bring herself into community to communicate.

Wells-Barnett is a model for developing a realistic womanist Christian social ethic. She was far from perfect. Her imperfections offer a practical guide for the difficulties and ordinary human qualities which must be contended with in living out a womanist social ethic of justice. Rather than a success story, hers is a human story. One forged out of the context of her time, her social and moral perspectives, and her commitment to a rigorous Christian lifestyle. In reading her diary, contemplating her autobiography, and sorting through her numerous articles, a frustrating picture emerges. The frustration comes, in large measure, because her life was not neatly scripted with well-rounded outcomes. Rather than appear to be a heroine larger than life, her life is writ large in its humanity. This humanity offers hope for those still struggling to articulate justice, however imperfectly.

Conclusion

In her 1974 essay, Theressa Hoover states "To be a woman, black and active in religious institutions in the American scene is to labor under triple jeopardy."[110] This state of affairs has not changed. In United States society, African-American women are at the bottom of the economic ladder when ranked with white men and women and African-American men. Women compose nearly 75% of the traditional Black Church, yet the higher levels of decision-making do not reflect this statistic in proportionate numbers.

There are increasing numbers of African-American women in seminaries, the ordained ministry, and in the ranks of lay professionals. A growing body of literature and reflection is emerging from African-American women in academic theological circles on the nature of the Black Church and church universal; the mission, identity, and scope of ministry; social and theological ethics; and biblical hermeneutics. Lay professionals and laywomen join in the chorus of resonant voices in articulating the experience as well as the gifts of African-American women in the church.

Wells-Barnett's life and witness provide rich resources for a contemporary womanist Christian social ethic. This ethic must articulate an understanding of authority, suffering, liberation, reconciliation, and obedience which seeks to promote the full partnership of women and men in creation with God. A womanist social ethic, like that of Wells-Barnett, searches for the possibilities, for justice.

Ida B. Wells-Barnett was a womanist. She did engage in outrageous, audacious, courageous or *willful* behavior. She wanted to know more and in greater depth than was considered good for one. She was responsible, in charge, and *serious*.

NOTES

[1] Alice Walker, *In Search of Our Mothers' Gardens* (New York: Harcourt Brace Jovanovich, Publishers, 1983), xi.

[2] *Ladies Magazine*, 3 (1830), 83-84; quoted in Ann Douglas, *The Feminization of American Culture*, (New York: Avon Books, 1977), 52.

[3] Michelle Zimbalist Rosaldo, "Woman, Culture, and Society: A Theoretical Overview," chap. in *Woman, Culture and Society*, ed. Michelle Zimbalist Rosaldo and Louise Lamphere (Stanford: University of California Press, 1981), 17-42.

[4] Diane K. Lewis, "A Response to Inequality: Black Women, Racism, and Sexism," in *The Signs Reader: Women, Gender and Scholarship*, ed. Elizabeth Abel and Emily K. Abel (Chicago: University of Chicago Press, 1983), 171.

[5] Ibid., 172.

[6] Aileen Kraditor, *The Ideas of the Woman Suffrage Movement, 1890-1920* (New York: W.W. Norton & Company, 1981) is an excellent analysis of the suffrage movement of this country.

[7] Hazel V. Carby, "On the Threshold of Woman's Era: Lynching, Empire and Sexuality in Black Feminist Theory," *Critical Inquiry* (Autumn 1985): 263.

[8] Ibid., 264.

[9] Katie G. Cannon, "Moral Wisdom in the Black Women's Literary Tradition," *Annual of the Society of Christian Ethics* (1984), 172.

[10] Cannon, *Black Womanist Ethics* (Atlanta: Scholars Press, 1988), 2. Cannon goes on to state that this "proved null and void in situations of oppression."

[11] Ibid.

[12] Ibid., 3.

[13] Cannon, "Moral Wisdom," 174.

[14] Luther P. Gerlach and Virginia H. Hine, *People, Power, Change: Movements of Social Transformation* (Indianapolis: The Bobbs-Merrill Company, Inc., 1970), xii.

[15] Joe Holland and Peter Henriot, S.J., *Social Analysis: Linking Faith and Justice*, rev. and enl. ed. (Maryknoll: Orbis Books, 1980), 34.

[16] Gerlach and Hine, xii.

[17] Ibid., xiii.

[18] Ibid.

[19] Wells, Diary, 11 April 1887.

[20] The working definition of authority used is that of legitimated power. Letty M. Russell, *Household of Freedom: Authority in Feminist Theology* (Philadelphia: The Westminster Press, 1987), 21 and Richard Sennett *Authority* (New York: Vintage Books, 1981), 16-27 have helpful insights into this understanding of authority. Sennett's work is extremely helpful in presenting a

clear and concise definition of authority and the emotional bonds elicited by and through authority.

[21] Russell, *Household of Freedom*, 33-36.

[22] Joanna Rogers Macy, *Despair and Personal Power in the Nuclear Age* (Philadelphia: New Society Publishers, 1983), 30.

[23] Ibid.

[24] The riot erupted when Black farmers in Elaine refused to sell their cotton below the market price. They had organized and determined that such an economic course would be counterproductive. White officials and farmers in Elaine were angered by such resistance and descended upon the Black community. Several men were lynched and the "ring leaders of the riot" where imprisoned, charged, and sentenced to death for inciting the insurrection. These so-called ring leaders were leaders in the Black farmers' organization. No whites were arrested or charged in the riot which they started.

[25] *Ida B. Wells, Crusade for Justice*, ed. Alfreda Duster (Chicago: University of Chicago Press, 1970), 400.

[26] Ibid.

[27] Russell, *Household of Freedom*, 18.

[28] Wells, *Crusade for Justice*, 283.

[29] Wells, *Crusade for Justice*, 286.

[30] Ibid., 287.

[31] Bontemps and Conroy, 82.

[32] Wells, *Crusade for Justice*, 273.

[33] Ibid., 226.

[34] Ibid., 227.

[35] Dorothee Soelle, *Beyond Mere Obedience* (New York: The Pilgrim Press, 1982), 11-17.

[36] Ibid., 15-16.

[37] Wells, editorial in the *Free Speech*, printed in Memphis *Weekly Avalanche*, 13 July 1889.

[38] Wells, Diary, Special Collections, Joseph Regenstein Library, University of Chicago, Chicago, 3 January 1887.

[39] Wells, *Crusade for Justice*, 299.

[40] James M. Gustafson, *Theology and Christian Ethics* (New York: Pilgrim Press, 1974), 129. The chapter "The Place of Scripture in Christian Ethics: A Methodological Study" is an exceedingly helpful methodological framework for the place of scripture in ethical reflection.

[41] Wells, *Crusade for Justice*, 299.

[42] Ibid., 222.

[43] Ibid., 311-12.

[44] Robert K. Merton, *Social Theory and Social Structure*, enl. ed. (New York: The Free Press, 1968), 73. Merton lists three features of functional analysis:

theory, method, and data. Wells-Barnett's approach to ending the lynch law contain these three key features.

[45] Wells, Diary, 3 January 1887.

[46] Russell, *Future of Partnership*, 102.

[47] Russell, *Household of Freedom*, 33. Russell discusses this in terms of authority as domination. In her work, she refers to hierarchy or pyramid. I have reframed the language in an attempt to focus more on the mentality of being first or in control. This anticipates my later discussion of leadership.

[48] Marcia Ann Gillespie, "The Myth of the Strong Black Woman," in *Feminist Frameworks: Alternative Theoretical Accounts of Relations Between Men and Women*, 2d, ed. Allison M. Jaggar and Paul S. Rothenberg (New York: McGraw-Hill Book Co., 1984), 33.

[49] Ibid., 35.

[50] Joyce Ladner, "Racism and Tradition: Black Womanhood in Historical Perspective," in *The Black Woman Cross-Culturally*, ed. Filomena Chioma Steady (Cambridge: Schenkman Publishing Co., Inc., 1981), 247.

[51] Bell Hooks, *Ain't I A Woman* (Boston: South End Press, 1981), 6.

[52] John Richardson and John Bowden, ed., *The Westminster Dictionary of Christian Theology* (Philadelphia: Westminster Press, 1983), 555.

[53] Ibid.

[54] Ibid.

[55] Wells, *Crusade for Justice*, 299.

[56] Ibid., 303.

[57] Dorothee Soelle, *Suffering* (Philadelphia: Fortress Press, 1975), 13.

[58] Ibid., 11.

[59] Ibid.

[60] Ibid., 17.

[61] Ibid., 19.

[62] Ibid., 22.

[63] Ibid.

[64] Ibid., 24.

[65] Ibid., 26.

[66] Ibid., 41.

[67] Ibid., 81.

[68] Ibid., 130.

[69] Ibid., 132.

[70] James Cone, *God of the Oppressed* (New York: Seabury Press, 1975), 165.

[71] Ibid., 174.

[72] Ibid., 178.

[73] Ibid., 177.

[74] Ibid., 181.

[75] Ibid., 191.

[76] Ibid., 194.

[77] Audre Lorde, "Eye to Eye: Black Women, Hatred, and Anger," in *Sister Outsider*, (Trumansburg, NY: The Crossing Press, 1984), 171-72.

[78] *The Fellowship Herald*, 22 June 1911.

[79] Wells, *Crusade for Justice*, 357.

[80] Ibid., 403.

[81] Wells, "Lynch Law in All Its Phases," *Our Day* 11, no. 64 (May 1893): 347.

[82] Wells, *Crusade for Justice*, 368.

[83] Ibid.

[84] Ibid., 360-65. This committee, appointed by Governor Dunne, had three white men, one white woman, and three Black men. The white woman, Mrs. Jorgan Dahl, eventually had to resign due to illness in her family. The absence of a Black woman on the committee was a slap in the face to the Women's Federation. The Federation, composed of Black women from various women's clubs in the state of Illinois, lobbied the Springfield legislature over Jim Crow bills. Through their work, the idea of marking Emancipation arose.

[85] Ibid., 364.

[86] The best sources of her confusion and disappointment are in her autobiography and her early diary from 1885-1887. She was simply unable to accept that despite her best efforts there were Afro-Americans who held her in contempt and refused to engage in social or political uplift in United States society.

[87] Low and Clift, 233-34. This riot occurred in 1919, one of the bloodiest years in United States history. The summer of this year was named Red Summer. There were 78 Blacks lynched during this year with ten victims being war veterans, several of them still in uniform. Eleven Black men were burned at the stake. Also in 1919, the East St. Louis, Houston, Philadelphia, and Chicago riots all occurred.

[88] W.E.B. DuBois, *The Souls of Black Folk* (Greenwich, CT: Fawcett Books, 1961), 16-17.

[89] Russell, *Household of Freedom*, 93. Sennett, *Authority*, 165-90.

[90] Cone, *God of the Oppressed*, 138-41.

[91] Ibid., 228-34.

[92] Ibid., 228

[93] Wells, Diary, 1 January 1886, Special Collections, Joseph Regenstein Library, University of Chicago, Chicago.

[94] Ibid., 233.

[95] Wells-Barnett, "Lynching and the Excuse for It," *The Independent* 53 (16 May 1901): 1136.

[96] This category of pastoral is an attempt to appeal to the African-American religious experience of the role of the pastor as comforter. Max Weber's classic essay, "Politics As A Vocation," offers the categories of an ethic of ultimate ends and an ethic of responsibility. These are helpful categories in reframing the question of leadership. See Weber, "Politics As A Vocation," in *From Max*

Weber: Essays in Sociology, ed. and trans. H.H. Gerth and C. Wright Mills (New York: Oxford University Press, 1946), 120-128.

[97] Wells, *Crusade for Justice*, 298.

[98] Jacquelyn Grant, "Tasks of a Prophetic Church" in *Detroit II Conference Papers*, ed. Cornel West, Caridad Guidote, and Margaret Coakley (Maryknoll: Orbis Books, Probe Edition, 1982), 137-38. Grant's essay points to a broader understanding of the prophetic church. I expand her categories to Black leadership which is crucial to a coherent womanist Christian social ethic.

[99] Wells, Ida B. Wells Papers, Special Collections, Joseph L. Regenstein Library, University of Chicago, Chicago.

[100] Merton, 105; 114-18. Merton defines manifest functions as "those objective consequences contributing to the adjustment or adaptation of the system which are intended and recognized by participants of the system." Latent functions are "those which are neither intended nor recognized."

[101] Dorothy Sterling, *Black Foremothers: Three Lives* (Old Westbury, NY: The Feminist Press, 1979), 79.

[102] Ibid., 80.

[103] Carby, 268.

[104] J. Helen Goldbeck, ed., *A Survey of the Blacks' Response to Lynching* (New Mexico Highlands University Media Material Center, 1973), 7.

[105] Carby, 268.

[106] Ida B. Wells-Barnett, *Southern Horrors: Lynch Law in All Its Phases* (New York: The New York Age Print, 1892; reprint, New York: Arno Press, *On Lynching: Southern Horrors, A Red Record, Mob Rule in New Orleans*, 1969), 5.

[107] Wells, "Lynch Law in All its Phases," *Our Day* 11, no. 64 (May 1893): 338.

[108] Wells, *Crusade*, 220.

[109] Examples of this from her autobiography are her break with Mary Church Terrell and the National Association of Colored Women's Clubs (*Crusade*, 258-60). She also details an early attempt to develop an Afro-American theater in a former amusement hall which brought the condemnation of local black pastors (*Crusade*, 289-95).

[110] Theressa Hoover, "Black Women and the Churches: Triple Jeopardy," in *Black Theology: A Documentary History, 1966-1979*, ed. Gayraud S. Wilmore and James H. Cone (Maryknoll: Orbis Books, 1979), 377.

SELECTED BIBLIOGRAPHY

Abel, Elizabeth and Emily K. Abel, eds. *The Signs Reader: Women, Gender and Scholarship*. Chicago: University of Chicago Press, 1983.

Ahlstrom, Sydney E. *A Religious History of the American People*. Vol 1. Garden City, New York: Image Books, 1975.

Andrews, William L. *To Tell a Free Story: The First Century of Afro-American Autobiography*, 1760-1865. Urbana: University of Illinois Press, 1986.

_____. ed. *Sisters of the Spirit: Three Black Women's Autobiographies of the Nineteenth Century*. Bloomington: Indiana University Press, 1986.

Benson, Adolph B., ed. *America in the Fifties: Letters of Fredrika Bremer*. New York: The American-Scandinavian Foundation, 1924.

Bigsby, C.E.E. *The Second Black Renaissance: Essays in Black Literature*. Westport: Greenwood Press, 1980.

Bontemps, Arna and Jack Conroy. *They Seek A City*. Garden City, New York: Doubleday, Doran and Co., Inc., 1945.

Braxton, Joanne Margaret. "Autobiography by Black American Women: A Tradition Within a Tradition." PhD diss., Yale University, 1984.

Brooks, Evelyn. "The Women's Movement in the Black Baptist Church, 1880-1920." PhD diss., The University of Rochester, 1984.

Bruce, Philip A. *The Plantation Negro as Freeman*. New York: n.p., 1889.

Butterfield, Stephen. *Black Autobiography in America*. Amherst: University of Massachusetts Press, 1974.

Cannon, Katie G. "Moral Wisdom in the Black Women's Literary Tradition." *Annual of the Society of Christian Ethics*. 1984.

_____. *Black Womanist Ethics*. Atlanta: Scholars Press, 1988.

Carby, Hazel V. "On the Threshold of Woman's Era: Lynching, Empire and Sexuality in Black Feminist Theory." *Critical Inquiry.* Autumn 1985: 262-277.

Clarke, Erskine. *Wrestlin' Jacob: A Portrait of Religion in the Old South.* Atlanta: John Knox Press, 1979.

Coleman, Willie Mae. "Keeping the Faith and Disturbing the Peace Black Women: From Anti-Slavery to Women's Suffrage." PhD diss., University of California, Irvine, 1982.

Cone, James H. *The Spirituals and the Blues: An Interpretation.* New York: Seabury Press, 1972.

_____. *God of the Oppressed.* New York: Seabury Press, 1975.

Cott, Nancy F. *The Bonds of Womanhood: "Woman's Sphere" in New England, 1780-1835.* New Haven: Yale University Press, 1977.

Crawford, Floyd W. "Ida B. Wells: Her Anti-Lynching Crusades in Britian and Repercussions From Them in the United States, 1958" TMs. Special Collections, Joseph Regenstein Library, University of Chicago, Chicago.

_____. "Ida B. Wells: Some American Reactions to Her Anti-Lynching Crusades in Britian, 1963" TMs. Special Collections, Joseph Regenstein Library, University of Chicago, Chicago.

Cross, F.L. and E.A. Livingstone, eds. *The Oxford Dictionary of the Christian Church.* 2d ed. Oxford: Oxford University Press, 1974.

Davis, Angela. *Women, Race, and Class.* New York: Random House, 1981.

Davis, Elizabeth Lindsay, ed. *The Story of the Illinois Federation of Colored Women's Clubs.* n.p., 1922.

Degler, Carl N. *At Odds: Women and the Family in America from the Revolution to the Present.* New York: Oxford University Press, 1980.

Douglas, Ann. *The Feminization of American Culture.* New York: Avon Books, 1977.

DuBois, W.E.B. *Souls of Black Folk.* New York: McClurg and Co., 1903; reprint, New York: New American Library, 1982.

_____. *Darkwater: Voices From Within the Veil*. New York: Schocken Books, 1920.

_____. *Against Racism: Unpublished Essays, Papers, Addresses, 1887-1961*. Edited by Herbert Aptheker. Amherst: University of Massachusetts Press, 1985.

Earhart, Mary. *Frances Willard: From Prayers to Politics*. Chicago: University of Chicago Press, 1944.

Farley, Margaret A. *Personal Commitments: Beginnings, Keeping, Changing*. San Francisco: Harper and Row, Publishers, 1986.

Faulkner, William John, ed. *The Days When the Animals Talked: Black American Folktales and How They Came to Be*. Chicago: Follett Publishing Company, 1977.

Foner, Eric. *Reconstruction: America's Unfinished Revolution, 1863-1877*. New York: Harper and Row, Publishers, 1988.

Foner, Philip S. *Women and the American Labor Movement: From Colonial Times to the Eve of World War I*. New York: The Free Press, 1980.

_____. *Women and the American Labor Movement: From World War I to the Present*. New York: The Free Press, 1980.

Foner, Philip S. and Ronald L. Lewis, eds. *The Black Worker from 1900-1919*. Volume V, *The Black Worker, A Documentary History from Colonial Times to the Present*. Philadelphia: Temple University Press, 1980.

Fredrickson, George M. *The Black Image in the White Mind: The Debate of Afro-American Character and Destiny, 1817-1914*. New York: Harper and Row, Publishers, 1971.

_____. *White Supremacy: A Comparative Study in American and South African History*. New York: Oxford University Press, 1981.

Giddings, Paula. *When and Where I Enter: The Impact of Black Women on Race and Sex in America*. New York: William Morrow and Company, 1984.

Goldbeck, H. Helen. *A Survey of the Blacks' Response to Lynching*. New Mexico Highlands University Media Center, 1973.

Goss, Margaret T. "Ida B. Wells Leadership Example for Women of Today."
    Sunday Chicago Bee, n.d.

Grant, Jacquelyn. "Tasks of a Prophetic Church." In *Detroit II Conference
    Papers*, eds. Cornel West, Caridad Guidote, and Margaret Coakley, 136-
    42. Maryknoll: Orbis Books, Probe Edition, 1982.

Gustafson, James M. *Theology and Christian Ethics*. New York: Pilgrim Press,
    1974.

Harley, Sharon and Rosalyn Terborg-Penn, eds. *The Afro-American Woman:
    Struggles and Images*. Port Washington, New York: Kennikat Press,
    1978.

Harper, Frances Ellen Watkins, Mary W. Howe, Mrs. W.T. Anderson, and Ida
    B. Wells, "Symposium--Temperance." *A.M.E. Church Review* 7 (April
    1891): 372-381.

Haygood, Atticus G. "The Black Shadow in the South." *Forum*. October, 1893.

Henri, Florette. *Black Migration: Movement North 1900-1920*. Garden City,
    New York: Anchor Press, 1975.

Herskovits, Melville J. *The Myth of the Negro Past*. Boston: Beacon Press, 1958.

*A History of the Club Movement Among the Colored Women of the United
    States of America, As Contained in the Minutes of the Conventions,
    Held in Boston, July 29, 30, 31, 1895, and of the National Federation of
    Afro-American Women, Held in Washington, D.C., July 20, 21, 22, 1896*.
    n.p., 1902.

Hine, Darlene Clark, ed. *The State of Afro-American History: Past, Present, and
    Future*. Baton Rouge: Louisana State University Press, 1986.

Hooks, Bell. *Ain't I A Woman*. Boston: South End Press, 1981.

"How Miss Wells' Crusade is Regarded in America." *Literary Digest*. 28 (July
    1894): 366-367.

Hurston, Zora Neale. *The Sanctified Church*. Berkeley: Turtle Island, 1983.

Irvin, Helen B. *The Negro at Work During the World War and During
    Reconstruction: Statistics, Problems, and Policies Relating to the Greater*

Inclusion of Negro Wage Earners in American Industry and Agriculture.
Washington: United States Department of Labor, Division of Negro
Economics, 1920.

Isaac, Rhys. *The Transformation of Virginia: 1740-1790.* Chapel Hill: University
of North Carolina Press, 1982.

Jaggar, Allison M. and Paul S. Rothenberg, eds. *Feminist Frameworks:
Alternative Theoretical Accounts of Relations Between Men and
Women.* 2d ed. New York: McGraw-Hill Book Co., 1984.

Jelinek, Estelle C., ed. *Women's Autobiography: Essays in Criticism.* Bloomington: Indiana University Press, 1984.

Jenkins, Maude T. "The History of the Black Woman's Club Movement in
America." PhD diss., Teachers College, Columbia University, 1984.

Johnson, Paul E. *Shopkeeper's Millennium: Society and Revivals in Rochester,
New York 1815-1837.* New York: Hill and Wang, 1978.

Jones, Jacqueline. *Labor of Love, Labor of Sorrow: Black Women, Work and
the Family, From Slavery to the Present.* New York: Vintage Books,
1985.

Jones, Maldwyn A. *The Limits of Liberty: American History 1607-1980.* New
York: Oxford University Press, 1983.

Kessler-Harris, Alice. *Out to Work: A History of Wage-Earning Women in the
United States.* New York: Oxford University Press, 1982.

Kraditor, Aileen. *The Ideas of the Woman Suffrage Movement, 1890-1920.* New
York: W.W. Norton & Company, 1981.

Lebsock, Karen. *The Free Women of Petersburg: Status and Culture in a
Southern Town, 1784-1860.* New York: W.W. Norton and Company,
1984.

Lefkowitz, Rochelle and Ann Withorn, eds. *For Crying Out Loud: Women and
Poverty in the United States.* New York: Pilgrim Press, 1986.

Levine, Lawrence W. *Black Culture and Black Consciousness: Afro-American
Folk Thought From Slavery to Freedom.* New York: Oxford University
Press, 1977.

Lincoln, C. Eric. *Race, Religion, and the Continuing American Dilemma.* New York: Hill and Wang, 1984.

Litwack, Leon F. *North of Slavery: The Negro in the Free States 1790-1860.* Chicago: University of Chicago Press, 1961.

Loewenberg, Bert James and Ruth Bogin, eds. *Black Women in Nineteenth-Century American Life: Their Words, Their Thoughts, Their Feelings.* University Park: The Pennsylvania State University Press, 1976.

Lorde, Audre. *Sister Outsider.* Trumansburg, New York: The Crossing Press, 1984.

Lovell, John Jr. *Black Song: The Forge and the Flame, The Story of How the Afro-American Spiritual Was Hammered Out.* New York: The Macmillan Company, 1972.

Low, W. Augustus and Virgil A. Clift, eds. *Encyclopedia of Black America.* New York: McGraw Hill, 1981; reprint, New York: Da Capo Press, 1981.

Macy, Joanna Rogers. *Despair and Personal Power in the Nuclear Age.* Philadelphia: New Society Publishers, 1983.

Mathews, Donald G. *Religion in the Old South.* Chicago: University of Chicago Press, 1977.

Moses, Wilson Jeremiah. *The Golden Age of Black Nationalism, 1850-1925.* New York: Oxford University Press, 1978.

Mossell, Mrs N.F. [Gertrude E.H. Bustill Mossell]. *The Work of the Afro-American Woman.* 2nd ed. Philadelphia: Geo. S. Ferguson Company, 1908; reprint, New York: Oxford University Press, 1988.

National Association for the Advancement of Colored People, *Thirty Years of Lynching in the United States, 1889-1918.* NAACP, 1919; reprint, New York: Negro Universities Press, 1969.

Niebuhr, H. Richard. *The Responsible Self: An Essay in Christian Moral Philosophy.* New York: Harper and Row, Publishers, 1963.

Ofari, Earl, ed. *Let Your Motto Be Resistance: The Life and Thought of Henry Highland Garnet.* Boston: Beacon Press, 1972.

Olney, James, ed. *Autobiography: Essays Theoretical and Critical.* Princeton: Princeton University Press, 1980.

Penn, I. Garland. *The Afro-American Press, and Its Editors.* Springfield, Massachusetts: Willey and Co. Publishers, 1891.

Raboteau, Albert J. *Slave Religion: The "Invisible Institution" in the Antebellum South.* New York: Oxford University Press, 1978.

Richardson, John and John Bowden, eds. *The Westminster Dictionary of Christian Theology.* Philadelphia: The Westminster Press, 1983.

Rosaldo, Michelle Zimbalist and Louise Lamphere, eds. *Woman, Culture and Society.* Stanford: University of California Press, 1981.

Rudwick, Elliot M. and August Meier. "Black Man in the 'White City': Negroes and the Columbian Exposition, 1893." *Phylon: The Atlanta Universty Review of Race and Culture,* 26: 354-361.

Russell, Letty M. *The Future of Partnership.* Philadelphia: The Westminster Press, 1979.

_____, ed. *Feminist Interpretation of the Bible.* Philadelphia: The Westminster Press, 1985.

_____. *Household of Freedom: Authority in Feminist Theology.* Philadelphia: The Westminster Press, 1987.

Schultz, Elizabeth. "To Be Black and Blue: The Blues Genre in Black American Autobiography." Albert E. Stone, ed. *The American Autobiography: A Collection of Critical Essays.* Englewood Cliffs, New Jersey: Prentice-Hall, Inc., 1981.

Sennett, Richard. *Authority.* New York: Vintage Books, 1981.

Shapiro, Herbert. *White Violence and Black Response: From Reconstruction to Montgomery.* Amherst: The University of Massachusetts Press, 1988.

Sobel, Mechal. *Trabelin' On: The Slave Journey to an Afro-Baptist Faith.* Princeton: Princeton University Press, 1988.

Soelle, Dorothee. *Suffering.* Philadelphia: Fortress Press, 1975.

_____. *Beyond Mere Obedience*. New York: The Pilgrim Press, 1982.

Spacks, Patricia Meyer. "Stages of Self: Notes on Autobiography and the Life Cycle." Albert E. Stone, ed. *The American Autobiography: A Collection of Critical Essays*. Englewood Cliffs, New Jersey: Prentice-Hall, Inc., 1981.

Spero, Sterling D. and Abram L. Harris. *The Negro and the Labor Movement*. New York: Columbia University Press, 1931.

Steady, Filomea Chioma, ed. *The Black Woman Cross-Culturally*. Cambridge: Schenkman Publishing Co., Inc., 1981.

Sterling, Dorothy. *Black Foremothers: Three Lives*. Old Westbury, New York: The Feminist Press, 1979.

Stone, Albert E., ed. *The American Autobiography: A Collection of Critical Essays*. Englewood Cliffs, New Jersey: Prentice-Hall, Inc., 1981.

Stuckey, Sterling. *Slave Culture: Nationalist Theory and the Foundations of Black America*. New York: Oxford University Press, 1987.

Thompson, Mildred. "Ida B. Wells-Barnett: An Exploratory Study of an American Black Woman, 1893-1930." MPh diss., George Washington University, 1979.

Thompson, Robert Farris and Joseph Corner. *The Four Moments of the Sun: Kongo Art in Two Worlds*. Washington, District of Columbia: National Gallery of Art, Washington, 1981.

Tucker, David M. "Miss Ida B. Wells and Memphis Lynching." *Phylon: The Atlanta University Review of Race and Culture*. Vol. 32, no. 2 Second Quarter, (Summer 1971): 112-122.

_____. *Black Pastors and Leaders: Memphis 1819-1972*. Memphis: Memphis State University Press, 1975.

Wade-Gayles, Gloria. *No Crystal Stair: Visions of Race and Sex in Black Women's Fiction*. New York: The Pilgrim Press, 1984.

Walker, Alice. *In Search of Our Mothers' Gardens: Womanist Prose*. New York: Harcourt Brace Jovanovich, Publishers, 1983.

Wells, Ida B. Unpublished diary, 1885-1887. Special Collections, Joseph Regenstein Library, University of Chicago, Chicago.

_____. "Afro-Americans and Africa." *The A.M.E. Church Review.* Vol. 9, No. 1. July 1892.

_____. *Southern Horrors. Lynch Law in All Its Phases.* New York: The New York Age Print, 1892; reprint, New York: Arno Press, *On Lynching: Southern Horrors, A Red Record, Mob Rule in New Orleans,* 1969.

_____. *A Red Record: Tabulated Statistics and Alleged Causes of Lynching in the United States, 1892-1893-1894.* Chicago: Donohue and Henneberry, Printers, Binders and Publishers, 1894; reprint, New York: Arno Press, *On Lynching: Southern Horrors, A Red Record, Mob Rule in New Orleans,* 1969.

_____. "Lynch Law in All Its Phases." *Our Day.* Vol XI, no. 64. May, 1893: 333-347.

_____. *The Weekly Call.* Topeka, Kansas. 22 April 1893.

_____. *The Weekly Call.* Topeka, Kansas. 15 July 1893.

_____. "Lynch Law in America." *The Arena.* January 1900: 15-24.

_____. "The Negro's Case in Equity." *The Independent.* 26 April 1900, 52:1010-1011.

_____. "Lynching and the Excuse for It." *The Independent.* 16 May, 1901, 53:1133-1136.

_____. "Ida B. Wells Speaks." September 2. n.d, n.p., Special Collections, Joseph Regenstein Library, University of Chicago, Chicago.

_____. Undated and anonymous biographical sketch. Ida B. Wells Papers, Special Collections, Joseph Regenstein Library, University of Chicago, Chicago.

_____. Unpublished diary, 1930. Special Collections, Joseph Regenstein Library, University of Chicago, Chicago.

_____. *Crusade for Justice.* Edited by Alfreda Duster. Chicago: University of Chicago Press, 1970.

Wells-Barnett, Ida B. "Booker T. Washington and His Critics." *World Today*. April 1904: 518-521.

_____. "How Enfranchisement Stops Lynching." *Original Rights Magazine*. Vol.1, no. 4, (June 1910).

_____. "Our Country's Lynching Record." *Survey*. 1 February 1913: 573-574.

White, Deborah Gray. *Ar'n't I a Woman: Female Slaves in the Plantation South*. New York: W.W. Norton and Company, 1985.

Willard, Frances. *Glimpses of Fifty Years: The Autobiography of an American Woman*. Chicago: Woman's Temperance Publication Association, 1889.

Wilmore, Gayraud S. *Black Religion and Black Radicalism: An Interpretation of the Religious History of the Afro-American People*. 2d ed. Maryknoll: Orbis Books, 1983.

Wilmore, Gayraud S. and James H. Cone, eds. *Black Theology: A Documentary History, 1966-1979*. Maryknoll: Orbis Books, 1979.

Wood, The Reverend Norman B. *The White Side of a Black Subject*. Chicago: American Publishing House, 1897.

Emilie M. Townes

Emilie Maureen Townes, an ordained American Baptist clergywoman, is a native of Durham, North Carolina. She holds a Doctor of Ministry degree from the University of Chicago Divinity School and a Ph.D. in Religion in Society and Personality from the Joint Garrett-Evangelical Theological Seminary/Northwestern University Program in Religious Studies.

Townes is assistant professor of Christian social ethics at Saint Paul School of Theology in Kansas City, Missouri. She has served as an instructor in the Department of Religious Studies at DePaul University, an adjunct professor of ethics and society at Garrett-Evangelical and was a member of the field education staff. She has also been an adjunct professor at Chicago Theological Seminary and McCormick Theological Seminary in Chicago, Illinois. In addition to her teaching responsibilities, she served as interim pastoral leader of Christ the Redeemer Metropolitan Community Church for three years. She is currently the vice-chair/chair-elect of the Board of Directors of reStart, Inc.—an interfaith agency for the homeless.

Townes served on the Commission on Life and Theology of the American Baptist Churches and the National Commission on the Ministry. She is a member of the Society of Christian Ethics, the National Women's Studies Association, the American Academy of Religion, and the Ministers Council of the American Baptist Churches. She has served on the Women in Ministry Coordinating Committee of the National Council of Churches and the board of directors of the Ecumenical Women's Center. Townes served a term of chair in both organizations. While a member of the Chicago Baptist Association, she served on its ordination commission and its long range planning committee.

She is editor of a forthcoming anthology entitled *A Troubling in My Soul: Womanist Perspectives on Evil and Suffering.*